Introduction to Information Systems Project Management

THE IRWIN/MCGRAW-HILL SERIES
Operations and Decision Sciences

OPERATIONS MANAGEMENT

Bowersox and Closs
Logistical Management: The Integrated Supply Chain Process
First Edition

Chase, Aquilano, and Jacobs
Operations Management for Competitive Advantage
Ninth Edition

Chu, Hottenstein, and Greenlaw
PROSIM for Windows
Third Edition

Cohen and Apte
Manufacturing Automation
First Edition

Davis, Aquilano, and Chase
Fundamentals of Operations Management
Third Edition

Dobler and Burt
Purchasing and Supply Management
Sixth Edition

Flaherty
Global Operations Management
First Edition

Fitzsimmons and Fitzsimmons
Service Management: Operations, Strategy, Information Technology
Third Edition

Gray and Larson
Project Management: The Managerial Process
First Edition

Hill
Manufacturing Strategy: Text & Cases
Third Edition

Hopp and Spearman
Factory Physics
Second Edition

Lambert and Stock
Strategic Logistics Management
Third Edition

Leenders and Fearon
Purchasing and Supply Chain Management
Eleventh Edition

Moses, Seshadri, and Yakir
HOM Operations Management Software for Windows
First Edition

Nahmias
Production and Operations Analysis
Fourth Edition

Nicholas
Competitive Manufacturing Management
First Edition

Olson
Introduction to Information Systems Project Management
First Edition

Pinedo and Chao
Operations Scheduling
First Edition

Sanderson and Uzumeri
Managing Product Families
First Edition

Schroeder
Operations Management: Contemporary Concepts and Cases
First Edition

Schonberger and Knod
Operations Management
Seventh Edition

Simchi-Levi, Kaminsky, and Simchi-Levi
Designing and Managing the Supply Chain: Concepts, Strategies, and Case Studies
First Edition

Sterman
Business Dynamics: Systems Thinking and Modeling for a Complex World
First Edition

Stevenson
Production/Operations Management
Sixth Edition

Vollmann, Berry, and Whybark
Manufacturing Planning & Control Systems
Fourth Edition

Zipkin
Foundations of Inventory Management
First Edition

BUSINESS STATISTICS

Alwan
Statistical Process Analysis
First Edition

Aczel
Complete Business Statistics
Fourth Edition

Bowerman, O'Connell, and Hand
Business Statistics in Practice
Second Edition

Bryant and Smith
Practical Data Analysis: Case Studies in Business Statistics, Volumes I and II
Second Edition
Volume III
First Edition

Butler
Business Research Sources
First Edition

Cooper and Schindler
Business Research Methods
Seventh Edition

Delurgio
Forecasting Principles and Applications
First Edition

Doane, Mathieson, and Tracy
Visual Statistics
Second Edition, 2.0

Doane, Mathieson, and Tracy
Visual Statistics: Statistical Process Control
First Edition, 1.0

Gitlow, Oppenheim, and Oppenheim
Quality Management: Tools and Methods for Improvement
Second Edition

Lind, Mason, and Marchal
Basic Statistics for Business and Economics
Third Edition

Mason, Lind, and Marchal
Statistical Techniques in Business and Economics
Tenth Edition

Merchant, Goffinet, and Koehler
Basic Statistics Using Excel for Office 97
Second Edition

Neter, Kutner, Nachtsheim, and Wasserman
Applied Linear Statistical Models
Fourth Edition

Neter, Kutner, Nachtsheim, and Wasserman
Applied Linear Regression Models
Third Edition

Siegel
Practical Business Statistics
Fourth Edition

Webster
Applied Statistics for Business and Economics: An Essentials Version
Third Edition

Wilson and Keating
Business Forecasting
Third Edition

QUANTITATIVE METHODS AND MANAGEMENT SCIENCE

Bodily, Carraway, Frey, Pfeifer
Quantitative Business Analysis: Casebook
First Edition

Bodily, Carraway, Frey, Pfeifer
Quantitative Business Analysis: Text and Cases
First Edition

Bonini, Hausman, and Bierman
Quantitative Analysis for Business Decisions
Ninth Edition

Hesse
Managerial Spreadsheet Modeling and Analysis
First Edition

Hillier, Hillier, Lieberman
Introduction to Management Science: A Modeling and Case Studies Approach with Spreadsheets
First Edition

Introduction to Information Systems Project Management

David L. Olson

Texas A&M University, College Station, Texas

Boston   Burr Ridge, IL   Dubuque, IA   Madison, WI   New York   San Francisco   St. Louis
Bangkok   Bogotá   Caracas   Lisbon   London   Madrid
Mexico City   Milan   New Delhi   Seoul   Singapore   Sydney   Taipei   Toronto

McGraw-Hill Higher Education ✕

*A Division of The **McGraw-Hill** Companies*

INTRODUCTION TO INFORMATION SYSTEMS PROJECT MANAGEMENT

Published by Irwin/McGraw-Hill, an imprint of The McGraw-Hill Companies, Inc., 1221 Avenue of the Americas, New York, NY 10020. Copyright © 2001 by The McGraw-Hill Companies, Inc. All rights reserved. No part of this publication may be reproduced or distributed in any form or by any means, or stored in a database or retrieval system, without the prior written consent of The McGraw-Hill Companies, Inc., including, but not limited to, in any network or other electronic storage or transmission, or broadcast for distance learning.

Some ancillaries, including electronic and print components, may not be available to customers outside the United States.

This book is printed on acid-free paper.

1 2 3 4 5 6 7 8 9 0 FGR/FGR 0 9 8 7 6 5 4 3 2 1

ISBN   0-07-229498-1

Publisher: *Jeffrey J. Shelstad*
Senior sponsoring editor: *Scott Isenbert*
Editorial assistant: *Christina Sanders*
Marketing manager: *Zina Craft*
Project manager: *Paula Krauza*
Production supervisor: *Gina Hangos*
Coordinator freelance design: *Mary Christianson*
Supplement coordinator: *Mark Sienicki*
Media technology producer: *Edward Przyzycki*
Freelance cover designer: *Didona Design*
Cover photographs: © *PhotoDisc/Volumes 21, 55, 43, 29, 57, and 54; middle row, first image*
    © *Crescenzo Mazza/FPG*
Compositor: *GAC Indianapolis*
Typeface: *10/12 Times Roman*
Printer: *Quebecor Printing Book Group/Fairfield*

Library of Congress Cataloging-in-Publication Data

Olson, David Louis.
    Introduction to information systems project management / David L. Olson.
        p.   cm.
    ISBN 0-07-229498-1 (softcover : alk. paper)
    1. Information resources management. 2. Management information systems.
    I. Title
    T58.64.O47   2000
    658.4'038'011dc—21   00-27782

http://www.mhhe.com

To Daria

Brief Contents

Contents

About the Author

David L. Olson is Lowry Mays Professor of Business in the Department of Information and Operations Management at Texas A&M University. He received his PhD in Business from the University of Nebraska in 1981. He has been at Texas A&M University since then, promoted to full professor in 1995. He has published research in more than 50 refereed journals, primarily on the topic of multiple objective decision making. He teaches in the management science, management information systems, and operations management areas. He has authored the book *Decision Aids for Selection Problems*, and co-authored the books *Decision Support Models and Expert Systems, Introduction to Management Science, Introduction to Simulation and Risk Analysis, Business Statistics: Quality Information for Decision Analysis*, and *Statistics, Decision Analysis, and Decision Modeling*. He has made more than 80 presentations at international and national conferences on research topics. He is a member of the Decision Sciences Institute, the Institute for Operations Research and Management Sciences, and the Multiple Criteria Decision Making Society. He has coordinated the Decision Sciences Institute Dissertation Competition, Innovative Education Competition, chaired the Doctoral Affairs Committee, served twice as nationally elected vice president, and as National Program Chair. He has received a Research Fellow Award from the College of Business and Graduate School of Business at Texas A&M University, and he has held the Business Analysis Faculty Excellence Fellowship for two years. He is a Fellow of the Decision Sciences Institute.

Preface

Project management is one of the fastest growing career fields in business today. Most of the growth in this field is in the information systems area, where there are widespread reports about most projects being late, many over budget, and all-too-often not satisfying design specifications. This book is about information systems project management, although the principles apply to projects in any field. Many chapters demonstrate current practice taken from published reports about project management.

The need to trade off time, cost, and quality is encountered throughout the book. Three factors consistently cited in published studies as factors related to project success are top management support, user involvement, and clear project objective statements. These three factors are emphasized, but other factors are presented as well.

An introductory chapter discusses project features in general. The systems perspective provides a useful framework for project analysis. The systems view is a concept useful for better understanding project purposes. Systems theory is important in project management because of the unintended consequences often encountered in projects as a result of complex interrelationships of system components. By viewing projects as systems, some of these unintended consequences may be anticipated, and prepared for.

Part I discusses two processes involved in the initial project definition stage. Chapter 2 discusses issues concerning the adoption of proposed projects. Practice in the commercial field is reviewed. A number of quantitative methods are demonstrated, including a detailed demonstration of one company's method in Appendix 2A. Chapter 3 discusses aspects of requirements definition—a more complete study of what resources would be required to complete projects that have passed the approval stage. Risk analysis at the initial stage of project development is reviewed, along with the use of the systems failure method to reduce risk by anticipating problems.

The planning stage involves specific identification of how projects are going to be accomplished and is discussed in Part II. Chapter 4 discusses standards and methodologies, and different types of information projects. Chapter 5 reviews project estimation practice. Some of the quantitative methods used are demonstrated.

In Part III, scheduling techniques sort out project complexity, considering the interrelated nature of project activities. Chapter 6 presents and demonstrates deterministic critical path methods and discusses resource leveling and constraining. Chapter 7 deals with probabilistic aspects of project scheduling, with tools to assess risk of project completion times.

Part IV deals with project implementation. Alternative forms of organization are discussed in Chapter 8, focusing on those that have successfully been applied to project management. The abilities of various alternative organizational forms to deal with project uncertainty are discussed. Project implementation issues are examined in Chapter 9, including detailed discussion of critical success factors. Chapter 10 discusses other project control features and means of assessing project success. Techniques to deal with a variety of risks involved in software project development are reviewed.

The Appendix provides a very basic introduction to *Microsoft Project,* a leading commercial software product for support of project planning and management. Project management software continues to advance rapidly, and more detailed description would be outdated by publication. The intent of the Appendix is not to make the reader an expert, but rather to allow the reader to start working with the software, an extremely useful tool for project planning as well as communicating plans to others. Problems using *Microsoft Project* are included in Chapters 3, 4, 6, 7, 9, and 10.

Each chapter includes some suggested problems that could be used in a course. Field trip ideas are included in Chapters 2 through 5. There is sufficient material for a three-hour credit course. Project planning, as emphasized in the book, involves high levels of uncertainty, and rarely do projects proceed according to plan. The book provides a view of projects as systems, along with tools to make project planning and implementation more successful.

Professor Olson would like to thank his colleagues: David Paradice and Ahmed Shabana. Also, all the reviewers: Michael Godfrey–Indiana State University; Raymond Crepeau–Indiana University Purdue University; Richard Irving–York University; Francois Bergeron–Universite Laval; Edward Pascal–University of Ottawa; William Moylan–Lawrence Technical University; R. Anthony Inman–Louisiana Technical University; William Sherrard–San Diego State University; Satish Mehra–Memphis State University; Theodore Klastorin–University of Washington; and Wade Shaw–Florida Tech.

## Chapter 1

Introduction to Project Management

Chapter Outline

Main Ideas Discussed

- Projects as unique activities with a definable purpose
- Project management, or getting a new complex activity accomplished
- Project success
- Critical success factors in project management
- Key competing project dimensions of cost, time, and quality

Today almost every organization gets involved in many projects. One reason projects are so important is the fast pace of change; another is the more specialized nature of modern business. Many of these projects involve information systems, a distinctive type of project. Firms have to try to stay close to the cutting edge to harness the power of computers in almost every aspect of business. Large accounting firms have enlarged their information systems consulting operations, almost all of which involves information systems projects. This means that there are more and more unique activities drawing people together from diverse locations and diverse organizations with diverse, specialized skills.

Like other projects, information systems projects involve output from a variety of sources. Projects come in all shapes and sizes. One of the largest, most recent projects involved a major airport hub, utilizing the latest in technology. The Denver International Airport is an impressive accomplishment. But it could be viewed as a failure from a strict project management viewpoint. It is a success in that it now provides the Denver metropolitan area with air service. But as a project, the airport was criticized frequently in newspapers with respect to time and budget performance, as well as whether it met specifications. The baggage-handling problem is outlined in the accompanying box. That and other problems resulted in a delayed opening, thus making original budgets insufficient. Other problems included failure of the airport passenger trains shuttling people between concourses and failure to take into account the long road to the city that is very susceptible to heavy snows. Overall, construction of the Denver International Airport demonstrates the pitfalls involved when undertaking any project.

The Denver International Airport

Projects involve ample opportunities for things to go wrong. One of the most publicized recent projects with problems is the Denver International Airport.[1] The project's original cost was estimated at $1.7 billion, and it was scheduled to open October 1993. The subsequent pre-construction budget was $2.08 billion. A report dated August 22, 1994,[2] stated that the airport had cost the city of Denver about $3.2 billion as of that time, not including airline and Federal Aviation Administration costs. Delays were costing $1 million per day, which included operations costs and about $500,000 for interest on bond issues. The airport opening was held up because of a malfunctioning computerized baggage system, which was supposed to provide baggage handling for all airlines at the airport. The automated system, which directed 4,000 baggage carts over a 20-mile automated cart system, cost $193 million. However, there was a flaw. The system damaged baggage and sometimes directed luggage to the wrong flights. The bugs in the system proved difficult to find.

Ultimately, the Denver International Airport opened. While it is a monument to civilization on the Great Plains, it is also a point of debate to many of the citizens of Denver. It was very expensive at its original price, but it ended up costing far more. Various estimates of cost were calculated, one version ending up at $4.8 billion.

Project management has long been associated with operations management and is an important topic in the operations management curriculum. There has been an explosion of projects in the field of information systems. Although information systems project management involves some characteristics different from those found in operations management, many of the same tools can be applied. This is primarily due to the number of new projects organizations have adopted to implement ever-changing computer technology. There are many useful things that information technology can do for organizations, but the information technology environment involves high turnover of personnel, turbulent work environments, and rapidly changing technology, resulting in high levels of uncertainty with respect to time and cost. Despite this more volatile environment, project management principles applicable to operations management can often be transferred to the information systems environment.

What Is a Project?

A **project** involves getting a new, complex activity accomplished. Many activities qualify as projects. Building the Golden Gate Bridge, transporting the Statue of Liberty across the Atlantic, and the attempt to elect George McGovern as President of the United States were all major projects. The development of the atomic bomb and sending men to the moon were major research and development projects in the field of science. Each political campaign is a marketing project, just like other marketing projects to sell new products. You have each written a paper, which was assigned as a "project." These projects involved researching some topic and then organizing your ideas into a cohesive, rational whole. In football, developing a promising young quarterback prospect is often a multiyear project, including intensive coaching. Quarterbacks must learn the team's offense, learn the style of teammates, develop their leadership skills, develop their passing techniques, and build endurance and strength. What television viewers might view as natural talent may have involved the closely planned and coordinated activities of quite a large number of people. Thus, projects

- Involve a definable purpose.
- Cut across organizational lines.
- Are unique activities.

The construction or repair of structures such as the Golden Gate Bridge can be considered a project due to its unique nature, definable purpose, and ability to cut across organizational lines.

Projects are purposeful, in that they are designed to accomplish something for the organization undertaking them. Projects usually cut across organizational lines, drawing people from a variety of functional specialties. Constructing automobiles on an assembly line is no longer a project once the assembly line is developed because it becomes a closed, repetitive activity that continues as long as anyone can foresee. Making a series of sales calls is not a project because it is not a unique activity. However, just like the first assembly line, the first round of sales calls is a project, until a desired level of competence is attained. Projects include the following:

- Constructing something—a road, a dam, a building, an information system.
- Organizing something—a meeting, an election campaign, a symphony, a movie.
- Doing anything the first time.
- Accomplishing a new, complex activity.

Project Characteristics

Because projects involve new activities, they typically involve high levels of uncertainty and risk. One of the reasons assembly-line operations are so efficient is that workers perform the same function over and over, hour after hour, day after day, year after year. This repetitiveness allows high degrees of specialization, which, in turn, enables greater productivity. The activities of many different people and machines can be balanced for maximum efficiency in an assembly-line operation. Projects, however, involve lower degrees of efficiency and thus are more uncertain.

Because of this higher degree of uncertainty, it is much more difficult to estimate the level of resources required to accomplish a project than it is for other forms of productive organizations. It is also more difficult to estimate the time required (which amounts to another resource). Many projects are late, but not all projects take longer than estimated. The Russian atomic bomb project was completed ahead of schedule,[3] and about the same time, the U-2 airplane project was finished in about one-tenth of the estimated time in the United States. Yet projects finished ahead of schedule are still rare. *Projects are collections of activities.* If one activity is late, other activities are delayed. If an activity is ahead of schedule, workers tend to slow down to meet the original completion date. Following activities often can't start early anyway, because the people and materials for following activities may not be available until their originally scheduled start time. For these and other reasons, it is far more common for projects to be late than to be finished early.

Because of their temporary nature, projects inevitably involve gathering together a diverse group of specialists to accomplish a variety of tasks. Project team members usually do not know each other very well, at least at the beginning of the project. They tend to be quite different people, with different skill sets and interests. *The primary feature of a project is that it is a set of temporary activities conducted by ad hoc organizations.*

Information systems projects have many similarities to generic projects. They consist of activities, each with durations, predecessor relationships, and resource requirements. They involve high levels of uncertainty and often suffer from time and cost overruns, while rarely experiencing time and cost underruns. However, information systems projects are different from generic projects in some aspects. While each project is unique, there are usually many, many replications of information system project types. Most are served by a standard methodology, with the need to identify user requirements, followed by design of a system, production of the system, testing of the system, training and implementation, and, ultimately, maintenance of the system. These steps are not always serial; there are often many loops back to prior stages. They involve the need for specialists in different areas of the information systems field, but these specialties are not as distinctly different as carpentry and electrical work. Systems analysts usually know how to program, and testers know all of the other functions involved in a project. Project team members from the development side usually understand each other well. Information systems projects, of course, involve computers, a distinct characteristic that has more effect than initially might be apparent.

Dimensions of Complexity

Projects can differ in a number of aspects, including the number of people involved and the diversity of skills involved. Some projects are individual efforts to accomplish something. Others, such as a major military campaign, can involve hundreds of thousands of people. The more people involved, the greater the need to organize into subunits, requiring a higher proportion of managers and thus a lower proportion of productive people. In general, the more complex the project, the more time and resources required.

Group size dimensions can vary over extremes. A few examples of projects for different sized groups, ranging from individual effort through three general group levels, are given in Table 1–1 for comparison.

Projects can also differ on the dimensions of uncertainty. It is much more difficult to predict how much time is going to be required the first time you do something. Because projects usually involve an operation performed for the first time, they usually take longer than expected or estimated. Currently, information systems are in very high demand, outstripping their supply. Another possible bias is introduced by the practice of making initial estimates intentionally low to get work. This bias improves the probability of getting work, which is often negotiated on a cost-plus basis. This practice is not at all recommended; it leads to a bad reputation when initial promises are not kept. An additional factor in project lateness is that large government projects are the most commonly reported. These projects tend to be very complex and often run over in time and budget. How many times have you read about a government project of significant magnitude taking less time or money than estimated (other than the U2)? Because there is a

Table 1–1 Project Size by Size of Group

Individual	A term paper is often an individual effort. Making an oil painting of a landscape is an individual project.
Group	Organizing a wedding can be a major project for a small group. Implementing a computer system may involve a small group project. Each audit is a project conducted by auditing specialists.
Organization	Construction organizations are created to develop efficient skills at building structures of one type or another. As each project is completed, there is often a great deal of change in personnel, although the organization will retain some of its people for the next project. Information systems consulting organizations follow a similar pattern.
Multiorganization	The space shuttle involves coordinated activities of many people. Probably the most involved projects known to mankind are also the most wasteful. World War II involved the radical reorganization of entire countries, relocating entire industries in the Soviet Union, long marches in China, the rebuilding of entire industries in Germany and England, and developing entire new industries in the United States.

strong correlation between time and money, late projects almost always cost more than expected.

General project management is a field that has developed primarily since World War II.[4] With more complex undertakings, many project management principles have developed. Many of these principles apply to information systems project management. Information systems projects, however, have some unique features. They typically involve a cost/time/quality trade-off, which can be simplistically stated as follows:

In the field of information systems, there is an old adage that you can have any two of three things in a project. You can get it done on time, you can get it done within budgeted cost, or you can get it done well. If you are willing to wait, you can get the job done right within cost. If you are willing to spend the money, you can get a good job done quickly. Or, you can get the job done on time and within budget, with the only reservation being that it won't perform as specified.[5]

This adage is not presented as a recommended way to treat all projects. We all like to think that we can do better than anyone else, and accomplish all three tasks. But over and over, in the fields of construction, government projects, and in information systems, problems completing projects on time, within budget, and within specifications have been encountered. Project management cannot be blamed for all of these reported failures. The point is that we should understand the difficulties involved in a project environment and seek to understand the project as a system so that we keep it on target with respect to accomplishing what it is intended to do, in the most timely and efficient manner possible. Bringing in a project on time, within budget, and within specifications is tough. Project managers need to expect difficult challenges.

Modern Business

Business has grown much more complex, with interrelated currencies and stock markets. The pace of business is at the speed of light, as stock trading is conducted electronically, often by artificial intelligence systems. Information technology markets are less predictable. The outputs of many companies are tied together through just-in-time systems with dedicated suppliers. At the output end of production, producers and retailers are often connected through electronic data interchange. The international aspect of business is typified by new arrangements such as the General Agreement on Tariffs and Trade, the North American Free Trade Association, and the European Economic Community. The rapid pace of change has resulted in the disappearance of many companies, age-old organizations (such as the Southwest Conference), and entire countries (such as the Soviet Union).

In the rapidly changing world of business today there is a growing need to manage projects intelligently. Project management advanced a great deal in the defense, aerospace, and construction industries. Techniques developed for controlling the interrelated activities of many different organizations and crews can be applied to the field of information systems, which includes many projects to install new applications or to tie old applications together.

Viewing Projects as Systems

Systems are collections of interrelated parts working together to accomplish one or more objectives. There are many systems of interacting parts where viewing the whole tells us more than simply looking at the system's components. In systems, output is not simply the sum of component parts. Components are affected by other parts of the system. System components are affected by being in the system, and the sum of the system output is greater than the sum of individual outputs without being a part of the system. Systems are purposeful and meant to do something.

Information projects are systems. Subsystems found in project management systems include a technical core, a control subsystem, and a project information subsystem. The *technical core* includes the technical expertise and equipment that gives the system the ability to accomplish what it needs to do. Expertise can include systems analysis, program development, testing, installation, and user training skills. Equipment in a broad sense can include software, such as CASE tools and subroutines that improve productivity. The *control subsystem* is the means by which management controls operations. Within an organization, this control subsystem coordinates the technical core with the outside environment. In an institution, an example of a control subsystem is the board of directors, which approves goals and strategies for the organization (which are usually generated by top management). In a project management system, control includes procedures specified for specific tasks, milestones to mark completion of project phases, and the expertise available within the project team to solve problems when they are encountered. *The project information subsystem* provides management with measures of how the system is accomplishing its objectives. Project information systems need to record the current status of activities and list responsibilities, planned and actual durations of activities, and cost expenditures.

The value of viewing information systems projects as systems is that the total view of the project in light of its intended purpose is clearer. Projects consist of many interrelated tasks, performed by different people with different skills. If each task was accomplished in isolation, many suboptimalities would occur. Specific tasks could possibly be performed faster or at less expense if the rest of the project was disregarded. But the focus of each member of the project team should be to accomplish project objectives and not to optimize production of specific tasks. If trade-offs exist between task accomplishment and project accomplishment, the systems view makes it clear that overall project considerations come first.

Systems provide a useful framework within which to view projects. To make projects work, project managers need to be able to anticipate the consequences of planned actions. They need to develop a system organization—through hiring and training appropriate, qualified people—within budget. They need to be able to know who they have to deal with outside of the system for supplies, materials, regulation compliance, and so forth. They need to understand how to measure how the project is going and what controls are available if the project is not going as planned. Understanding the concept of systems makes it much easier to see the effect of the principles of project management.

Project Entities

A number of people are needed to make projects work. The **project manager** coordinates the efforts of people coming from a variety of functional areas. Project managers also need to integrate planning and control costs by assigning tasks and schedules to the members of the project team.

The **project team** is a group of people with the required skills to accomplish the project. They will often come from different places with radically different skills and backgrounds. Oftentimes these project team members will enter the project (and leave) at different times, making for an even greater degree of turbulence. People who work on projects need to be very flexible and learn to work with a variety of other people.

The **project management system** is the organizational structure used by the project manager to get things done. The project management system includes the information system to provide project team members with necessary information, because coordination between groups is critical to integrate activities. Organizational structure involves procedures to ensure accurate communication and completeness of activities.

The Information Systems Project Environment

The application of information technology has led to remarkable progress in all walks of life, including business. Many information systems projects are generated in almost all business and governmental organizations. Wateridge[6] pointed out that many of these projects fail, despite decades of research. DeMarco[7] reported that about 15 percent of software development work delivered nothing, and overruns of 100 to 200 percent were common. Ten years later, Winsburg and Richards[8] reported a system scheduled to be completed in 1987 with a budget of $8 million was completed in 1993 at a cost of $100 million. These writers also reported a billing system canceled after expenditure of $1 million, with project completion expected to be far into the future. Many more current references agree about the chronic state of information systems projects missing budgets, time schedules, and expected project performance.[9]

Defining project success is in itself difficult. There are many views of what makes a project successful.

Project Success and Failure

Successful implementation has been found to require mastery of the technical aspects of systems along with understanding key organizational and behavioral dynamics.[10] There has been a great deal of research into information system **project failure.** Failure can arise when design objectives are not met. Projects also can fail when time and budget constraints are not held. Seemingly successful projects may fail because the intended users don't use them. And finally, systems may not meet the expectations of stakeholders.

The accompanying boxes discuss two information systems projects. The first is an example of interaction failure. The IRIS project is a good example of a system. The project made economic sense when viewed solely on economic grounds. But the total effect of the project on all components of the organization was not realized when the project was started. Failure to see negative consequences led to wasted expenditure on a project that was late, over budget, and far less useful than originally intended.

The Integrated Requisitioning Information System (IRIS)

Kirby[11] reported his experiences observing the development of a large information system. The Integrated Requisitioning Information System (IRIS) was intended as an integrated system to change requisitioning, purchasing, receiving, disbursement, and employee expense reporting procedures. The system was designed to electronically transfer all required information, substantially reducing paper documents. IRIS needed to interface with more than 36 information systems in use at the firm, ultimately affecting more than 3,000 employees as well as suppliers. Additional goals were to eliminate some accounting staff (not widely publicized by management) and bring suppliers online (increasing their dependence upon the company).

Project Description

The project was initiated in late 1990. Early in 1992 four contracting firms were brought in to oversee the design, production, and implementation of the new system. Fifteen people worked full time on the project, with another 35 people contributing on a part-time basis. Full-scale development was under way by May 1992.

Design meetings were held in early 1992 to define requirements and functional specifications. These meetings involved up to 50 people, from every functional area that would be affected. Meetings were held about every six weeks. A comprehensive manual, defining system functional requirements, was developed. Original cost estimates were about $3 million, including development, implementation, hardware, and training costs.

Phase 1, including check requests, check writing, on-demand checks, and travel expense reporting, was to begin November 1992. However, it became apparent that programmers were having difficulty meeting functional specifications, so development of the training program was delayed. There was a high degree of turnover of personnel assigned to the project. Cost estimates were revised to $5 million, and some functional features were scaled back. Much of the blame was attributed to the contractor who was to deliver the software. This contractor was terminated in June 1993, and it was decided to write the needed software using internal programmers. This led to additional delays while these people received project orientation. In early 1994, a considerably scaled back version of the Phase 1 system was pilot tested. Further details on this scaled back version are not known. But the overall project must be considered a failure, as it proved impossible to implement as intended within original budget.

Failure Causes

Management cited poor systems analysis, programming errors, inaccurate forecasting, and other causes for the failure of the IRIS implementation. Kirby contended that the failure was not due to these causes, but rather to failure to recognize the total systems nature of project management. The company focused on the financial effect of the system's development. It was believed that streamlining business functions would lead to increased profits, thus justifying system development. Cost reduction in the form of layoffs and lower operating costs were expected. However, as system prototyping was being conducted, accounting personnel were asked to give feedback on ways to improve the system. Management saw the prototyping as eliminating potential bugs and improving the interface between users and the system, thus increasing system efficiency. The accounting clerks soon realized the threat to their jobs—or at least radical changes in their assigned tasks.

The Integrated Requisitioning Information System (concluded)

IRIS was also intended to improve organizational communication and control. Efficiency was to be improved by reducing duplication of effort. However, plant representatives saw the system as a means for headquarters to increase its control over their operations. IRIS was supposed to provide faster and more efficient expense reports and reimbursement for regional sales offices. Sales representatives were to complete travel reports online. However, a number of sales representatives thought the system decreased flexibility and tied up their office computers. Because not all sales representatives were computer literate, some saw the project as a plan to force sales reps to learn to use computers or lose their jobs.

Conclusions

Kirby noted that people can interpret events in many different ways. Information technology offers a great deal, but it can also threaten many people. In this project, a great deal of effort was put forth by the company to involve members of the organization in developing the system. But management made the mistake of assuming that employees would focus their view of the project on the economic perspective of efficiency, just as management did. By understanding threats to others (more apparent if the project is viewed as a system), management can understand some of the negative effects that might be involved. If these negative effects are insurmountable, projects that would otherwise seem economically attractive can be avoided before such projects ultimately fail.

The second project was reported as a success. It appears to have been a very effective implementation of information technology to aid business. The TRW digital network installation shows a successfully implemented project plan, indicating that it is possible. It is impossible to know if long-term success continued.

Voice and Data Digital Network Installation

In the 1980s, the management team of TRW's Space and Defense Sector was concerned with high communication cost inflation. TRW needed faster response capabilities to keep up with turbulent markets and shorter product cycles. A new network infrastructure was proposed with integrated voice, data, and image capability. Planning the new system took more than two years. Installation took another two years. The project was completed on schedule at a cost of $45 million, which was 10 percent under budget. The system was housed in 65 buildings with more than 20,000 employees. The system consisted of a 30,000-line digital private branch exchange, 25,000 integrated voice and data digital lines, security video services, and 200 communications rooms. Railing and Housel[12] described the planning, procurement, and implementation processes that enabled TRW to develop their system at the best price.

The business problem facing TRW's Space and Defense Sector was a yearly cost of $5 to $10 million to move voice and data lines. Each voice and data line that had to be moved cost $500. There was a similar, less precisely measurable cost in lost productivity while waiting for lines to be adjusted. The company used many different types of data processing systems. Reliance on AT&T for network service was problematic because AT&T was undergoing its divestiture, and local telephone costs were increasing rapidly.

An integrated digital network was expected to provide faster response at lower cost. It would also make reconfiguration easier, leading to faster response and reduction of lost productive time. Formidable technical obstacles were dealt with, but organizational culture was found to be a major problem. Each project unit wanted control over its information resources, which resulted in many underutilized and isolated data networks. The project would allow unused computing resources to be utilized over high-speed digital lines, which could also transfer data more rapidly. To comply with user needs, the integrated network would allow user teams to access computer resources without controlling how these resources were used. Project goals included reducing cost, promoting movement of information rather than people, sharing excess computing capacity, development of a flexible network configuration, and providing employees with the best available information technology.

A **cost/benefit analysis** was completed, and top management authorized a detailed analysis of current network needs. The needs analysis formed the basis for requests for information, a promotional program to gain user support for the project, and a request for proposal to produce the system. A project management team consisting of technical, engineering, and project personnel was created. The large-scale integrated digital network was broken into smaller subprojects to make each component more manageable. Budgets were allocated, with regularly scheduled meetings for progress and cost reviews. A **baseline schedule** was maintained to allow the project management team to monitor how closely they were keeping to their schedule. This was credited with forcing subproject management to fix problems as they arose.

The **requirements analysis** was the first task accomplished by the project management team. The requirements analysis established criteria for network evaluation, provided data on user population characteristics, and provided a basis for estimating the types and number of devices needed. Final cost estimates indicated a minimum benefit of an 8 percent cost reduction relative to current operations, as opposed to a 30 percent increase if the project were not adopted. Savings were projected to be $100 million plus over a 10-year period, with an additional $30 million in productivity increases.

A series of requests for information inviting vendor input on various parts of the new network were published. Detailed **requests for proposals** followed. Vendors had to show how their proposed systems would meet specific data and voice communications standards, as well as how they could adapt to future standards. Testing

---

Voice and Data Digital Network Installation (concluded)

and verification of each hardware and software element was specified as components were installed. Vendors had to specify the availability of resources needed.

Final evaluation of proposals included a **risk evaluation** to consider the ability of vendors to provide needed resources and to deliver quality system components. Bid costs were compared against hard dollar cost savings. Detailed proposals and requirements analysis were used to develop a detailed implementation plan.

To limit project cost escalation, the project management team created a configuration control board to limit modifications to original contracts. This kept changes to a minimum and was credited as leading to a 10 percent savings over the original project budget. Processes credited with leading to project success were proactive strategic planning, detailed requirements analysis, and cost/benefit analysis. Detailed specifications and rigorous evaluation also contributed to this project's success.

The difference between successful and failed information systems projects often lies in planning and implementation. The steps commonly applied to successful information systems projects include the following:

- Perform a cost/benefit analysis
- Develop a baseline schedule.
- Perform a requirements analysis.
- Solicit requests for proposal, thereby inviting vendor input.
- Test and verify all hardware and software.
- Perform a risk evaluation of all proposals.

Most information systems projects have been reported to be much less successful, reflecting in part a very turbulent environment where many changes are needed. Quite often, management gives up and changes direction. This was not the case with TRW, which stuck with their plan in a very controlled manner for more than four years. This is not always possible to do.

A great deal of research has been performed to identify factors that lead to project success. These factors include planning, user involvement, good communication, and sound monitoring of projects. Additional factors that are reported as important in information systems project success repeatedly include top management support and clear statement of project objectives.

Project Critical Success Factors

A **critical success factor** is a feature that must be performed well in order for the activity as a whole to succeed. Belassi and Tukel[13] examined published studies of project critical success factors. Table 1–2 indicates which factors were included in each of the seven studies.

Table 1–2 Comparison of Critical Success Factors

Critical Success Factors	Studies[a]						
	S&C71	*Mar76*	*BMF83*	*C&K83*	*Loc84*	*M&H87*	*P&S89*
Goal Definition							
Define goals		x	x			x	
Operational concept				x			
Project commitments known					x		
Top Management Support							
Continuing involvement in project	x						
Top management support		x		x	x		x
User Involvement							
Client consultation							x
Project Manager							
Competent project manager	x				x		x
On-site project manager			x				
Other Selected Factors							
Project team selection		x					x
Project team commitment			x				
Adequate project team capability			x				
Manpower and organization				x			
Accurate initial cost estimates			x				

Notes:
[a]S&C71   Sayles and Chandler[14]
Mar76   Martin[15]
BMF83   Baker, Murphy and Fisher[16]
C&K83   Cleland and King[17]
Loc84   Locke[18]
M&H87   Morris and Hough[19]
P&S89   Pinto and Slevin[20]

Source: Reorganized from W. Belassi and O. I. Tukel, "A New Framework for Determining Critical Success/Failure Factors in Projects," *International Journal of Project Management* 14, no. 3 (1996), pp. 141–51.

The factors listed are grouped to help identify the critical success factors necessary to information systems. A number of cited studies referred to different aspects related to defining goals. For each of the seven studies cited, the terms used to represent a concept are indicated by an 'x.' For general projects, user involvement is not as big a factor, because in construction or product development, user involvement is not usually required in systems design. But clear project objective statements and top management support are clearly important in all projects. Clear lines of communication are also important (a concept related to user involvement). The difference is that the users are key players in information systems projects, while in construction, technical features are more crucial.

Primary Reasons for Information Systems Project Failure

Ewusi-Mensah and Przasnyski[21] distinguished among total abandonment (complete termination of project activity before implementation), substantial abandonment (major simplification resulting in a project radically different than original specifications), and partial abandonment (reduction in original project scope without major changes in original specifications). Total abandonment was found to be the most common case. Keil[22] found that managers sometimes became too committed to projects, extending a project's life when it should be canceled. The causes of this type of failure were categorized by economic payoff, psychological factors (managerial persistence in expecting positive project prospects when they feel personally responsible), escalation factors (throwing good money after bad), social factors (including competitive rivalry), and organizational factors related to political support for a project. These conclusions closely matched those of Newman and Sabherwal.[23]

In the Engler[24] survey of information systems executives, the primary reason cited for project failure was lack of user involvement. This was followed by lack of top executive support and lack of a clear statement of business objectives. Yoon, Guimaraes, and O'Neal[25] investigated eight factors in expert systems success, finding that user involvement, top management support, and skill development were all important in project success.

Three factors have consistently appeared as success factors in studies such as those reported earlier:

- Client involvement.
- Top management support.
- Clear statement of project objectives.

We briefly discuss each of these factors here. A more complete discussion follows in Chapter 9.

Amoako-Gyampah and White[26] reported the system development of a project at a large manufacturing firm. The project was not a success. Four months after the system was installed, more than 1,000 requests for changes in the system had been received. Even though many means of encouraging user involvement had been applied, poorly defined lines of responsibility and communication resulted in failure of communication between users and system designers. Users grew to feel that their input wasn't valued; thus, they stopped contributing.

Top-management commitment has long been believed to be an important factor in information systems project success.[27] Projects have a very difficult time succeeding if they are not "fostered" by top management.[28] Project leadership is important too, but favorable views at the top, where control over purse strings lies, is probably more necessary for projects to succeed.

Another key role is the **project champion.** Graham[29] noted that project managers are seldom part of a firm's top management; to ensure access to required resources, then, the support of at least one project champion is required. Graham concluded that wise project managers needed to build a coalition of senior managers external to the project for support. Keil[30] proposed project champions (strong advocates who provided continued funding and protection) as important in the success of information technology projects. Project champions often have no authority, but they are crucial to the success of projects. While project champions do a great deal in maintaining project effort, Keil also found that they sometimes kept projects going even after they obviously were going to fail.

A detailed project plan needs to be developed that defines the system, user requirements, and system requirements. Part of this plan is a clear statement of the business objectives of the proposed system.[31] Because a project system is a coordinated effort of interrelated actors, the overall purpose of the project needs to be kept in mind by all participants. There also needs to be a great deal of coordination, because the output of one group affects what other groups are doing. Without a clear statement of purpose of the overall project—as well as what each project team component is to do—this coordinated effort will not mesh.

Pinto and Slevin[32] examined more than 400 projects, finding the following critical success factors (listed in order of number of appearances):

- Project mission—clear goals and directions provided.
- Top management support—to assure needed resources were provided.
- Plan/schedule—include detailed specifications.
- Client consultation—all affected parties given a hearing.
- Personnel—good people assigned to the project team.
- Technical tasks—needed expertise available.
- Client acceptance—sell the product of the project to the users.
- Monitoring and feedback—timely control during all stages of the project.
- Communication—network and data required are available.
- Troubleshooting—deal with crises and deviations.

Among the first four entries are the three factors of clear objectives, top management support, and user involvement (client consultation). User involvement reappears in the form of client acceptance. Stakeholder analysis can be very helpful in identifying the interests (and organizational power) of people within the user organization. It is necessary to recognize that all organizations are political entities. Projects proceed better—and have a much higher probability of acceptance—if those with significant political power are satisfied. Additionally, continuous planning, review, and authorization are key in information systems project implementation. The following application demonstrates the benefits of paying attention to these critical success factors. Clear goals and directions were established, strong top management support was present, and users were involved.

Perceptions of Project Success

Fowler and Walsh[33] discussed project success from the perspective of different stakeholders. A new information system was developed for a major British nuclear firm. The nuclear power generating firm had been formed as a private operation after a history as a state-owned monopoly with the strategic goal of technical excellence. In 1989 the firm developed a strategy based on strategic business units, with the goal of providing products and services that customers would pay for. However, many in management felt that the small business units had become too independent and were not considering overall organizational goals. Therefore, business development directors were appointed with companywide responsibility for marketing and sales in different market segments. Key corporate objectives were to increase international sales, and to increase diversification between nuclear and nonnuclear business.

A major information systems project was initiated to support a nuclear power generating firm's emphasis on commercial, nonnuclear, international, and self-reliant business growth.[34] The system was supposed to satisfy local financial information requirements for all strategic business units along with the needs of corporate headquarters. Future organizational changes were to be considered.

An external consultant was hired to guide project development and serve as project manager. A number of available products were evaluated through phases of requirements definition, purchase, installation, modification, procedures and data conversion, training, and documentation.

In the project initiation and system specification phase, it was apparent that a system imposed by the central headquarters would not be acceptable. Therefore, each strategic business unit would continue to "own" their own data and retain management responsibility. An information systems project team was formed; the team then toured the organization to establish requirements based on heavy user input. This resulted in policies to implement the new system in a distributed manner. Existing hardware and communications were to be used unless inappropriate. A common project management process of acceptance testing, data conversion, interfacing, training, hardware and networking, installation, and implementation was to be applied. A number of packages were assessed for functionality, ease of use, technical capability, and supplier acceptability. Demonstrations of packages were arranged. A particular commercial package was selected for companywide use. While this package received the highest overall evaluation, it also was identified as the riskiest with respect to implementation success.

Systems design and development of a common accounting structure, reports, and inquiries were adopted. Software modules for accounting functions were selected. Applications outside the scope of the software package were developed outside of the package. Implementation included a pilot test for each of the 15 sites. A thorough training plan was implemented.

The reasons given for the change in information systems varied considerably across stakeholder groups. Within the information systems team, stated reasons focused on the need to change from site-based to business-based accounting. Outside of the information systems team, there was much less clarity about project

---

Perceptions of Project Success (concluded)

objectives. Other than the informational tour, there was little evidence of a change in management, nor were the systemic effects of the project considered. The focus seemed to have been on getting the software and hardware right, with little emphasis on organizational and human effects, which included changes in task requirements, computer skills required, and contingency planning.

Strong top management support was present, and provided continued impetus for the project. However, it was perceived that many users were convinced that the system would fail. The reasons for this general perception were that in recent organizational restructuring, the information systems group was viewed as less powerful, the information systems group was viewed as having failed in several earlier system implementations, and users felt that they had not received adequate feedback about project progress.

The informational tour had been adopted to ensure user involvement. However, it apparently oversold the system. Unrealistic expectations arose.

There also was confusion between the information systems team and the strategic business units about the intended use of the system. The development team felt that every effort had been made to ensure end-user involvement in requirements specification. However, after the fact it was apparent that there was not a meeting of the minds.

A key factor that was lacking was clearly stated project objectives. Because of the variety of requirements from the different strategic business units, the project management group faced a spectrum of project requirements.

The information systems team was dominated by accountants, due in part to the financial features of the proposed system. However, other users were intended in addition to accountants. The lack of representation of these other users led to significant mismatches in perceptions of what the system was to do.

The system was widely viewed as undersized. This was blamed on a focus on cost rather than business requirements. The undersized system was very slow in responding at initiation, although subsequent improvements were made. The human interface was considered to be lacking by users. The system was accounts oriented and not particularly intuitive.

The project was completed on time and, officially, within budget. From the information systems team perspective, the system was viewed as satisfying stated specifications. However, users found it difficult to implement the system. Expectation failure was clearly present. The project demonstrates how aspects of the key factors of user involvement, top management support, and project objective definition affect the perception of success.

Summary

Project management has many features different from those of repetitive operations. These include:

- Lower degrees of efficiency.
- Operating in a much less predictable market with more rapidly changing technology.
- The need to coordinate more parties and organizations.
- A highly dynamic environment involving temporary tasks.

Information systems project management has its own unique features. The market for information systems products is growing very rapidly but is also extremely volatile. Each year sees radical new opportunities to harness computer technology to do our jobs better and for business to be conducted in better ways. This means, however, that we must constantly expect change, and we need to keep mastering new skills.

Projects are systems consisting of interrelated parts working together to accomplish project objectives. There are a number of important roles within information systems projects. Project managers have to balance technical understanding with the ability to motivate diverse groups of people (the project team) brought together on a temporary basis. Managing this team requires organizing in such a way that groups can coordinate their diverse activities. Project champions play an important role in obtaining organizational commitment to projects.

While there are many valuable information systems projects that have been completed, the development environment is very difficult. Rarely do information systems projects finish on time, within budget, and within specifications simultaneously. Top management support to projects has repeatedly been found to be critical to information systems project success. User groups need to be consulted to find out just what systems will be required to do. Systems designers need to be involved to make sure that new systems fit in with the overall organizational information system. Programmers need to be involved to ensure realistic production rates. End users need to be involved to ensure the quality of systems by making sure that they are usable and useful. After planning is completed, there need to be many meetings to coordinate the project through completion and acceptance.

Key Terms

Baseline schedule   12
Cost/benefit analysis   12
Critical success factor   13
Project   3
Project champion   15
Project failure   9
Project management system   8

Project manager   8
Project team   8
Request for proposal   12
Requirements analysis   12
Risk evaluation   13
System   7

Exercises

1. What is a project? What are typical characteristics of projects?
2. What are the dimensions of project complexity?
3. Look up information related to the budget and time frame at the initial stages of the Denver International Airport project. Were there any approval issues involved?
4. What are the relationships among cost, time, and project quality in information systems projects?
5. What features of projects differ from conventional operations?
6. What is the general state of information systems project success? If a particular information systems project's results are less than optimal, is that clear grounds for firing the project manager?
7. What features of management information systems projects differ from other kinds of projects?
8. What were the causes of failure of the Integrated Requisitioning Information System?
9. Describe the project management steps involved in the IRIS system and the TRW project.
10. Discuss the major project critical success factors identified by past research.
11. Describe the role of a project champion. How can a project champion be a positive feature? How might a project champion be a negative feature?
12. Look up a project on the Internet, in the library, or in other publications. Identify problems encountered in managing the project.
13. Look up projects on the Internet, in the library, or in other publications that report time, cost, or specification results. What is the general trend? You may be able to find some statistics, such as from the Standish Group, on overall project performance. Of real project reports, what bias would you expect, and why?

Endnotes

1. M. Zetlin, "A Slow Takeoff," *Management Review*, July 1996, pp. 24–29.
2. J. S. Bozman, "Baggage System Woes Costing Denver Airport Millions," *Computerworld*, August 22, 1994, http://www.computerworld.com.
3. E. M. Goldratt, *Critical Chain* (Great Barrington, MA: The North River Press, 1997).
4. P. W. G. Wright, *The Management of Projects* (London: Thomas Telford, 1994).
5. This conventional wisdom is encountered in a number of venues, including information systems.
6. J. Wateridge, "IT Projects: A Basis for Success," *International Journal of Project Management* 13, no. 3 (1995), pp. 169–72.
7. T. DeMarco, *Controlling Software Projects* (New York: Yourdon Press, 1982).

8. P. Winsburg and D. Richards, "Why Do Software Projects Fail?" *InfoDB* 6, no. 3 (1991/1992), pp. 13–21.

9. E. Booker, "No Silver Bullets for IS Projects," *Computerworld,* July 11, 1994, http://www.computerworld.com; R. Cafasso, "Few IS Projects Come in on Time, on Budget," *Computerworld,* December 12, 1994, http://www.computerworld.com; W. W. Gibbs, "Software's Chronic Crisis," *Scientific American* 271, no. 3 (September 1994), pp. 86–95; J. Johnson, "Chaos: The Dollar Drain of IT Project Failures," *Application Development Trends* 2, no. 1 (January 1995), pp. 41–47; and J. King, " 'Tough Love' Reins in IS Projects," June 19, 1995, "IS Reins in Runaway Projects," February 24, 1997, "Project Management Ills Cost Businesses Plenty," September 22, 1997, *Computerworld,* http://www.computerworld.com.

10. E. Oz, "Information Systems MIS Development: The Case of Star*Doc," *Journal of Systems Management* 45, no. 5 (1994), pp. 30–34.

11. E. G. Kirby, "The Importance of Recognizing Alternative Perspectives: An Analysis of a Failed Project," *International Journal of Project Management* 14 no. 4 (1996), pp. 209–11.

12. L. Railing and T. A. Housel, "A Network Infrastructure to Contain Costs and Enable Fast Response: The TRW Process," *MIS Quarterly* 14, no. 4 (1990), pp. 404–19.

13. W. Belassi and O. I. Tukel, "A New Framework for Determining Critical Success/Failure Factors in Projects," *International Journal of Project Management* 14, no. 3 (1996), pp. 141–51.

14. L. R. Sayles and M. K. Chandler, *Managing Large Systems* (New York: Harper and Row, 1971).

15. C.C. Martin, *Project Management* (New York: Amoco, 1976).

16. B. N. Baker, D. C. Murphy, and D. Fisher, "Factors Affecting Project Success," in *Project Management Handbook* (New York: Van Nostrand Reinhold, 1983).

17. D. I. Cleland and W. R. King, *Systems Analysis and Project Management* (New York: McGraw-Hill, 1983).

18. D. Locke, *Project Management* (New York: St. Martin's Press, 1984).

19. P. W. Morris and G. H. Hough, *The Anatomy of Major Projects* (New York: John Wiley and Sons, 1987).

20. J. K. Pinto and D. P. Slevin, "Critical Success Factors in R&D Projects," *Research in Technology Management,* 1989, pp. 31–35.

21. K. Ewusi-Mensah and Z. H. Przasnyski, "On Information Systems Project Abandonment: An Exploratory Study of Organizational Practices," *MIS Quarterly* 15, no. 1 (1991), pp. 66–86.

22. M. Keil, "Pulling the Plug: Software Project Management and the Problem of Project Escalation," *MIS Quarterly* 19, no. 4 (1995), pp. 420–47.

23. M. Newman and R. Sabherwal, "Determinants of Commitment to Information Systems Development: A Longitudinal Investigation," *MIS Quarterly* 20, no. 1 (1996), pp. 22–54.

24. N. Engler, "Bringing in the Users," *Computerworld,* November 25, 1996, http://www.computerworld.com.

25. Y. Yoon, T. Guimaraes, and Q. O'Neal, "Exploring the Factors Associated with Expert Systems Success," *MIS Quarterly* 19, no. 1 (March 1995), pp. 83–106.

26. K. Amoako-Gyampah and K. B. White, "When Is User Involvement Not User Involvement?" *Information Strategy,* Summer 1997, pp. 40–45.

27. M. J. Ginzberg, "Key Recurrent Issues in the MIS Implementation Process," *MIS Quarterly* 5, no. 2 (June 1981), pp. 47–59; S. L. Jarvenpaa and B. Ives, "Executive

Involvement and Participation in the Management of Information Technology," *MIS Quarterly* 15, no. 2 (1991), pp. 204–57; T. H. Kwon and R. W. Zmud, "Unifying the Fragmented Models of Information Systems Implementation," in *Critical Issues in Information Systems Research*, eds. R. J. Boland and R. A. Hirschheim (New York: Wiley, 1987); H. C. Lucas, Jr., *Implementation: The Key to Successful Information Systems* (New York: Columbia University Press, 1981); M. L. Markus, "Implementation Politics: Top Management Support and User Involvement," *Systems, Objectives, Solutions* 1, no. 4 (1981), pp. 203–15; and Newman and Sabherwal, "Determinants of Commitment to Information Systems Development."

28. Ewusi-Mensah and Przasnyski, "On Information Systems Project Abandonment."
29. J. H. Graham, "Machiavillian Project Managers: Do They Perform Better?" *International Journal of Project Management* 14, no. 2 (1996), pp. 67–74.
30. Keil, "Pulling the Plug: Software Project Management and the Problem of Project Escalation."
31. P. Weill, "The Relationship between Investment in Information Technology and in Performance: A Study of the Western Manufacturing Sector," *Information Systems Research* 3, no. 4 (1992), pp. 307–33.
32. Pinto and Slevin, "Critical Success Factors in R&D Projects."
33. A. Fowler and M. Walsh, "Conflicting Perceptions of Success in an Information Systems Project," *International Journal of Project Management* 17, no. 1 (1999), pp. 1–10.
34. Ibid.

Project Selection and Approval

Chapter Outline

Main Ideas Discussed

- Factors important in project selection decisions
- Project selection methods
- Methods of project evaluation
- Value analysis
- Multiple objective analysis
- Optimization models with budget constraints

The project process begins with a project proposal generated by users or management. The first step is an initial selection of projects, either on a case-by-case basis or by periodic selection by committees. A related decision of great importance is to keep track of the progress of a project so that those that are not going to provide value to the organization can be canceled.

This chapter discusses the decision problem of project selection and shows how the most commonly used methods work. Analytic methods support this selection process in two ways: (1) They provide decision makers with analysis of expected outcomes from adopting specific projects, and (2) they provide a basis for communication so that the reasoning behind a selection decision can be explained to others.

Measurement of Project Effect

Information systems projects typically involve benefits that are difficult to measure in terms of concrete monetary benefits. This vastly complicates sound management because cost/benefit analysis, the ideal tool for evaluating project proposals, will not always accurately reflect project benefits. Hinton and Kaye[1] cited cost and benefit intangibility, hidden outcomes involved in information technology investment, and the changing nature of information technology systems as important issues:

- *Intangible factors.* Both costs and benefits tend to have intangible features. The tangible costs and benefits tend to be historical and are backed by data or solid price quotations from vendors. Many of the benefits are expected in the future, however, and are very difficult to measure. Such benefits include expected increases in market share, improved customer service, and better corporate image. These would all have a significant effect on the corporation's bottom line, but guessing exactly what that effect would be is challenging at best.

- *Hidden outcomes.* Other aspects of information technology projects often involve unexpected results. Information technology projects can affect organizational power. New projects can change the power specific groups may have held in the past, which can have a negative effect on the teamwork of the organization. Information technology also includes components of the organization's communications network. Different elements of the organization can often adopt projects that affect the organizational communications network without this effect being considered. This can result in duplication of efforts or development of barriers between groups within the organization. Computers can make work more productive and more attractive. But they also can change work roles to emphasize skills in which specific employees have no training, making them feel less productive.

    Often times, failure to identify the effect of projects is not noticed until project implementation. At that stage, the problems created are more difficult to deal with. It is important to consider the systems aspects of projects and try to predict how the project will change how people do their jobs. Thorough user involvement can make project effect more obvious, as well as easier to reconcile and convince users of the project's benefits.

- *The changing nature of information technology.* There are many excellent applications of computer technology to aid businesses. But a major problem is that technology is highly dynamic. Some information systems projects take years to implement. This can, and often has, resulted in installation of a new system after it is outdated by even newer technology. McLeod and Smith[2] suggest a maximum of nine months between management approval and project component construction in information systems projects.

Selection Practice

Hinton and Kaye[3] surveyed 50 members of a professional organization whose members were responsible for appraising key organizational investments. Methods used for information technology projects were appraised and compared with projects in other areas (e.g., operations, marketing, training). Treatment of a project as a capital investment involves cost/benefit analysis to establish profitability. Treatment as a revenue-related project does not require cost/benefit analysis, because the project is expected to foster key organizational goals and the benefits are recognized as being difficult to measure accurately. Table 2–1 gives the results of this survey.

Information technology projects tended to be treated as a capital investment. The following financial techniques have often been used:

1. Payback.
2. Discounted cash flow.
3. Cost/benefit analysis.

Each of these methods will be demonstrated in this chapter. Decision makers treat information technology investment more like operations projects with measurable profitability requirements, or **tangible benefits,** than the revenue-based appraisals appropriate for training and marketing. *Operations investments focus on efficiency-related measures. Conversely, marketing investments are usually viewed in terms of their expected effect on improving competitive position or increasing*

TABLE 2–1   Project Investment Treatment by Environment

| | Investment Treated as | | |
Investment Type	Capital (%)	Mixed (%)	Revenue (%)
Training	0	1	99
Marketing	4	9	87
Information technology	**39**	**41**	**20**
Operations	58	31	11

Source: Adapted from M. Hinton and R. Kaye, "Investing in Information Technology: A Lottery?" *Management Accounting* 74, no. 10 (November 1996), p. 52.

market share. For example, the capital approach was found very appropriate for hardware proposals, but difficulties were encountered when justifying software purchases. **Intangible benefits** such as competitive advantage or improved practices tended to be disregarded because they are hard to quantify. The most commonly cited justification for project adoption was reduction in expenses, usually in payroll. The second most common justification involved the subjective aspect of accomplishing some strategic objective. For example, in the health care industry, intangible benefits cited were enhanced patient care and satisfaction, quicker response times to customers, and the need to satisfy governmental regulations.

Simms[4] argued that focus on bottom-line justification misleads companies with respect to evaluation of information technology investment. Net present value masks some of the true value of information technology proposals. On the other hand, some projects that have a low effect on corporate performance often appear attractive in cost/benefit analyses because cost/benefit analysis emphasizes those features most easily measured. The value of information technology projects is in making organizations more competitive, increasing customer satisfaction, and operating more effectively. These are the sometimes intangible strategic benefits that are often disregarded because they were not measurable.[5]

Information systems projects involve risks from a number of sources. Most of these risks have to do with estimating the time for a specific organization to accomplish required work. The amount of time needed for a project, on average, depends on a number of factors, including the following:

1. Project manager ability.
2. Experience with this type of application.
3. Experience with the programming environment.
4. Experience with the language or system used.
5. Familiarity with modern programming practices.
6. Availability of critical equipment, software, and programming language.
7. Completeness of project team (all team members on board).
8. Personnel turnover.
9. Project team size.
10. Relative control of project manager over project team.[6]

Of these factors, probably the most important is the ability of the project manager. Experience can take a variety of forms, as indicated by items 2 through 4. Familiarity with modern programming practices concerns exposure to current best practices. These items are a checklist of characteristics that should be at minimum acceptable levels. If satisfactory ratings are not assigned for all items, there may be doubt about this organization's ability to complete this particular project.

Cost/benefit analysis should consider costs over the entire life cycle of the project. Simms stated that life-cycle costs are roughly four times the development costs for most information systems projects.[7] But these long-range costs are much less predictable and therefore often not included in cost/benefit analyses.

Simms also noted that many companies tie up valuable developmental resources on low-cost, unevaluated projects. A comprehensive information technology management program needs to evaluate the costs and benefits, strategic
effects, risk, and life-cycle costs of all of its projects. Simms saw an evolutionary
progression in information technology management, with firms starting with conventional cost/benefit evaluation.[8] When this stage is mastered, firms tend to implement risk analysis along with cost/benefit analysis. Finally, firms add
consideration of strategic, intangible benefits. This final approach was said to provide up to 50 percent higher returns.

Corcoran[9] argued that more accurate cost estimates would be obtained if the
information technology department estimated costs, and more accurate benefits
would be obtained by having the users estimate benefits. Letting users know the
costs of proposed projects could lead to more rational decision making because
users will weed out projects that are not worth the cost. Further, users have been
seen to be more realistic in their expectations after seeing the costs of various levels of performance.

Another issue involves who should do the estimating. In construction, a common practice is to have those who will be responsible for implementing the project do the estimation. This is in a competitive bidding environment, where there
is great danger inherent in estimates that are too low. The motivation is for these
estimators to be very cautious. This tends to result in safe estimates considering
every possible risk, which is another way of saying that it results in inflated estimates. (Inflating estimates is how you cope with risk at the estimation stage.) In
the information systems field, there is far more work to do than capacity to do it.
Therefore, the environment is less competitive. While information systems consulting is rapidly growing, in the private sector competition is based more on negotiation and perceived quality than competitive bidding on price. Therefore,
estimators do not have the motivation to consider all risks. De Marco[10] reported
that software developers who estimate their own performance tend to be optimistic. De Marco suggested having one group estimate a project and a different
group build it, which would avoid personal biases. This system may not catch as
much of the risk associated with a project unless some performance pressure were
put on the estimator.

Reasons for adopting an information technology project, according to
Corcoran,[11] are as follows:

- Cost cutting
- Cost avoidance
- Revenue maintenance
- Revenue enhancement
- Entering a new market
- Gaining market share

These reasons include soft benefits that are important but difficult to accurately
quantify, such as developing market share. Federal Express uses a system to cate-

gorize its information technology projects for different evaluative treatment.[12] Projects with a strategic effect were recognized as being at a disadvantage when cost/benefit analysis is applied. Strategic projects were critical to business improvements, however, so they were viewed as necessary investments. Required projects are tasks that the company has to do to stay in business, such as calculating payroll and complying with regulations, and must be adopted regardless of cost. The remaining project proposals are rigorously analyzed for their return on investment (ROI) using cost/benefit analysis. Projects in this category that fail to meet the firm's ROI standard are held in limbo until better ways of implementing them are found.

Information systems projects involve significant investment on the part of firms. Efficient management of these investments is critical to a firm's success. However, it is very difficult to accurately assess the costs and benefits involved in most information technology projects. Many companies simply disregard important intangible factors because they involve high levels of uncertainty and even speculation. But there are many important intangible factors involved in assessing the worth of information technology project proposals. Value analysis or multiple criteria analysis offer means of considering such factors.

Project Evaluation Techniques

A number of methods exist to evaluate project proposals: Selecting the best option available, designing an ideal option, and rank-ordering options are several such methods. This section demonstrates some of the most widely used methods and shows how other methods can be used to consider other factors describing expected project performance.

General Project Selection

Cabral-Cardoso and Payne[13] surveyed research and development decision makers in the United Kingdom about their use of formal selection methods in project selection decisions. The study, based on 152 samples, asked each decision maker to identify familiarity based on use for 18 different methods. Table 2–2 lists the most commonly cited methods in the survey (methods rank ordered by percentage use). Economic and financial analyses include payback (determining the expected time until investment is recovered) and cost/benefit analysis. Net present value and internal rate of return extend cost/benefit analysis to consider the time value of money, which is appropriate when projects are lengthy (three years or more).

Checklists describe criteria of importance and their minimum acceptable levels of requirement. Screening is a variant of checklists and eliminates projects that do not meet minimum estimated performance standards on specific measures. Project profiles describe the performance of each project based on certain criteria so that the decision maker can see each project's strengths and weaknesses. Scoring and rating models are a simple form of multicriteria analysis in which measures are obtained on each criterion of importance and then combined in some

TABLE 2–2   Common Methods Used in Project Selection Decisions

Method	Percentage of Users
Economic and Financial	
Payback analysis	68
Cost/benefit analysis	63
NPV/IRR	40
Multifactor Techniques	
Checklist	38
Project profile	26
Scoring rating models	26
Multicriteria decision models	11
Mathematical Programming	
Goal programming	18
Expert Systems	6

fashion. **Multicriteria decision models** are, in general, more formal than scoring and rating models, but they operate on essentially the same principle—identify criteria that are important, measure how well each project meets the criteria, and combine the results into some value score that can be used for ranking.

The last two types of methods are more specialized. Mathematical programming provides optimal solutions for a portfolio of projects, on any specific measure, subject to constraints, such as budget limits. Expert systems are usually sets of rules that implement a checklist approach in a thorough, systematic manner.

Information Systems Project Approval

Bacon[14] conducted a survey of 80 American, British, Australian, and New Zealand companies' practices in approving information systems technology projects. He provided a list of 15 criteria divided into financial, management, and development groupings. *Financial criteria* included net present value, internal rate of return, and payback methods as discussed earlier, as well as a profitability index and a budgetary constraint method. The accounting rate of return method, like payback, does not consider the time value of money. Its attractiveness is due in all likelihood to its being very simple and easy to understand. Another reason accounting rate of return is used is that managerial bonuses are often based on accounting rates of return.[15] Bacon's survey also included a profitability index, which is a variant of net present value analysis (as are rates of return).[16] The budgetary constraint method would adopt projects in order of rate of return until some budget limit was exceeded. This method can be optimized by using mathematical programming.

Five *management criteria* were listed: support of business objectives, response to competition, seeking better support to management decision making, consideration of probability, and satisfaction of legal requirements. Project proposals that support business objectives may not always be quantifiable, and accurate measurement of the impact on net present value is usually impractical. Support of management decision making reflects the importance of information technology as an objective in itself. Probability can sometimes be included with other criteria (in the form of expected value), but risk represents a fundamental consideration.

There were three *development criteria:* technical system requirements (projects needed for effective operation of the organization), introduction of new technology, and probability of project completion. We saw in Chapter 1 that probability of project completion on schedule is highly problematic.

The results of Bacon's survey of 203 companies are displayed in Table 2–3. The percentage of companies and percentage of projects are self-explanatory. The column for ranking by total project value compiled the responses of the ranking of a criterion in terms of overall value of projects to which it applies. This was intended to reflect each method's value in important cases.

TABLE 2–3

Criteria	Companies Using (%)	Projects to Which Applied (%)	Ranking by Total Project Value
Financial			
Budgetary constraint	68	64	8
Payback	61	51	5
Internal rate of return	54	54	2
Net present value	48	58	4
Accounting rate of return	16	47	10
Profitability index	8	47	14
Management			
Explicit business objectives	88	57	1
Support decision making	88	29	7
Legal/government requirements	71	13	13
Implicit business objectives	69	44	3
Response to competition	61	28	6
Probability of achieving benefits	46	63	9
Development			
Technical/system requirements	79	25	12
Introduce/learn new technology	60	13	15
Probability of project completion	31	62	11

Source: Adapted from C. J. Bacon, "The Use of Decision Criteria in Selection Information Systems/Technology Investments," *MIS Quarterly* 16, no. 3 (1992), pp. 335–53.

Among the financial criteria, the budgetary constraint method was reported to be used most often. Payback was the second most widely reported method. Firms with more projects used net present value (NPV) and internal rate of return (IRR) more often, providing one possible explanation for their higher ranking in the percentage of projects in which the method was applied and their higher ranking by total project value. Bacon found that 25 percent of these large organizations did not report any use of the **discounted cash flow** (net present value) methods. Among those firms that did use it, it was used primarily for evaluating large projects. IRR was used more often than NPV, despite the theoretical superiority of NPV. Bacon concluded that managers may be able to grasp the significance of IRR and that NPV involves many assumptions about discount rates that are not accurate. IRR and NPV were ranked highest, however, in the value of the projects analyzed. This indicates that their use tends to be reserved for larger projects. Accounting rate of return and profitability index were used by a small proportion of the companies.[17]

Of the management criteria, explicit business objectives was ranked first on all three measures. Many companies reported the criterion of support to decision making. The survey also indicates that information technology projects are often adopted to keep up with competition or to satisfy legal requirements. The need to keep up with competition is often expressed by the statement, "We cannot afford not to invest." The risk-related criterion of the probability of achieving benefits was reported by less than half of the companies surveyed. But of those who reported its use, Bacon stated that it was applied to 83 percent of the projects analyzed.[18]

The most commonly reported development criterion was technical/system requirements. Organizations may invest in upgraded information technology because their existing systems might be outdated or of insufficient capacity. A danger is that technical managers may deem it necessary to have state-of-the-art systems, an opinion possibly not shared by business managers. Companies in this case will have invested more in information technology than was merited by business needs. Justification based on introducing new technology can be subject to the same criticism. Often the probability of project completion is used as the basis for project adoption. While only 31 percent of the companies reported using probability of completion as a justification criterion, those who did were reported to apply it to more than 60 percent of their projects.

The rest of this chapter demonstrates most of the basic methods reported. The first method demonstrated is screening, a common form of the checklist method that can be and often is combined with other criteria.

Screening

Screening is a process that is very useful in cutting down the dimensions of the decision problem. The way in which screening operates can vary widely in details, but it essentially involves identifying those factors that are important, establishing a minimum level of importance, and eliminating those projects that fail on any one of these minimum standards. Obviously, if the standards are set too high, the decision problem disappears because no projects survive the screening. This is appropriate if the minimum standards reflect what management demands in return for their investment.

To demonstrate screening, assume that 100 information systems project proposals are received in a designated month. All of the projects were evidently worthwhile in someone's mind, but management must consider budgets and other resource limitations. Table 2–4 lists the criteria and minimum performance levels for acceptable projects. If any of the 100 proposed projects failed to meet all four of these standards, they would be rejected preemptively, which then reduces the number of proposed projects requiring more detailed analysis. This approach can be implemented by checklists, which give clearly defined standards on those areas of importance to management.

Screening is good at quickly weeding out those projects with unacceptable features. The negative side of screening is that trade-offs between very good features and these unacceptable features are disregarded. The willingness of decision makers to accept a lower ROI for projects with strategic importance is disregarded. For projects for which such trade-offs are not important, screening is a very efficient way to reduce the number of proposals to a more manageable number.

Earlier in the chapter, we gave a list of risk factors for information system projects. These could be implemented as a **checklist** by management to specify the minimum acceptable measures to be used to screen individual projects. Not all risk elements might apply for a given organization's checklist. An example checklist is given in Table 2–5. Checklists ensure implementation of policy limits. Checklists are a way to implement screening from the perspective of features management feels are important. The next step in analysis is to more directly compare alternative project proposals.

The intent of a **project profile** is to display how the project proposal compares with standards, as well as how the project compares with other proposals. Profiles have a benefit over screening limits because poor performance on one factor can be compensated for by strong performance on another factor. For instance, match with company strategic programs can be an important factor. There could be other project proposals that contribute nothing to the firm's strategic program, yet have an outstanding cost improvement for administrative work. This would be reflected in very strong performance on ROI. Conversely, another project may have a slightly negative ROI calculation but may involve entering a new field in which the firm wants to gain experience.

To demonstrate project profiles, assume a firm has a number of information projects proposed. This is generally a large list because of the many beneficial things information technology can do for organizations. Table 2–6 is a short list of six proposals, measured on resources used as well as benefits expected.

A profile displays the characteristics of individual projects. Estimated cost is needed to determine if available budget can support a project. The same is true for

TABLE 2–4   Screening

Expected return on investment	At least 30 percent
Qualified project team leadership	Available
Company has expertise in this area	Either company is experienced in this work, or company desires to gain this experience
Project completion time	Within 12 months

TABLE 2–5   Checklist

Factor	Minimum Standard
Project manager ability	Qualified manager available
Experience with this type of application	Have experience, or application is a strategically key new technology
Experience with the programming environment	Personnel with experience can be obtained
Experience with the language or system used	Personnel with experience can be obtained
Familiarity with modern programming practices	If not, training is available
Availability of critical equipment, software, and programming language	Each critical component available
Completeness of project team (all team members assigned)	Key personnel identified and agree to work; support personnel widely available

TABLE 2–6   Project Profiles

Project Identifier	Estimated Cost	Systems Analysts	Cash Flow This Period	NPV/Cost Ratio	Key to Strategy
A265	$230,000	3	$100,000	0.43	No
A801	370,000	4	− 190,000	0.51	Yes
A921	790,000	5	360,000	0.46	No
B622	480,000	3	− 52,000	0.11	Yes
B837	910,000	7	− 200,000	0.22	Yes
C219	410,000	3	170,000	0.41	No

other scarce resources, such as systems analysts in this case. Although Table 2–6 presents the results in tabular form, graphical displays and ratios are often valuable to give a measure with which relative performance can be measured. For measures such as NPV/cost ratio, cutoff levels can be used to screen out projects. For instance, a 40 percent return on estimated cost in net present terms might be desired. Projects B622 and B837 are both below this limit and thus might be screened out. However, both of these projects are listed as key to the organization's strategy, and management might be willing to accept lower return for the potential for advancing organizational strategy. When resources are potentially scarce, such as budget limits and systems analysts in this example, optimization can be used, as in Santhanam and Kyparisis[19]

Cost/Benefit Analysis

Cost/benefit analysis seeks to identify accurate measures of benefits and costs in monetary terms, and uses the ratio of benefits to costs. (The term "benefit/cost ratio" seems more appropriate and is sometimes used, but most people refer to "cost/benefit analysis.") For projects involving long time frames, considering the net present value of benefits and costs is important.

Cost/Benefit Example

Assume that a firm is considering the purchase of a new automated machine, which they expect to be more efficient. The firm produces 20,000 units per year of a product that sells for $2 per unit. There is an expected demand that would allow the firm to sell up to 30,000 units per year in a growing market, but existing machinery (obtained 10 years ago and totally depreciated) is only capable of producing 20,000 units per year. The quality of the existing machine has declined, and about 10 percent of production must be discarded as waste. This existing machinery produces the product at a unit cost of $1.50. It could be used for another 10 years, with an expected rejection rate of 10 percent.

The benefits of owning the new machine are an expected reduction in unit cost to $1.20, with no rejected product due to the application of computer technology. The new automated machine has a capacity of 40,000 units per year. Purchase price is $90,000, with an expected life of 10 years. Operating the machinery would involve the same overhead and labor expense as the old machine, but there would be an installation and training expense of $10,000, incurred within three months of initial operations. The company has a marginal value of capital of 15 percent per year.

The cost/benefit calculation for the new machine requires identification of benefits in monetary units. Use of net present value requires identification of the timing of monetary exchanges. The benefit from the new machine consists of increased production at lower unit cost. Adopting the new machine would increase production because its nominal capacity is double that of the old machinery, and its quality performance is such that there are no discarded products. This would enable the new machine to easily meet the annual demand of 30,000 units per year.

A comparison of the old operation versus the new is given in Table 2–7. The increased contribution to profit per year would be $24,000 − $6,000 = $18,000 for 10 years. Using the new machine would result in added costs of $100,000, incurred at the outset of the project.

The nominal cost/benefit ratio (disregarding the time value of money) is 10 × $18,000/$100,000 = 1.8. This indicates that the project is worthwhile, in that the extra initial expenses of $100,000 would be exceeded by expected benefits by 80 percent. The cost/benefit ratio is easily interpreted. If the ratio exceeds 1.0, the project would be profitable. The ratio can be used as a basis for rank-ordering projects, with higher ratios more attractive.

Payback

Another measure of value is to identify the time for an investment to be repaid. In this case, the investment of $100,000 (viewing the installation as part of the investment) would be recovered in $100,000/18,000 = 5.6$ years. **Payback** is a rough estimate, but it presents a view of the transaction that is very understandable and important to managers.

Another time-related factor is the need for cash flow. One alternative may be superior to another on the net present value of the total life cycle of the project. However, cost/benefit analysis does not consider the effect of negative cash flow. For instance, in our machinery example, the cash flow by machine would be as given in Table 2–8. The Net Benefit column is calculated by subtracting the old machine's cash flow from the new machine's cash flow. In the first year, this is negative because of the high investment cost of the new machine. In Years 2

TABLE 2–7   Comparison of Old and New Machinery

Benefits	Old Machine	New Machine
Revenues	20,000 units/year × (1 − .1 waste) × $2 = $36,000 per year	30,000 units/year × (1 − 0 waste) × $2 = $60,000 per year
Less unit costs	20,000 units × $1.50 = $30,000 per year	30,000 units × $1.20 = $36,000 per year
Net	+ $6,000 per year	+ $24,000 per year
Costs		
Purchase	0	$90,000
Setup	0	$10,000

TABLE 2–8   Payback

Year	Old Machine	New Machine	Net Benefit	Cumulative
1	$6,000	$24,000 − $100,000	−$82,000	−$82,000
2	6,000	24,000	+ 18,000	− 64,000
3	6,000	24,000	+ 18,000	− 46,000
4	6,000	24,000	+ 18,000	− 28,000
5	6,000	24,000	+ 18,000	− 10,000
6	6,000	24,000	+ 18,000	+ 8,000

through 6, however, the new machine provides a positive net benefit relative to the old machine. The new machine gains a nominal advantage by the end of Year 6, but $100,000 has been sacrificed at the beginning. One of the most common reasons for business failures in the United States is lack of cash flow. Webb[20] examined the trade-off between cash flow and net present value in economic analysis. In this case, if the firm has cash flow difficulties, the investment would be less attractive than if it had adequate cash reserves.

The Time Value of Money

We can modify the cost/benefit ratio by considering the **time value of money** (discounted cash flow). In this project, for instance, the nominal expected gains of $180,000 are spread out over 10 years, while the extra costs of $100,000 are all incurred at the beginning. This is not an attractive situation; using the $100,000 up front would mean that the company would not be able to adopt some other investments (and maybe even force the firm to borrow money). The marginal value of money for the firm is 15 percent per year. **Net present value** converts a time stream of money back to its worth in today's terms (or in terms of the project's start, or any other specific time of reference).

Table 2–9 shows the changes in cash flow between the old machine and the new machine (shown in the net difference column, calculated as the new machine value minus the old machine value). Each year's net change in cash flow is discounted by the discount rate of 1.15 per year to the t'th power, where t is the time period. Note that initial expenses are treated as occurring at the end of Year 0. This has the effect of dividing by $1.15^0 = 1$, or stating that the net value of initial expenses is equal to their current value.

Viewed in this light, relative to obtaining a return of 15 percent per year on alternative investments, obtaining the new machine would be unattractive; it

TABLE 2–9   Net Present Value

Year (t)	Old Machine	New Machine	Net Difference	Divide by 1.15^t
0	0	−$100,000	−$100,000	−$100,000
1	$6,000	24,000	+ 18,000	+ 15,652
2	6,000	24,000	+ 18,000	+ 13,610
3	6,000	24,000	+ 18,000	+ 11,835
4	6,000	24,000	+ 18,000	+ 10,292
5	6,000	24,000	+ 18,000	+ 8,949
6	6,000	24,000	+ 18,000	+ 7,782
7	6,000	24,000	+ 18,000	+ 6,767
8	6,000	24,000	+ 18,000	+ 5,884
9	6,000	24,000	+ 18,000	+ 5,117
10	6,000	24,000	+ 18,000	+ 4,449
			Net present value	−$ 9,662

would be equivalent to writing a check for $9,662 today. If there were some alternative investment on which the company could obtain 15 percent on their $100,000 initially invested, they would be ahead by adopting the alternative investment to the tune of almost $10,000 over a 10-year period.

The cost/benefit ratio using net present values of benefits and costs requires decomposing the net present value into its components for benefits and costs. The net present value of the benefits would be the sum of discounted values for Years 1 through 10 in this case, or +$90,338. The discounted costs are $100,000, because all of the costs were incurred at the beginning of the project. The ratio of benefits to costs is therefore $90,338/$100,000 = 0.90. Because this ratio is less than 1.0, the investment is not attractive at a discount rate of 1.15.

A related concept is **internal rate of return (IRR),** which is the marginal value of capital for which the net present value of a stream of cash flow would break even, or equal zero. In this case, the internal rate of return amounts to 1.124, or a 12.4 percent average return. Therefore, the net present value at 15 percent is negative, and the new machine does not appear to be attractive.

Other Factors

There are a number of complications that can be brought into the calculation of cost/benefit ratios. One of the most obvious limitations of the method is that benefits, and even costs, can involve high levels of uncertainty. The element of chance can be included in cost/benefit calculations by using expected values. For instance, the demand for production output appears to be increasing. Therefore, using an expected demand of 30,000 units per year is probably conservative. Demand could very well continue to increase. The expected value calculation can be quite complicated in its purest form, consisting of identifying all possible demands for a given year and associating accurate probabilities to each outcome. Instead of getting involved in such a speculative and detailed exercise, most managers do what we did—assume a conservative value. But it should be recognized that there is added benefit to the new machine in its ability to expand. If this expansion capacity is not considered in the cost/benefit calculation, the new machine option is not accurately evaluated.

For instance, if growth in demand is expected to increase at the rate of 1,000 units per year, this form of benefit for the new machine could be reflected as follows, where an extra ($2 − $1.20) × 1,000 units/year = +$800 in gain is obtained each year. As before, net difference is calculated as the new machine cash flow minus the old machine cash flow (see Table 2–10). This would involve a cost/benefit ratio in net present value terms of $103,921/$100,000 = 1.04, and an ROI of 1.160, greater than the company cost-of-capital of 15 percent.

The cost/benefit ratio does not reflect intangible benefits unless they are presented in monetary terms. Cost/benefit analyses have included measurements for intangible items, but they tend to be given lower values because of the uncertainty involved in their estimates. Detailed analyses of the decision maker's willingness to pay for intangible factors have been conducted, but they can be time

TABLE 2–10   Net Present Value

Year (t)	Old Machine	New Machine	Net Difference	Divide by 1.15^t
0	0	−$100,000	−$100,000	−$100,000
1	$6,000	24,000	+ 18,000	+ 15,652
2	6,000	24,800	+ 18,800	+ 14,216
3	6,000	25,600	+ 19,600	+ 12,887
4	6,000	26,400	+ 20,400	+ 11,664
5	6,000	27,200	+ 21,200	+ 10,540
6	6,000	28,000	+ 22,000	+ 9,511
7	6,000	28,800	+ 22,800	+ 8,571
8	6,000	29,600	+ 23,600	+ 7,715
9	6,000	30,400	+ 24,400	+ 6,936
10	6,000	31,200	+ 25,200	+ 6,229
			Net present value	+$ 3,921

consuming and less than convincing. Governments have encountered some problems in applying cost/benefit analysis to public works such as: (1) evaluating the benefit of recreational facilities and (2) placing a dollar value on human life.[21] For example, when a dam is built, there clearly is benefit obtained from providing many citizens much improved fishing and water sports. (There is also added cost if citizens are deprived of the opportunity to view some historical sites that will be flooded because of the dam's construction.) The approach usually taken has been to place some dollar value on recreation, based on some very insubstantial measures. The evaluation of human life has also been tackled by economists, who have applied things such as the net present value of the expected earnings of those whose lives are expected to be lost in some proposed investment project. This of course involves high levels of speculation as well, because the calculation assumes certain ages, assumes that the only value of a human is what they earn, and disregards who pays and who benefits.

If a firm was threatened with a severe monetary penalty for not complying with a governmental regulation with respect to environmental pollution or safe working conditions, a net present value analysis might well lead to the conclusion that it would be rational to pay the penalty and avoid improving operations. For instance, assume that a blast furnace is pouring out black matter at a phenomenal rate that the government finds terribly offensive. Governmental regulations call for a penalty of $10,000,000 if the pollution source is not cleaned up within one year. Hard-core cost/benefit analysis would identify the cost of cleaning up the facility, which might involve an expense of $12,000,000 in equipment and installation and an added cost of operations of $5,000,000 per year over the next eight years, the remaining life of the equipment. At a discount rate of 12 percent per year, the net present value of benefits and costs would be as shown in Table 2–11. The Net column shows discounted values for benefits and costs. Totals are given at the bottom of the table.

Companies must examine cost/benefit ratios in respect to issues such as environmental pollution from factories. They must compare the cost of paying government penalties versus facility renovation.

TABLE 2–11   Net Present Value

Year	Benefits	Net	Costs	Net
1	$10,000,000	$8,928,571	$17,000,000	$15,178,571
2	—		5,000,000	3,985,969
3	—		5,000,000	3,558,901
4	—		5,000,000	3,177,590
5	—		5,000,000	2,837,134
6	—		5,000,000	2,533,156
7	—		5,000,000	2,261,746
8	—		5,000,000	2,019,416
Total		$8,928,571		$35,552,483

The table shows that the ratio of net present benefits to net present costs is $8,928,571/ $35,552,483 = 0.25, well below 1.0, indicating that the rational decision maker would pay the fine and keep operating as is. But the government did not impose the fine limit for the purpose of raising money. They imposed the fine as a means to coerce polluters to clean up operations. The U.S. Congress has no trouble adding extra zeroes to penalties. If the firm continues to pollute, it is not too hard to imagine the penalty being raised in the future to some much larger figure. There have been actual cases similar to this scenario, where within three years the penalty was raised to much larger values, providing a much different cost/benefit ratio. Benefits are often difficult to forecast.

To demonstrate intangible benefits in our machine investment case, one of the clear advantages the new system has is in its higher level of quality output. The loss of discarded products is included in the analysis. But poor production quality results in more than just identification of products not passing testing limits and rejecting them. Quality comes on a continuous scale. The older machine will, in all likelihood, include production of a number of products that barely pass test limits and don't contain desired levels of quality. The customer will accept them, but slowly over time a reputation for inferior workmanship will result. The new machine should improve the company's image with respect to quality. Placing a dollar value on image is pure speculation. Rigorous proponents of cost/benefit analysis disregard such immeasurable benefits as "soft" and not worthy of hard-core analysis. Managers with more vision recognize that there is a relative advantage for the new machine that is not reflected in the cost/benefit analysis.

An additional benefit of the new machine is that it is more flexible. It has the capacity to respond to larger markets because it has added capacity. At the moment of analysis, there is just the one customer. We have just considered the effect of increased demand on the part of this customer, but there might be additional sources of sales in the future. This again would be highly speculative. A hard approach would require the decision maker to identify a specific expected increase in demand. A soft approach would list flexibility as a measure of importance. There could also be other advantages that are intangible, such as safety of workers, effect on market share, or replenishing capital equipment so that old facilities do not fall apart, disrupting the ability of the firm to conduct business.

Value Analysis

Keen[22] proposed **value analysis** as an alternative to cost/benefit analysis in the evaluation of proposed information system projects. These projects, clearly attractive to business firms, suffer in that their benefits are often heavily intangible. For instance, decision support systems are meant to provide decision makers with more complete information for decision making. But what is the exact dollar value of improved decision making? We all expect the success of firms to be closely tied to effective decision making, but there is no rational, accurate measure of better decision makeup.

Value analysis was presented as a way to separate the benefits measured in intangible terms from costs, which are expected to be more accurately measurable. Those tangible benefits as well as costs can be dealt with in net present terms, which would provide a price tag for proposed projects. The value of the benefits would be descriptive, with the intent of giving the decision maker accurate descriptions of what they were getting, along with the net present price. The decision would then be converted to a shopping decision. Many of us buy automobiles, despite the fact that the net present cost of owning an automobile is negative. We need automobiles in many areas for transportation. But small economy vehicles provide that utility. Most automobiles are sold for other reasons. Automobiles provide many intangible benefits, such as making the driver look very sporty, letting

TABLE 2–12   **Value of Intangible Benefits**

	Old Machine	*New Machine*
Working conditions with respect to safety	Risky	Very safe
Effect on market share	Vulnerable on quality	High quality
Capital equipment	Deteriorating	In good condition
Net present cost of other factors	0	$9,662

the driver speed over the countryside, and letting the driver transport those they would like to impress. The dollar value of these intangible benefits is a matter of willingness to pay, which can be identified in monetary terms by observing the purchasing behavior of individuals. This measurement requires some effort and is different for each individual.

In terms of our machine project, the intangible values can be identified by criterion, or measure of value to the decision maker, as shown in Table 2–12. Value analysis would consist of presenting the decision maker with the intangible comparisons in performance and then placing the decision in the context of whether or not the decision maker thought the improvements provided by the new machine were worth about $10,000. If, in the decision maker's judgment, these intangible benefits were clearly worth $10,000 or more, the new machine should be acquired. On the other hand, if the decision maker is unwilling to pay $10,000 for these improvements, the old machine should be retained. Taking value analysis one more step, to quantify these intangible benefits in terms of value (not in terms of dollars) takes us to multiple criteria analysis.

Multiple Objectives

Profit has long been viewed as the determining objective of a business. However, as society becomes more complex, and as the competitive environment develops, businesses are finding that they need to consider multiple objectives. While short-term profit remains important, long-term factors such as market maintenance, product quality, and development of productive capacity often conflict with measurable short-term profit.

Conflicts

Conflicts are inherent in most interesting decisions. In business, *profit* is a valuable concentration point for many decision makers because it has the apparent advantage of providing a measure of worth. Minimizing *risk* becomes a second dimension for decision making. There are cash flow needs that become important in some circumstances. Businesses need developed markets to survive. The effect of *advertising expenditure* is often very difficult to forecast, yet decision makers must consider it. *Capital replenishment* is another decision factor that requires consideration of trade-offs. The greatest short-term profit will normally be obtained by delaying reinvestment in capital equipment. Many U.S. companies have been known to cut back capital investment to appear reasonably profitable to investors.

Labor policies can also have an effect on long-range profit. In the short-term, profit will generally be improved by holding the line on wage rates and risking a high labor turnover. There are costs that are not obvious, however, in such a policy. First, there is a training expense involved with a high turnover environment. The experience of the members of an organization can be one of its most valuable assets. Second, it is difficult for employees to maintain a positive attitude when their experience is that short-term profit is always placed ahead of employee welfare. Innovative ideas are often provided by the people involved with the grass roots of an organization—the work force.

This variety of objectives presents decision makers with the need to balance conflicting objectives. We present the simple multiattribute rating technique (SMART), an easy-to-use method to aid selection decisions with multiple objectives.

Multiple Criteria Analysis

Multiple criteria analysis considers benefits on a variety of scales without directly converting them to some common scale such as dollars. The method is not at all perfect (there are many variants of multiple criteria analysis[23]), but it does provide a way to demonstrate to decision makers the relative positive and negative features of alternatives, and it provides a means of quantifying the preferences of decision makers.

Perhaps the easiest application of multiple criteria analysis is the **simple multiattribute rating theory (SMART)**,[24] which identifies the relative importance of criteria in terms of weights and then measures the relative performance of each alternative on each criterion in terms of scores. We first explain the scoring process.

Scores.   Scores in SMART can be used to convert performances (subjective or objective) to a 0 to 1 scale, where 0 represents the worst acceptable performance level in the mind of the decision maker and 1 represents the ideal, or possibly the best, performance desired. Note that these ratings are subjective, or a function of individual preference. Scores for the criteria given for our machine decision are listed in Table 2–13.

The safety score was assigned assuming that the new machine would provide working conditions as ideal as possible. The score for the old machine is an evaluation expressing the decision maker's judgment of just how unsafe the old machine is. A rating of 0.3 indicates that it is very unsafe. With respect to market share, the new machine would provide as good an effect on market share as any machine the decision maker could imagine. The old machine would involve significant risk of losing market share, rated at 0.5. Obtaining the new machine would place the company in an excellent position with respect to capital equipment, while the old machine would be much worse. Finally, the cost of the old machine is much better, and in fact lower than any imaginable alternative, while the new machine's net present cost of $10,000 is rated as fair.

TABLE 2–13   Machine Example Criteria Scores

	Old Machine	New Machine
Working conditions with respect to safety	0.3	1.0
Effect on market share	0.5	1.0
Capital equipment	0.4	1.0
Net present cost	1.0	0.6

TABLE 2–14   First Estimate of Weights for Machine Example

	Worst Measure	Best Measure	Assigned Value
Section I, Rank Order			
Effect on market share	Poor quality product	High quality	
Net present cost	Worst expected	0	
Working conditions with respect to safety	Very risky	Very safe	
Capital equipment	Need replacement now	In mint condition	
Section II, Assigned Value			
Capital equipment	Need replacement now	In mint condition	10
Working conditions with respect to safety	Very risky	Very safe	15
Net present cost	Worst expected	0	25
Effect on market share	Poor quality product	High quality	40
Section III, First Estimate			
Capital equipment	$10/90 = 0.11$		
Working conditions with respect to safety	$15/90 = 0.17$		
Net present cost	$25/90 = 0.28$		
Effect on market share	$40/90 = 0.44$		

Weights.   The next phase of the analysis ties these ratings together into an overall value function by obtaining the relative weight of each criterion. In order to give the decision maker a reference about what exactly is being compared, the relative range between best and worst on each scale for each criterion should be explained.[25]

There are many methods that can be used to determine these weights. In SMART, the process begins with rank-ordering the four criteria. A possible ranking for a specific decision maker might be as given in Table 2–14. Two estimates of weights can be obtained. The first assigns the least important criterion 10 points and assesses the relative importance of each of the other criteria on that basis.

These add to 90. The first estimate of weights would divide each relative importance by 90, yielding the results shown in Section III. The total will of course add to 1.0. The implication is that effect on market share (over the range of values considered) is four times as important as maintaining capital equipment and about 1.5 times as important as net present cost.

The second estimate of weights (Table 2–15) is obtained by looking at relative importance from the opposite perspective. The most important criterion is assigned 100 points, and the others are evaluated on that basis. This is supposed to be an independent check of the prior estimate, although relative order should be maintained in both assessments. This total is 200. The second estimate of weights is therefore obtained by dividing each value by 200. Again, the total will add to 1.0. the next step is to compromise if necessary between these two estimates as shown in Table 2–16. The last criterion can be used to make sure that the sum of the compromise weights adds to 1.00.

Value Score.   The next step of the SMART method is to obtain value scores for each alternative by multiplying each score on each criterion for an alternative by that criterion's weight, and adding these products by alternative (see Table 2–17).

TABLE 2–15   Second Estimate of Weights

	Worst Measure	*Best Measure*	*Assigned Value*
Sections I and II			
Effect on market share	Poor quality product	High quality	100
Net present cost	Worst expected	0	50
Working conditions with respect to safety	Very risky	Very safe	30
Capital equipment	Need replacement now	In mint condition	20
Section III			
Effect on market share	100/200 = 0.50		
Net present cost	50/200 = 0.25		
Working conditions with respect to safety	30/200 = 0.15		
Capital equipment	20/200 = 0.10		

TABLE 2–16   Compromise between Estimates

	First Estimate	*Second Estimate*	*Compromise*
Effect on market share	0.44	0.50	0.47
Net present cost	0.28	0.25	0.26
Working conditions with respect to safety	0.17	0.15	0.16
Capital equipment	0.11	0.10	0.11

This value score provides a relative score that can be used to select (take the alternative with the highest value score) or to rank order (by value score). In this case, the new machine would be indicated as better fitting the preferences of the decision maker.

Hobbs and Horn[26] compared cost/benefit analysis and multiple criteria analysis (see Table 2–18).

Other Multiple Criteria Methods.   Note that there are many other approaches implementing roughly the same idea. The best known is multiattribute utility theory,[27] which uses more sophisticated (but not necessarily more accurate) methods

TABLE 2–17   Value Scores for Each Criterion

Criterion	Weight	Old Machine	New Machine
Working conditions with respect to safety	0.16	× 0.3 = 0.048	× 1.0 = 0.160
Effect on market share	0.47	× 0.5 = 0.235	× 1.0 = 0.470
Capital equipment	0.11	× 0.4 = 0.044	× 1.0 = 0.110
Net present cost	0.26	× 1.0 = 0.260	× 0.6 = 0.156
Value score by alternative (sum)		0.587	0.896

TABLE 2–18   Comparison of Cost/Benefit and Multiple Criteria Analysis

Cost/Benefit Analysis

Strengths	Based on well-developed economic theory
	Purports to measure values for public in general
	Results can be validated by repetition
	Values for intangibles can be established and applied generally
Weaknesses	Basic economic assumptions not universally accepted: Who pays? Who benefits?
	Fundamental value judgments (like the value of a life) made by analysts, not stakeholders
	Most valid methods difficult or impossible to apply in practice

Multiple Criteria Analysis

Strengths	Learning and user understanding emphasized
	Trade-offs more explicit
	Values obtained directly from stakeholders
	Dominated alternatives (another alternative as good or better on all measures, strictly better on at least one measure) easily identified
	Decision decomposed into manageable subcomponents
	Assumptions documented
Weaknesses	Too much data to digest
	Results difficult to validate by repetition
	Difficult to obtain stakeholders representing community at large
	Improper application of methods can distort results
	Inconsistencies in value judgments across stakeholders

to obtain both scores and weights. The analytic hierarchy process[28] is another well-known approach.

Budget Optimization

Optimization models are an additional class of analytic tools. *Linear programming models* can and have been used to identify a portfolio of projects, staying within specified budgets and resource limits. *Goal programming models* provide a way to incorporate managerial choices of trade-offs among competing objectives, such as maximizing net present value of the portfolio, maximizing after-tax profit, or distributing projects across various departments of the organization. Further information about project selection goal programming models can be obtained from Santhanam and Kyparisis.[29]

Detailed explanation of linear programming calls for far more space than is available here. There are many software tools available to support its application. In project management, the most commonly used approach is zero-one linear programming, where each project can be defined as a variable that either is or is not adopted (takes on a value of either 0 or 1). This form of linear programming model is very suitable for imposing a budget limit. In fact, limits of many resources can be included in the model, as demonstrated in the following example.

A company committee is in charge of administering new computer projects with a budget of $2,500,000 to fund projects. There are four company departments (A, B, C, and D) that have submitted project proposals. Each proposal includes estimates of total cost, number of systems analysts required, and number of systems programmers required. Benefit measures include estimated cash flow for the next year, estimated after-tax profit for the next year, and net present value. There are 12 systems analysts available, and six special programmers who could be devoted to these projects. The board of directors has given minimum required limits for next year's cash flow and after-tax profits. Cash flow from these projects is to be at least $300,000. After-tax profits from these projects is to be at least $200,000. The board would like to maximize the net present value of the selected projects, subject to the preceding limits, and the restriction that projects must be either adopted or not adopted. Table 2–19 summarizes this example.

The letter in the project name indicates the department that submitted the project. An additional limit, for political purposes (or fairness, if you prefer), is that each of these four departments receive funding for at least one project. Solutions can be generated for different budget levels (for instance, from $2.5 million down to $2 million in increments of $100,000) to maximize net present value, and measures for all other features the committee considered important can be obtained as well. The initial solution is for a budget of $2.5 million. The linear programming model is shown in Figure 2–1.

The linear programming solution obtains a net present value total of $1.1 million, expending only $2.3 million. Therefore, there is no need to run models with budget limits greater than $2.3 million. The solution with a budget limit of $2.2

TABLE 2–19   Proposed Projects with Measures

	Project Cost $(= \$ \times 10^3)$	Estimated Analysts (People)	Systems Programmers (People)	Cash Flow	After-Tax Profit $(= \$ \times 10^3)$	Net Present Value $(= \$ \times 10^3)$
A01	$230	3	0	50	$ 20	$100
A02	370	4	1	75	30	190
A03	180	2	0	40	20	80
A04	90	1	2	10	10	30
A05	570	4	1	160	70	220
B06	750	3	0	240	110	390
B07	370	3	1	100	40	180
B08	250	3	0	55	20	140
B09	190	2	0	30	10	90
B10	200	1	2	0	10	90
C11	310	2	0	50	20	70
C12	430	3	1	125	10	10
C13	680	3	0	205	100	170
C14	550	1	3	0	50	100
D15	290	1	1	100	40	140
D16	200	1	1	50	20	90
D17	150	1	2	0	10	110

million is given in Figure 2–2. This solution funds a lot more jobs, and gets almost as much net present value, for only $2.13 million in budget. The solution with a limit of $2.1 million is given in Figure 2–3. This solution generates $1.03 million in net present value for a budget of $2.02 million. The solution with a budget limit of $2 million is given in Figure 2–4.

Cutting the budget to $2 million reduces the number of projects to six. Twelve analysts are still required, but the number of programmers required is reduced to three. This solution has a slightly lower cash flow and after-tax profit than do the solutions with greater budgets. The maximum net present value obtainable with this budget is $1 million.

Summary

We have reviewed some of the primary methods used to evaluate project proposals. Screening provides a way to simplify the decision problem by focusing on those projects that are acceptable on all measures. Profiles provide information that display trade-offs on different measures of importance. Cost/benefit analysis (with net present value used if the time dimension is present) is the ideal approach from the theoretical perspective, but it has a number of limitations. It is very difficult to measure benefits, and it is also difficult to accurately measure some aspects of costs. One view of dealing with this problem is to measure more

FIGURE 2–1

Linear programming model, $2.5 million budget

Maximize   Σ project variable × npv   over all projects
subject to: Σ project variable × cost   ≤   2500 over all projects
             Σ project variable × analysts   ≤   12 over all projects
             Σ project variable × programmers ≤   6 over all projects
             Σ project variable × cash   ≥   300 over all projects
             Σ project variable × atp   ≥   200 over all projects
             Σ A project variables   ≥   1
             Σ B project variables   ≥   1
             Σ C project variables   ≥   1
             Σ D project variables   ≥   1
             project variables all 0 or 1

		cost	analysts	program	cash	atp	npv
A01	1	230	3	0	50	20	200
B06	1	750	3	0	240	110	390
C13	1	680	3	0	205	100	170
D15	1	290	1	1	100	40	140
D16	1	200	1	1	50	20	90
D17	1	150	1	2	0	10	110
	functions	2300	12	4	645	300	**1100**
		<	<	<	>	>	
		2500	12	6	300	200	
A	1 >		1				
B	1 >		1				
C	1 >		1				
D	3 >		1				

FIGURE 2–2

Budget limit, $2.2 million

		cost	analysts	program	cash	atp	npv
A01	1	230	3	0	50	20	200
B06	1	750	3	0	240	110	390
B10	1	200	1	2	0	10	90
C11	1	310	2	0	50	20	70
D15	1	290	1	1	100	40	140
D16	1	200	1	1	50	20	90
D17	1	150	1	2	0	10	110
	functions	2130	12	6	490	230	**1090**
		<	<	<	>	>	
		2200	12	6	300	200	
A	1 >		1				
B	2 >		1				
C	1 >		1				
D	3 >		1				

FIGURE 2–3

Budget limit,
$2.1 million

		cost	analysts	program	cash	atp	npv
A01	1	230	3	0	50	20	200
A04	1	90	1	2	10	10	30
B06	1	750	3	0	240	110	390
C11	1	310	2	0	50	20	70
D15	1	290	1	1	100	40	140
D16	1	200	1	1	50	20	90
D17	1	150	1	2	0	10	110
	functions	2020	12	6	500	230	**1030**
		<	<	<	>	>	
		2100	12	6	300	200	
A	2 >		1				
B	1 >		1				
C	1 >		1				
D	3 >		1				

FIGURE 2–4

Budget limit,
$2 million

		cost	analysts	program	cash	atp	npv
A01	1	230	3	0	50	20	200
B06	1	750	3	0	240	110	390
B09	1	190	2	0	30	10	90
C11	1	310	2	0	50	20	70
D15	1	290	1	1	100	40	140
D17	1	150	1	2	0	10	110
	functions	1920	12	3	470	210	**1000**
		<	<	<	>	>	
		2000	12	6	300	200	
A	1 >		1				
B	2 >		1				
C	1 >		1				
D	2 >		1				

accurately. Economists have developed ways to estimate the value of a life and the value of scenic beauty. However, it is difficult to persuade users to accept these measures.

A more common view is that it is wasted effort to spend time seeking a highly unstable and inaccurate dollar estimate for many intangible factors. Value analysis is one such alternative method. Value analysis isolates intangible benefits from those benefits and costs that are more accurately measurable in monetary terms; it relies upon the decision maker's judgment to come to a more informed decision. The SMART method, one of a family of multiple criteria decision analysis techniques, provides a way to quantify these intangible factors to allow decision makers to trade off values.

Cost/benefit analysis provides an ideal way to proceed if there are no intangible factors (or at least no important intangible factors). However, such factors are usually present. Intermediate approaches, such as payback analysis and value analysis, exist to deal with some cases. More complex cases are better supported by multiple criteria analysis. In cases of constraints, such as budgets, it is sometimes appropriate to optimize over some objective. Linear programming provides a means of generating the best portfolio of funded projects subject to constraint limits given that accurate measures of project performance are available.

Key Terms

checklist 32	payback 35
discounted cash flow 31	project profile 32
intangible benefits 26	screening 31
internal rate of return (IRR) 37	SMART 42
multiple criteria analysis 42	tangible benefits 25
net present value 36	time value of money 36
optimization models 46	value analysis 40

Exercises

1. Compare the ease of estimating costs and benefits of projects with the ease of estimating costs and benefits of repetitive operations. Why might they be different?

2. How did Hinton and Kaye find that managers treat information technology projects (in the context of investments)? What is the difference in treatment as capital or treatment as revenue generating?

3. According to Hinton and Kaye, what is the most commonly used method to evaluate information systems projects?

4. Two different views of project estimation bias were discussed. List factors favoring having those responsible for building a project doing the estimation. Then list the factors favoring the opposite view.

5. Describe Federal Express's approach to information system project funding.

6. Discuss the positive and negative features of outsourcing information technology projects.

7. Cabral-Cardoso and Payne surveyed research and development decision makers about their project selection methods. Compare the most commonly

identified methods found by Cabral-Cardoso and Payne with the list identified by Hinton and Kaye.

8. Describe the differences in evaluating project proposals by screening, a checklist, and a project profile.

9. Cost/benefit analysis is cited as the ideal evaluation method, but we have seen that it is not always used. What are the limitations of cost/benefit analysis?

10. Given the following data, estimate payback, net present value, and cost/benefit ratio. Use a discount rate of 10 percent per year.

Time	Outflow	Inflow
Begin Year 1	$10,000	$ 0
End Year 1	5,000	6,000
End Year 2	3,000	7,000
End Year 3	1,000	8,000

11. Estimate payback, net present value, and cost/benefit ratio for the data in Problem 10 using a discount rate of 7 percent per year.

12. Use a spreadsheet to calculate internal rate of return for the data in Problem 10.

13. When faced with penalties for ecology-damaging production, why is cost/benefit analysis dangerous?

14. Discuss the differences between value analysis and cost/benefit analysis.

15. Why are other objectives besides profit important in business?

16. Apply SMART analysis to the following data. Develop your own weights of relative importance for NPV, market share, and technical learning, as well as as scores for each of these measures with respect to each project.

Project	NPV Benefits	NPV Costs	Market Share	Technical Learning
1	$ 800	$ 700	Little impact	Minor gain
2	900	1,000	Significant	Minor gain
3	1,200	1,100	Average	Major gain
4	1,500	1,200	Average	Average gain

17. In Problem 16, apply managerially imposed weights of: CBR 0.4, market share 0.4, technical learning 0.2. Use the same scores for NPV, market share, and technical learning for the four projects that you developed in Problem 16.

18. (Requires linear programming.) A firm's project selection committee meets quarterly to decide on which project proposals to adopt. They have a $10

million quarterly budget available. NPV reported includes the expenditures for cost given. There are 360 person-months of staff support available. Identify the set of projects that will optimize the net present value contribution to the firm subject to budget and staff constraints.

Proposal	Estimated Costs	Person-Months	NPV
A1	$ 360,000	15	$ 846,000
A13	462,000	21	746,000
A23	375,000	14	382,000
B8	924,000	28	736,000
B12	853,000	32	715,000
B38	1,426,000	51	915,000
B62	1,368,000	46	1,256,000
C15	1,568,000	51	3,165,000
C22	1,385,000	58	2,512,000
C34	1,276,000	46	1,853,000

19. *Field trip:* Visit firms with information systems projects. Interview them about how their project selection process works.

Endnotes

1. M. Hinton and R. Kaye, "Investing in Information Technology: A Lottery?" *Management Accounting* 74, no. 10 (November 1996), p. 52.
2. G. McLeod and D. Smith, *Managing Information Technology Projects* (Cambridge, MA: Course Technology, 1996).
3. Hinton and Kaye, "Investing in Information Technology."
4. J. Simms, "Evaluating IT: Where Cost-Benefit Can Fail," *Australian Accountant,* May 1997, pp. 29–31.
5. Hinton and Kaye, "Investing in Information Technology."
6. Simms, "Evaluating IT."
7. Ibid.
8. Ibid.
9. C. T. Corcoran, "Cost-Benefit Analysis: IS Managers Need to Put a Price Tag on Productivity," *Infoworld,* May 26, 1997, pp. 65–66.
10. T. De Marco, *Controlling Software Projects: Management, Measurement and Estimation* (New York: Yourdon Press, 1982).
11. Corcoran, "Cost-Benefit Analysis."
12. Ibid.
13. C. Cabral-Cardoso and R. L. Payne, "Instrumental and Supportive Use of Formal Selection Methods in R&D Project Selection," *IEEE Transactions in Engineering Management* 43, no. 4 (1996), pp. 402–10.
14. C. J. Bacon, "The Use of Decision Criteria in Selecting Information Systems/Technology Investments," *MIS Quarterly* 16, no. 3 (1992), pp. 335–53.
15. S. C. Weaver, D. Peter, R. Cason, and J. Daleiden, "Panel Discussions on Corporate Investment: Capital Budgeting," *Financial Management* 18, no. 1 (1989), pp. 10–17.

16. Bacon, "The Use of Decision Criteria in Selecting Information Systems/Technology Investments."

17. Ibid.

18. Ibid.

19. R. Santhanam and J. Kyparisis, "A Multiple Criteria Decision Model for Information System Project Selection," *Computers and Operations Research* 22, no. 8 (1995), pp. 807–18.

20. D. C. Webb, The Tradeoff between Cash Flow and Net Present Value," *Scandinavian Journal of Economics* 95, no. 1 (1993), pp. 65–75.

21. R. F. Bordley, "Making Social Trade-Offs among Lives, Disabilities, and Cost," *Journal of Risk and Uncertainty* 9 (1994), pp. 135–49; and J. G. Cullis and P. R. Jones, "'What a Difference a Day Makes . . .': Concern about a New Approach to Valuing a Life," *Journal of Public Economics* 16 (1996), pp. 455–57.

22. P. G. W. Keen, "Value Analysis: Justifying Decision Support Systems," *MIS Quarterly* 5, no. 1 (1981), pp. 1–16.

23. See, for example, D. L. Olson, *Decision Aids for Selection Problems* (New York: Springer-Verlag, 1996).

24. W. Edwards, "How to Use Multiattribute Utility Measurements for Social Decisionmaking," *IEEE Transactions on Systems, Man, and Cybernetics* SMC-7, no. 5 (1977), pp. 326–40.

25. Ibid.; and B. F. Hobbs and G. T. F. Horn, "Building Public Confidence in Energy Planning: A Multimethod MCDM Approach to Demand-Side Planning at BC Gas," *Energy Policy* 25, no. 3 (1997), pp. 356–75.

26. Hobbs and Horn, "Building Public Confidence in Energy Planning."

27. R. L. Keeney and H. Raiffa, *Decisions with Multiple Objectives: Preferences and Value Tradeoffs* (New York: John Wiley & Sons, 1976).

28. T. L. Saaty, "A Scaling Method for Priorities in Hierarchical Structures," *Journal of Mathematical Psychology* 15 (1977), pp. 243–81.

29. Santhanam and Kyparisis, "A Multiple Criteria Decision Model for Information System Project Selection."

APPENDIX 2A

METHOD FOR IMPLEMENTING DESIGN TO BUDGET

Sharpe and Keelin[1] presented a procedure used by SmithKline Beecham to evaluate funding for their portfolio of research projects. This process combines the ideas of decision trees to evaluate risk with cost/benefit analysis and the ability to generate better alternatives. The process includes three steps:

1. *Generate alternatives.* Each proposed project is to be reevaluated by considering three modifications to the project: a version to buy up, a version to prune the project, and the alternative of canceling the project. The intent is to identify the best investment alternative.

2. *Value alternatives.* For each original project, all four versions are analyzed with decision trees that consider the extremes of each major uncertainty. The expected

value of each alternative is calculated, and that version of each project with the greatest expected value is selected for consideration of funding. The return on investment for the best version of each project is calculated.

3. *Rank projects by return on investment.* Projects are rank ordered and funded in net present value or return on investment order, thus ensuring the greatest expected payoff for the company's research budget.

This approach can be demonstrated using projects from Table 2A–1. We show detailed calculations for Project A1 in terms of expected net present value.

Original Proposal

Project A1 as proposed involves developing a group support system to enable employees to conduct meetings electronically. The main benefit is expected to be reduction of travel expenses, which have been estimated at roughly $500 per person per meeting. A low estimate of proposed system use is 50 meetings per year, with an average of five people required to travel for each of these meetings. A high estimate is 100 meetings per year. There is a 0.7 probability that the system will be successfully installed on time. If the system is successfully installed, there is an estimated 50 percent probability assigned to both the low (50 meetings per year) and high usage (100 meetings per year) scenarios of system use. The project is to be evaluated on a three-year basis. Net present value calculations use a discount rate of 12 percent per year. The expected availability of this system is estimated at 84

TABLE 2A–1   Calculation of Benefits and Costs for Current Group Support System Proposal

Development Costs		*Operating Effect*	*Benefits*	
$ 50,000	Software	Labor $68,000 Year 1 + fringes,	Availability is 84%	
10,000	Consultant	5% inflation/year	**Low usage**	**High usage**
30,000	Labor	Year 1: $81,600	$105,000	$210,000
6,000	Fringes	Year 2: $85,680	$105,000	$210,000
16,000	Hardware	Year 3: $89,964	$105,000	$210,000
$112,000				

Initial Investment
Low usage	−$112,000
High usage	−$112,000

Discounted Net Benefits
Year 1	($105,000 − $81,600)/1.12 = $20,893	($210,000 − $81,600)/1.12 = $114,643
Year 2	($105,000 − $85,680)/1.12^2 = $15,402	($210,000 − $85,680)/1.12^2 = $ 99,107
Year 3	($105,000 − $89,964)/1.12^3 = $10,702	($210,000 − $89,964)/1.12^3 = $ 85,439
NPV of net benefits	$46,997	299,189

Total NPV (net benefits − investment)   −$65,003 $187,189

Expected value if successful: −$65,003 × 0.5 + $187,189 × 0.5 = $61,093

There is a 0.7 probability that the system will be installed successfully.
Final expected value: $61,093 × 0.7 − $112,000 × 0.3 = +$9,165

percent. Low benefits are thus $50 \times 5 \times 500 \times 0.84 = \$105,000$. Management wants to be conservative and not inflate expected benefits in Years 2 and 3.

The current system involves development expenses of $50,000 to purchase software; $10,000 to hire a consultant to help with installing the system; and four information systems personnel for a six-week development period, with a labor cost of $30,000 (see Table 2A–1). Fringe benefits are 20 percent of labor, another $6,000. Eight personal computers would be required for the system, at an estimated cost of $2,000 each, for a hardware cost of $16,000. These estimated costs total $112,000 for the project, incurred at the beginning of the project.

Two people would be needed on a full-time basis to operate the system at an estimated labor cost of $68,000. With fringes, this amounts to $81,600, growing in Years 2 and 3 at the rate of 5 percent inflation per year. The currently proposed system is estimated to involve some downtime, as part of the nature of electronic equipment used across long distances.

The decision tree for the current system (see the top quarter of Figure 2A–1) involves two equally probable scenarios. If usage is low, the net present value of benefits minus expenses minus investment, all discounted at 12 percent per year, is $-\$65,003$, as benefits fail to cover investment and operating expense. If usage were high, on the other hand, the net present value is $+\$187,189$. Because low and high usage both have a probability of 0.5, the expected net present value if the system were to be installed successfully is $+\$61,093$. But there is only a 70 percent chance of successfully installing the system, and a 30 percent chance of a loss of $112,000 with no benefits. The expected value for the current proposal is therefore $+\$9,165$.

FIGURE 2A–1

Decision tree for installing group support system

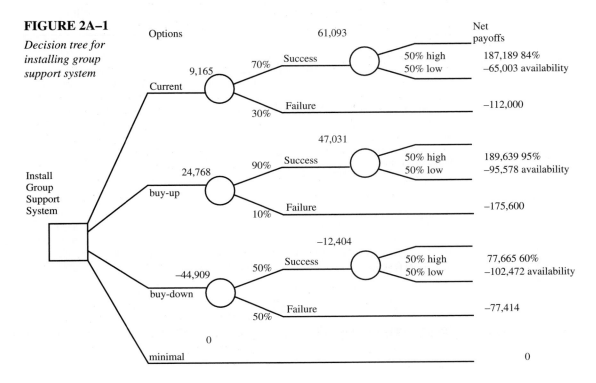

Buy-Up Proposal

The current proposal could be made more reliable by hiring a consultant to do most of the installation (increasing the probability of successfully implementing the system to 0.9). This is expected to increase the availability of the system to 95 percent in the case in which the system is successfully implemented. The cost elements would be the same ($50,000) for the software, but there would be an increased $100,000 for consultant fees. Information systems personnel would not have as much to do, so only three people would be needed for two weeks, at an estimated project cost of $8,000 (with $1,600 in fringe benefits). The same eight personal computers would be required at a cost of $16,000. Total investment is therefore $175,600.

For the low-usage scenario (see Table 2A–2), benefits of $125,000 × 0.95 = +$118,750 per year. The net present value of this option, after considering operating costs and investment, is −$95,578. If usage were to be high, the NPV would be +$189,639. Therefore, if the system were successfully installed, its expected net present value would be $47,031. There is a 90 percent probability of successful implementation with this system. If it failed (10 percent probability), the company would lose $175,600. The expected NPV of the buy-up alternative is therefore $24,768 due to the high cost of development.

Buy-Down Proposal

A cheaper version of the group support system can be obtained by buying a less expensive piece of software ($20,000) that requires no consulting expertise to install. This is a riskier

---

TABLE 2A–2   Calculation of Benefits and Costs for Buy-Up Group Support System Proposal

Development Costs		*Operating Effect*		*Benefits*	
$ 50,000	Software	Labor $68,000 Year 1 + fringes,		Availability is 95%	
100,000	Consultant	5% inflation/year		**Low usage**	**High usage**
8,000	Labor	Year 1: $81,600		$118,750	$237,500
1,600	Fringes	Year 2: $85,680		$118,750	$237,500
16,000	Hardware	Year 3: $89,964		$118,750	$237,500
$175,600					

Initial Investment
Low usage	−$175,600
High usage	−$175,600

Discounted Net Benefits

Year 1	($118,750 − $81,600)/1.12 = $33,170	($237,500 − $81,600)/1.12 = $139,196
Year 2	($118,750 − $85,680)/1.12² = $26,363	($237,500 − $85,680)/1.12² = $121,030
Year 3	($118,750 − $89,964)/1.12³ = $20,489	($237,500 − $89,964)/1.12³ = $105,013
NPV of net benefits	$80,022	$365,239

Total NPV (net benefits − investment) −$95,578 $189,639

Expected value if successful: −$95,578 × 0.5 + $189,639 × 0.5 = $47,031

There is a 0.9 probability that the system will be installed successfully.
Final expected value: $47,031 × 0.9 − $175,600 × 0.1 = $24,786

---

proposition, and the information systems group is only willing to estimate a 0.5 probability of successful system installation. Company information systems personnel can install this version in eight weeks using four people at a labor cost of $40,000. Fringes are therefore $8,000. Only six personal computers would be required, at a cost of $1,569 each, for a hardware expense of $9,414. This totals to project development expenses of $77,414. This system is expected to be relatively unreliable, and available only 60 percent of the time (see Table 2A–3).

Annual benefits for the low-usage scenario are therefore $125,000 per year × 0.6 = $75,000. After operating expenses and investment, this yields a project NPV of −$102,472. The annual benefits of a high-usage scenario are estimated at $250,000 × 0.6 = $150,000. After operating expenses and investment, there is an estimated NPV for this case of +$77,665. Both low and high cases have an estimated probability of 0.5, yielding an expected NPV of −$12,404 should the system installation be successful. The cost of a failed system is −$77,414. Given a probability of 0.5 for both the successful and unsuccessful branches, the expected value of the buy-down option is −$44,909.

Minimal Alternative

The minimum required for this project is zero—do nothing. This would mean management would continue to spend travel money as they now do, but at no added operating cost or project development cost.

TABLE 2A–3   Calculation of NPV for Buy-Down Group Support System Alternatives

Development Costs		*Operating Effect*	*Benefits*	
$20,000	Software	Labor $68,000 Year 1 + fringes,	Availability is 60%	
0	Consultant	5% inflation/year	**Low usage**	**High usage**
40,000	Labor	Year 1: $81,600	$75,000	$150,000
8,000	Fringes	Year 2: $85,680	$75,000	$150,000
9,414	Hardware	Year 3: $89,964	$75,000	$150,000
$77,414				

Initial Investment

Low usage	−$77,414
High usage	−$77,414

Discounted Net Benefits

Year 1	($75,000 − $81,600)/1.12 = −$ 5,893	($150,000 − $81,600)/1.12 = $ 61,071
Year 2	($75,000 − $85,680)/1.12^2 = −$ 8,514	($150,000 − $85,680)/1.12^2 = $ 51,276
Year 3	($75,000 − $89,964)/1.12^3 = −$10,651	($150,000 − $89,964)/1.12^3 = $ 42,732
NPV of net benefits	−$25,058	$155,079

Total NPV (net benefits − investment) −$102,472 $77,665

Expected value if successful: −$102,472 × 0.5 + $77,665 × 0.5 = −$12,404

There is a 0.5 probability that the system will be installed successfully.
Final expected value: −$12,404 × 0.5 − $77,414 × 0.5 = −$44,909

Decision

The alternative selected for this project is therefore the buy-up proposal, based on expected net present value. While this can lead to different ranking of alternatives, in this case the ranking is the same (see Table 2A–4). On the basis of this analysis, the buy-up version of the group support system is selected for consideration of funding. The procedure in this case identified a better solution than the original proposal.

Table 2A–4   Comparison of Alternatives

	Expected NPV of Benefits
Original proposal	$ 9,165
Buy-up	24,768
Buy-down	− 44,909
Minimal alternative	0

Endnote

1. P. Sharpe and T. Keelin, "How SmithKline Beecham Makes Better Resource-Allocation Decisions," *Harvard Business Review,* March–April 1998, pp. 45–57.

## CHAPTER 3

Requirements Analysis

Chapter Outline

Main Ideas Discussed

- What requirements analysis is
- The life cycle of software projects
- Eliciting requirements from users
- Group support systems to foster communication
- Risk aspects of information systems projects
- How the systems failure method can assist in project risk identification

To see where we are in the overall project process, we can look at an overview of the activities required to make an information systems project work. Once project proposals are approved, the next step is to determine the resources required to complete the project. This is referred to as *requirements analysis,* and it precedes systems design. The purpose of requirements analysis is to determine specifically what the system is intended to do. An initial idea of this is, of course, available from the original project proposal that was used for the cost/benefit analysis. After project approval, however, a more detailed analysis of what the system needs to do is required.

Analysis of User Needs

Requirements analysis involves a thorough analysis of user information needs prior to systems design. This involves business requirements. Requirements analysis is the initial phase of systems development. Therefore, data requirements also need to be considered. Byrd, Cossick, and Zmud[1] give five features of requirements analysis:

- Working with end users to establish an understanding of organizational information processing needs (business needs).
- Developing information system objectives.
- Designing and evaluating information system alternatives.
- Communicating analysis results to superiors and end users.
- Performing a systems audit.

Requirements analysis identifies the data and information needed to automate some organizational task and to support achievement of organizational objectives. Many information systems failures have been attributed to a lack of clear and specific information systems requirements.[2] Accurate identification of requirements early in the process has been reported to lead to more successful systems and lower costs for error correction.[3]

Requirements analysis consists of four processes:[4]

- Conceptual design
- Logical design
- Validation
- Formal specification

Conceptual design is the process of developing a model of what the system should do. Critical factors such as the implementation environment, organization goals and policies, product and service flows, and anticipated problems need to be identified.

The **logical design** process is where strengths and weaknesses of the conceptual design are assessed. Organizational and technological factors both have to be considered. Organizational factors include resources required, organizational politics, and priorities. Organizational factors are better understood by viewing projects as systems collecting interacting components with a common purpose. Technological factors refer to existing system capabilities, the availability of needed data, and the availability of needed personnel. The logical design process is a system design considering the organization's strengths and weaknesses.

Validation is a process meant to ensure that a valid set of requirements has been developed. Features that need to be considered in the validation process include data entry methods, system outputs, and other impacts of the proposed project on the overall system.

The **formal specification** is the result of requirements analysis. An ideal formal specification clearly specifies a complete set of information requirements, includes inputs and outputs, and discusses what these elements are to do.

Planning determines what work must be done. The effort, time, cost, and resources needed to execute the project need to be estimated. Planning is iterative because many assumptions have to be made at the requirements analysis stage that will need to be modified.

Planning is often omitted, based on arguments that (1) the quality of the system is all that matters for the project to be successful; (2) existing planning models are inaccurate and unreliable; and (3) there is usually limited time available, and skipping the planning step can save valuable time. Chatzoglou and Macaulay[5] disputed all three of these arguments. Success of an information systems project has been found to rely as much on project management as on system quality. Although planning is difficult and perfect planning impossible, without a plan progress cannot be monitored. It is better to create a rough plan and incrementally improve the plan as new information is received. Finally, the greater the time pressure, the greater the need for planning.

Methods to Elicit User Requirements

Tamai[6] found that most requirement elicitation methods applied in practice are not formal but tend to be forms of human interaction that have worked in the past. Methodologies include meetings, interviews, and brainstorming, as well as some more structured methods. Technical aspects are coordinated in documentation reviews, workflow analysis, and joint development workshops. For the initial stages of project development, where the focus is on clarifying the process to be supported and/or to generate solutions, more generic meetings can be useful. Group support technology can be a useful tool to support these different forms of human interaction and more effectively focus on the requirements needed by users.

The early 1990s have seen the implementation of a number of **group support systems (GSSs).** They come in a variety of forms, ranging from use of e-mail to software to support meeting rooms, as well as **Extranet** (to expedite communication with suppliers, vendors, and customers) and **Intranet** (to expedite communication within an organization) systems. These systems have been given credit for saving tremendous amounts of organizational time. The accompanying box describes the use of a Extranet at Caterpillar. Kirkpatrick[7] said that GSSs helped cut Boeing team project times an average of 91 percent. It is also possible to hold electronic meetings across the country, or across continents, saving large amounts of time and travel expenses. Nunamaker et al.[8] noted that GSSs tend to be more effective in reaching consensus or saving time depending on a number of factors, such as the size of the group and the agreement of the group on goals.

Caterpillar Uses Extranet to Communicate with Customers

Caterpillar Inc. is the world's largest manufacturer of construction and mining equipment. It sells a great many of its products internationally and is a leading U.S. exporter. Caterpillar faces a continuous challenge to make its enhancements and product modifications available to customers in a shorter time. Not long ago, modifications to Caterpillar's tractors were taking too long to reach customers, and the firm wanted to significantly reduce the time from design to market for these enhanced products.

Caterpillar recently participated in a trial Extranet operation with eighteen other organizations with similar manufacturing needs. An Extranet has semi-private access for a group of closely related organizations. Internet technology is used in a bounded electronic environment. The Extranet was intended to enable manufacturers to work together online and to respond to customer needs anywhere in the world.

Many information technology applications work only on proprietary systems. This closed environment makes it difficult to link supply chain participants such as manufacturers, suppliers, dealers, and customers. Extranets provide an enormous advantage in communication compatibility in that it is faster and more efficient than other attempts at linkage. Through the Extranet, Caterpillar customers can retrieve information about their orders and make changes to specifications while the machine is still on the assembly line. The cycle from order placement to product delivery is shortened. Before the Extranet implementation, this cycle took about 50 business days. With the Extranet, the cycle is cut to about 5 business days.

Challenges dealt with by Caterpillar demonstrate some of the problems that Extranet implementation involves. The public Internet does not provide sufficient security for sensitive firm information. Virtual firewalls were created to protect sensitive information from access by anyone not authorized to view it. Advanced security protocols overcame most of the security issues.

Source: *I/S Analyzer Case Studies* 36, no. 2 (February 1997).

Intranets have also been widely applied, using web technology in a private setting. Intranets are relatively inexpensive, easy to implement, and relatively platform independent. As demonstrated in the Caterpillar example, they can also provide access to customers and vendors.

GSSs can aid the group decision process a number of ways. GSS anonymity can reduce individual inhibition and focus attention on ideas in the problem recognition phase of decision making. Simultaneous input provides more efficient means to generate information and avoids domination by influential group members. Electronic recording and display make information manipulation more efficient in the data-gathering phase, as well as providing enhanced group memory for alternative generation and alternative evaluation. Group process structuring techniques, such as the Delphi method or nominal group technique (discussed

---
TABLE 3–1   Forms of Group Support Systems

Computer conferencing
    Lower levels of software support (such as e-mail)
Whiteboards
    Comments accessible by group participants
Decision room
    Individual terminals
    Anonymous input
    Shared screen
    "Brainstorming" software
    Voting support
Teleconferencing
Internet/Extranet

---

later in the chapter), can be used in the evaluation phase to obtain more task-oriented interaction. The ability to easily access data, communications, and modeling tools helps all phases of the decision process. Finally, electronic voting provides quick aggregation of votes and makes anonymous voting possible for the evaluation phase.

Group Support Systems

There are a number of distinct forms of GSSs in practice (see Table 3–1). Electronic mail is widely used and can be a means of conducting group meetings, either in batch mode or interactively. This form of group support requires little investment in software, but it can still yield very effective results in terms of time savings. Whiteboard systems can be used to allow participants to post opinions and comments at their convenience, which are then read by the rest of the group participants at their leisure. This form of system provides support across time. Decision room software provides a meeting room with a means of entering comments for brainstorming sessions, evaluating comments, sorting out the comments with the greatest support, and voting on final results. Another type of GSS is teleconferencing, where group members across the continents can see each other on the screen and conduct their meeting as if they were in the same room. Additional forms of GSSs are more extensive, including Internet features as demonstrated in the Caterpillar system.

Commercially Available GSSs

A number of products are available on the market. Electronic mail has been utilized to support many group meetings. There have been a number of decision room software products developed specifically for group support. For example, Software Aided Meeting Management (SAMM) is a University of Minnesota product for 3 to 16 member groups. SAMM includes modules supporting

TABLE 3–2   Commercial GSSs

Group Systems
    Ventana
       Cost: tens of thousands of dollars
       20 users
Mindsight
    Center for Advanced Research (EDS)
DELAWARE
    Battelle Memorial Institute
    Delphi modeling, cross-impact modeling
SAMM
    University of Minnesota
    Multicriteria utility model support
COMMENTS
    University of Indiana
Option Finder
       Cost: high thousands of dollars
       Keypad system for up to 250 users
CM/1
       Cost: low thousands
       Organize brainstorming

brainstorming; decision tools to aid problem definition, stakeholder analysis, multicriteria analysis, and clustering; voting schemes to include preference weighting and ranking; electronic input and display of ideas and positions by each member; and public and private screen displays.[9] Table 3–2 gives some idea of the scope of products available, with prices showing the rough cost involved. The business environment has resulted in a number of products changing hands, and some being dropped, as happens with all forms of software. For current information about commercially available GSSs, a good place to start is the Internet.

The Nemawashi *Approach*

So far we have discussed systems to aid cooperative group meetings. The Japanese style of decision making is quite different from conventional Western approaches. Some of the cultural features of the Japanese approach appear to have the potential to help groups reach decisions that everyone in the group can support. There is much more emphasis on team coordination of effort, relying on everyone in the organization to work toward the same goal. To foster this cooperative effort, the Japanese place much more emphasis on avoiding conflict situations.

The ***nemawashi*** approach[10] utilizes a coordinator to visit group participants individually before the group meets, seeking to identify group member ideas about how the decision problem can be dealt with, as well as identifying the opinions and position of each group member. The literal meaning of *nemawashi* is to dig around the root of a tree before transplanting. In group decision making, it describes the careful and exhaustive efforts taken to incorporate participant opinions in the decision process and avoid potentially unhealthy conflicts among group members. The intent is to obtain a consensus and prepare a formal document detailing the proposal *before* the group meets.

The following five-step process is used in *nemawashi*.

1. *Information collection.* When a decision needs to be made, a person or small group is assigned as a coordinator group (or individual). The coordinator consults superiors and identifies those people in the organization concerned with the decision. Each of these people (or their staff) is asked their opinion and wishes relative to the decision.

2. *Data analysis and plan generation.* The coordinator analyzes the information collected in step 1 and generates alternative plans for the decision. These alternatives can come from the participants. Experts in various aspects of the decision decide on the criteria for comparing alternative decisions and evaluate each alternative on each criterion. These experts can come from outside the organization.

3. *Plan selection.* In light of the opinions of group members, the coordinator selects that plan that is considered most likely to be accepted.

4. *Negotiation and persuasion.* The coordinator prepares the plan for circulation and negotiates with the group participants one-on-one. If this fails to produce a consensus, the coordinator revises the document and tries to negotiate acceptance again. This is continued until a consensus is reached.

5. *Document circulation.* The formal document is circulated, starting at the bottom of the organizational hierarchy, and individual group members indicate either acceptance or that they have read the document. Disapproval can also be indicated. When the document reaches the top of the organization, it is adopted or rejected considering the opinions of all group members.

The advantages of this approach are that better quality decisions should arise, implementation will be much easier, and higher morale should result throughout the organization. Risk taking is shared, and each participant's wishes are considered. Participants have ample time to think about the decision. On the downside, it is sometimes very difficult to develop a mutually acceptable proposal, and the process is time consuming. However, the *nemawashi* approach provides a proven method to generate group decision consensus for many difficult problems.

In the United States, successful GSS products have focused on furthering the group process rather than on applying models of the decision problem. GSSs are interested in getting group members to share their ideas, with the intent of reaching a consensus. The *nemawashi* approach offers a different perspective of the group decision process. That different perspective can be used to generate systems more accurately matching user needs.

Risk Identification and Analysis

Information systems involve high levels of risk, in that it is very difficult to predict what problems are going to occur in system development. Barki, Rivard, and Talbot[11] cited runaway information system project examples. In 1982 a major insurance company began development of an $8 million computer system from a major software provider. This system was intended to serve all the computing needs of the insurance company and was due to be completed in 1987. However, a number of problems were encountered resulting in delays of completion until 1993, with a new estimated cost of $100 million. In 1985 another insurance company undertook what was to be a one-year project to help minimize risk of buying insurance policies held by other insurers. The system was estimated to cost $500,000. However, the project encountered problems, and in 1990 was not yet complete despite expenditures of $2 million.

All risks in information systems project management cannot be avoided, but early identification of risk can reduce the damage considerably. Kliem and Ludin[12] gave a risk management cycle consisting of activities managers can undertake to understand what is happening and where:

- Risk identification
- Risk analysis
- Risk control
- Risk reporting

Risk identification focuses on identifying and ranking project elements, project goals, and risks. It requires a great deal of pre-project planning and research. *Risk analysis* is the activity of converting data gathered in the risk identification step into understanding of project risks. Analysis can be supported by quantitative techniques, such as simulation, or qualitative approaches based on judgment. *Risk control* is the activity of measuring and implementing controls to lessen or avoid the effect of risk elements. This can be reactive, after problems arise, or proactive, expending resources to deal with problems before they occur. *Risk reporting* communicates identified risks to others for discussion and evaluation.

Kliem and Ludin[13] also emphasized that risk management was not a step-by-step procedure, done once and then forgotten. The risk management cycle was viewed as a continuous process, occurring throughout a project. As the project proceeds, risks are more accurately understood.

The primary means of identifying risk amount to discussing potential problems with those who are most likely to be involved. Chapman[14] suggested three distinct methods of risk identification: individual work by a risk analyst, interviewing the project team, and discussion with a broader class of those affected, especially users.

Successful risk analysis depends on the personal experience of the analyst, as well as access to the project plan and historical data. Interviews with members of the project team can provide the analyst with the official view of the project, but risks are not always readily apparent from this source. More detailed discussion with those familiar with the overall environment within which the project is implemented is more likely to uncover risks. Chapman[15] compared brainstorming, the nominal group technique, and the Delphi method.

Brainstorming

Brainstorming involves redefining the problem, generating ideas, and seeking new solutions. The general idea is to create a climate of free association through trading ideas and perceptions of the problem at hand. Better ideas are expected from brainstorming than from individual thought because the minds of more people are tapped. The productive thought process works best in an environment in which criticism is avoided, or at least dampened.

Group support systems are especially good at supporting the brainstorming process. The feature of anonymity encourages more reticent members of the group to contribute. Most GSSs allow all participants to enter comments during brainstorming sessions. As other participants read these comments, free association leads to new ideas, built upon the comments from the entire group. Group support systems also provide a valuable feature in their ability to record these comments in a file, which can be edited with conventional word-processing software.

An additional feature of most group support systems is the ability for all participants to evaluate the comments and ideas that have been generated by the brainstorming process. By its nature, many of the comments generated will not be useful. The evaluation feature works by allowing each participant to rate each of the other comments on a scale, such as from 1 (for bad) to 10 (for great). Software can average these ratings and sort comments by these averages. This identifies the most popular ideas.

Diverse groups encourage a gamut of ideas during the brainstorming process.

Brainstorming works best if the group is diverse—and thus more likely to bring different ideas into play. The size of the group should be large enough to allow diversity but not so large as to cause problems of generating too many comments to handle. The negatives of brainstorming involve the social aspects. Individuals with dominating personalities can take over brainstorming sessions. It is key for productivity to keep the session positive.

Nominal Group Technique

The **nominal group technique**[16] supports groups of people (ideally 7 to 10) who initially write down their ideas about the issue in question on a pad of paper. Each individual then presents their ideas, which are recorded on a flip chart. The group can generate new ideas during this phase, which continues until no new ideas are forthcoming. When all ideas are recorded, discussion opens. Each idea is discussed. At the end of discussion, each individual records their evaluation of the most serious risks associated with the project by either rank ordering or rating.

The silent generation of ideas and structured discussion are contended to overcome many of the limitations of brainstorming. Nominal groups have been found to yield more unique ideas, more total ideas, and better quality ideas than brainstorming groups.

Delphi Method

The **Delphi method** was developed at the RAND Corporation for technological forecasting, but it has been applied to many other problem environments. The first phase of the Delphi method is anonymous generation of opinions and ideas related to the issue at hand by participants. These anonymous papers are then circulated to all participants, who revise their thoughts in light of these other ideas. Anonymous ideas are exchanged for either a given number of rounds or until convergence of ideas.

The Delphi method can be used with any number of participants. Anonymity and isolation allow maximum freedom from any negative aspects of social interaction. On the negative side, the Delphi method is much more time consuming than brainstorming or the nominal group technique. There also is limited opportunity for clarification of ideas. Conflict is usually handled by voting, which may not completely resolve disagreements.

The idea behind the Delphi method can be implemented in a number of ways. For example, Chapman[17] recommended a formal risk management process at all stages of a project's life cycle (project risk assessment method or PRAM). This method was more completely described in Chapman and Ward.[18] Wyatt[19] addressed application of this approach to information systems projects. PRAM steps include identifying the risk, assessing the effect of risk if negative consequences are realized, and deciding how to mitigate the negative consequences should they be realized.

The Systems Failure Method for Information Systems Projects

Fortune and Peters[20] presented the **systems failure method,** a systematic method for analysis of failure that occurred in similar operations in the past. This approach has been applied in a wide variety of situations, including project management. The idea behind this approach is that by reviewing past failures, future failures can be avoided.

In the context of information systems, disasters are failures of systems that do not satisfactorily support users. As organizations rely more on computers, Fortune and Peters noted that there is a corresponding increase in significant business interruptions.[21] Fortune and Peters differentiated between negative and positive disasters. **Negative disasters** come from decisions resulting in a change of policy, where a project is substantially modified, reversed, or abandoned after commitment of substantial resources.

The End of a Solution

The biggest information system project attempted by the state of Washington ended in failure in March 1997 when the Information Services Board canceled the project. The system was intended to unify two databases: one for driver's licenses and the other for vehicle registrations. The project began in 1992 and was designed to create a relational, client-server system; it was budgeted at $16 million. The proposed system was to allow residents to fill out only one change-of-address form to update licenses and registrations, and it was developed to take advantage of new technology. However, a preliminary study underestimated the required scope of the project. New laws changed some of the functions of the system. After the fact, the project manager stated that a business reengineering design before coding started would have avoided many of the problems experienced. The project's cost had reached $40 million before cancellation, and it would have required an additional estimated $27.5 million to complete. Separate hierarchical databases continue to be used. One of the lessons cited from the experience was the value of keeping projects small and incremental.

Source: J. Angus, "State Scraps IS Project," *Computerworld* (March 24, 1997), Washington database, http://www.computerworld.com.

The Washington database is a prime example of a negative disaster—$40 million was wasted without any change in the operation of the organization. Apparently a major flaw was inaccurate estimation of the work involved in building the project. Then the problem was compounded by changes in the system environment, as new laws changed the work that needed to be done. The project took on a life of its own, steamrolling ahead despite changed requirements. Consideration of the overall system, keeping in mind the overall goal of the project rather than forging ahead with an outdated plan, would have saved considerable effort and expense. Keeping projects small makes it easier to change direction.

Positive disasters involve some uncertainty. These are systems that are implemented despite heavy criticism and are felt by many informed people to have been a mistake. While the project output works, it does not work to the satisfaction of key users (see the accompanying IRS box).

IRS Project Failure

Delays in overhauling federal tax systems were cited as causing the U.S. Treasury to lose as much as $50 billion per year. This figure was generated by calculating what the government could be collecting in additional taxes if the IRS had succeeded in its decade-long attempt to modernize its computer systems. These computer systems were developed in the 1960s. Hundreds of millions of dollars are annually expended in upgrading efforts, currently consisting of about 50 projects, including a compliance research information system database and statistical tools to spot suspicious returns. The current tax systems modernization program had an estimated cost of $8 billion at last report.

This project is designed to boost tax collections from today's estimated 87 percent to 90 percent by 2001. New computer systems that have been implemented spotted and rejected 4.1 million suspicious electronic returns, an increase of 400 percent over the prior year. Better computer checking of a million suspicious paper returns, followed up by IRS examiners, yielded $800 million in added revenues and reduced refunds.

The IRS has 2,000 staff assigned to the effort, along with an estimated 10 outside contractors for every internal staff member. A critic has claimed that $4 billion has been spent so far with no results to date. Less-than-optimal results have been attributed to failure to conduct a business process redesign before systems development, failure to develop an overall systems architecture or development blueprint, outdated software development methodologies, and other problems.

An IRS commissioner testified in January 1998 that IRS computer systems were extremely deficient in their ability to support IRS missions and goals. In March 1998 the IRS called for bids to outsource a 15-year modernization program expected to cost more than $8 billion. This operation was outsourced to a consortium of seven vendors in 1999.

Sources: G. H. Anthes, "IRS Project Failures Cost Taxpayers $50B Annually," *Computerworld* (December 19, 1997), http://www.computerworld.com; and M. Hamblen, "IRS Puts Outsourcing Effort Out to Bid," *Computerworld* (March 31, 1998), http://www.computerworld.com.

This set of projects is not necessarily a failure. Progress is being made. The IRS is everyone's target, especially during election years. Nonetheless, large sums of money have been expended with less-than-desired results. Project failure can arise in many forms. The IRS expended a great deal of money ($4 billion) and in at least one view attained no value whatsoever. Thibodeau[22] reported that the Government Accounting Office had issued dozens of reports detailing these problems. The outsourcing indicates a change in direction from managing a group of small outsourced projects to outsourcing the management of information technology.

Some projects, such as the state of Washington's database integration project, never work. Others are finished, but over budget, very late, or both. Projects can be completed on time and within budget but still be failures because they don't perform as designed. Others meet design specifications but are maintenance and enhancement nightmares.

The following example demonstrates a prolonged failure in attempts to implement an information systems project.

An Example of Project Failure

A joint venture of two international air freight firms was established in 1990 after 20 years of business cooperation.[23] The services of the joint venture varied from lightweight express parcel products to heavy air freight. One of the firms was from the United States and the other was Japanese, and all shipments entering either country were cleared through customs in advance. The joint venture specialized in moving large shipments. Its customers were predominantly manufacturing companies and van lines. There were 30 to 40 competitors; about 60 percent were European or other firms.

The parent U.S. firm is very bureaucratic, with tight controls emphasizing efficiency. The joint venture, on the other hand, had a relaxed form of management with free interaction and communication. The goals of the joint venture were to increase market share and revenue. Additional goals were to lower costs and to provide 50 percent of the total services to Japanese businesses while increasing business to Europe and South America by 15 percent.

The joint venture processed a high volume of shipments imported to the United States. Documents for such shipments included a master airway bill number (customer billing), a house airway bill number (shipment identifier), shipment size, shipment weight, destination, commodity description, customs information, and accounting information. The Star*Doc information system was intended to deal with problems including high document handling costs, loss of ability to track shipments, loss of ability to respond to changes, high error rates, and data redundancy. An increasing number of house airway bills created work because forms had to be filled out manually. House airway bills had to be transferred to regional offices in pouches, which took an average of four days. A business systems group of 20 qualified professionals was established to implement a computer system to deal with these problems.

The Star*Doc system took 18 months and $3.3 million to develop. The development team designed the system to meet the specifications of the parent U.S. firm. Specifications addressed packaging only. No prospective users were involved with the project until the constructed system was installed. Management was aware of the development effort but was not involved with the project.

A pilot demonstration was held in April 1992 in one of the regional offices. The system did not operate properly. The system was approved for production anyway. Input from users was used to change several features. The system was installed in six other locations. Users could request changes in the system through formal application by managers. The business systems group at its discretion made changes. Users complained that

- The system did nothing to support the master airway bill.
- The system did not incorporate order tracking.
- The system lacked report-generating features.
- The system did not provide accounting applications.
- The system did not support managerial decision making.
- The system locked up and frequently disconnected unexpectedly.
- All transactions had to be performed online.
- The system could not support additional terminals.
- The screen format was not user friendly.

The most critical success factor in the freight forwarding industry is accurate and timely communication between customers and expediters and between expediters and the airline companies. Star*Doc did not fulfill this need. The house airway bills still needed to be hand typed. Freight shipments still could not be tracked online. Thus, there was continued data redundancy in the system.

Oz cited the following lessons:

- Business units need to be the source of information-need statements. In this case, the parent firm commissioned the project for the joint venture, without consulting affected business units about what the system should do.
- Potential users need to be involved from the earliest stages of systems development. They were not in this case.
- Appropriate systems development approaches should be applied. In this case, a canned software package was purchased and adapted for the joint venture's needs. This combined the approaches of purchasing software and prototyping. Prototyping without additional systems analysis and design should be avoided in a structured environment as was the case here. The appropriate approach would have been a thorough systems development life-cycle approach.[24]

This case demonstrates the importance of the three factors commonly cited as necessary in successful projects. While systems objectives may have been stated, users were clearly not involved in this project, and management support was passive at best.

Features of Successful Projects

We have primarily focused on things that go wrong with projects. We do not want to give the impression that projects cannot be made to work. (We do want to give the impression that it is difficult to make them work.) This section examines characteristics present in successful projects.

Ingram[25] studied projects involving downsizing mainframe systems to open systems platforms (client/server, Unix, local area networks, and downsizing projects) over the period from 1982 to 1992. Open systems are those that allow easy access to people across organizational boundaries (people in one organization can work with people in another organization). There were 62 of these projects that were considered vital to the organizations. Of these 62 projects, 57 percent came in materially late, 72 percent were materially over budget, and 88 percent failed to meet some significant user expectations. Of the 20 projects rated as above average or excellent, those attributes that were present were identified. The seven most commonly found in successful projects are identified in Table 3–3.

Open systems projects involve multiple parties. When a work breakdown structure (which provides measurable milestones) is used, there is clear understanding of what third parties are expected to do. In the unsuccessful projects, third parties often skipped tasks and requirements. In successful projects, project managers ensured that third parties had the capacity and commitment to accomplish tasks as promised.

The primary mistake made in unsuccessful projects was to proceed with a new technology or concept without establishing objectives, scopes, deadlines, expectations, and budgets. Without these, project teams would often find frequently changing objectives, scope growing beyond realistic bounds (scope creep), arbitrary deadlines, and unrealistic expectations.

The most successful project teams put reliability and attaining objectives ahead of technical brilliance. Successful project teams identified necessary technical skills and acquired project team members who had these skills. Successful projects tended to have objectives based on strong business cases with large paybacks. In successful projects, management was skeptical about vendor claims and minimized risk by using pilot projects. Those project elements that would likely create delays and cost overruns were identified and managed very closely. Strong technical solutions were found in successful projects, but the emphasis was on

TABLE 3–3   Attributes Common to Successful Projects

Seven Common Attributes	Number of Projects Exhibiting the Attribute[a]
No material time or cost lost to third-party accountability	20/20
Objectives, scope, deadlines, expectations, and responsibilities agreed upon at beginning	19/20
Necessary skills were available	18/20
Project objectives remained clear throughout the project	18/20
Minimal time and cost were lost to network platform issues	18/20
Quality of technical approach was adequate	18/20
Application software issues were top priority and effective	18/20

[a]Total number of projects equals 20.

technology that benefited the business. In successful projects, the level of technical sophistication that was needed was applied rather than the most sophisticated level available.

The Ingram study also found a low correlation between technical excellence and project success.[26] Sound project management, on the other hand, is critical to project success. Open systems offer great flexibility and a multitude of choices. In a project environment, this leads to many difficult decisions about products and how open systems will be managed. This can result in increased project difficulties because there is less coordinated control over the interactions among different organizations. A large number of projects reported significant problems with third parties performing as promised. Ingram attributed this to the lack of third-party capacity to perform rather than to deception or negative intent.

The Systems Failure Method

Now that we have examined project failure and examined some features of successful projects, we present an approach that is designed to improve the success rate of complex projects. It is a use of the systems view that we discussed in Chapter 1, viewing projects as collections of coordinated and interrelated activities, bringing diverse skills together to accomplish a set of goals.

The systems failure method is an approach intended to improve the prospects of success by examining similar undertakings that have failed with the intent of avoiding those things that caused failure. The method consists of studying the process as a system, to enable modeling the system so that cause-and-effect relationships can be understood. Planned systems are compared with similar systems that have either succeeded or have failed.

The approach begins with gathering as many similar cases as possible. This is a data collection step. Then each case is analyzed with the intent of studying the system aspects similar to the subject. The history of each case is developed and examined to determine why the system failed. The systems failure approach is described in Table 3–4.

Pre-analysis involves conceptualizing the system being studied to include different viewpoints and perspectives. Information is gathered and analyzed to enable the systems components to be identified as well as their interaction to accomplish systems goals and the hierarchical structure of systems control.

TABLE 3–4   Systems Failure Method Processes

- Pre-analysis (Define purpose, perspectives, gather source material)
- Identify significant failures and select systems
- Modeling (Clarify the nature of the system)
- Comparison (Gain understanding)
- Analysis
- Synthesis

Significant failures of similar systems are identified. Failure is the focus of the study. This requires modeling the system in some detail. Many of the more advanced systems involving human interaction consist of ill-structured, messy situations. Soft-systems methodology was proposed by Checkland[27] as a way to study these systems. Instead of identifying the optimal solution for a system, the purpose of soft systems is to involve users in a learning process. First, understanding of the system is required. The background and history of the problem is useful in gaining understanding. Then, the system is described, and this model of the system can be used to predict the outcome of alternative decisions. Ormerod demonstrated the application of soft-system modeling to development of information systems strategies for a supermarket chain[28] and for a South African mine.[29]

Models represent the theory of the analyst about the results of available actions on the system. By studying similar systems, better understanding of the system under study can be gained. System components need to be described, as well as relationships. Structural relationships describing system behavior are included.

The soft-system methodology consists of seven stages:[30]

1. Identify the problem situation.
2. Structure the problem situation.
3. Identify human activity systems.
4. Conceptualize models of human activity systems.
5. Compare models with perceptions in the problem situation.
6. Identify feasible desirable changes.
7. Take action.

Stage 1 involves identifying the actors with interests in the situation. Stage 2 requires an analysis of the political aspects of the situation. Systems thinking leads to identification of the system relationships in stage 3. In stage 4, the analyst develops a model of the system capable of predicting the expected consequences of actions. Stage 5 uses the models to gain insight. Stage 6 involves developing and evaluating more refined alternatives, to include benefit/cost analysis. Finally, the approach leads to action in stage 7.

Comparison involves identifying what you think would happen with the system under study, given the model based on similar systems. This requires developing a model laying out the process of system operation, including the decision-making subsystem. For instance, a medical information system would need to capture the flow of information and decision making in a medical process. A patient arrives with a malady. Information about this patient's medical history is needed. Records are kept at each medical facility for each patient. Those in this medical facility system can be recalled by accessing the database records relating to this patient. The patient is questioned about medical history, and hopefully other sources that might have records are identified and additional records requested. The physician then examines the patient, and diagnoses the causes of the current malady in light of the historical data available relating to the patient, as well as the physician's knowledge about similar cases. Another database, organized by symptoms, can be accessed by the physician to obtain greater understanding of probable causes. The physician then prescribes a treatment plan, which is closely monitored for results. The overall process requires support in the way of data by patient and data by symptom. That portion of the information system focuses on the patient. Another portion of the information system monitors billing information and includes charges and payment arrangements. The focus of comparison is on decision making and control. Relationships between this particular system and the wider system are needed, as well as understanding of the effects resulting from the external environment.

Analysis uses model output to draw inferences about the relationship of actions within the system and expected outcomes. In a medical information system, the administration may use the system to monitor productivity aspects by physicians in attempts to control costs. Physicians can use the system professionally by developing databases by disease and symptom that can be used to determine better treatment plans. *Synthesis* is obtained when the analyst feels that learning about the system has been gained.

According to Fortune and Peters,[31] failure of systems is commonly a result of the following:

- Deficiencies in organizational structure and lack of performance control.
- Lack of a clear statement of purpose.
- Subsystem deficiencies.
- Lack of effective communication between subsystems.
- Inadequate design.
- Insufficient consideration of environment, and insufficient resources.
- Imbalance of resources and inadequate testing.

Fortune and Peters were interested in the failure of all types of systems, not just information systems. Lack of a clear statement of purpose appears on their list of causes of failure, further confirming its importance in projects.

Systems Control.   Control is action taken to reach or maintain a desired state. Classical feedback control monitors the output of the system. When a difference is identified between desired performance levels, such as the size of a ballbearing being produced or the characteristics of a microchip, then action is taken by throwing out the inferior product and adjusting machinery so that future production will be within specifications. A common example of feedback control is a thermostat. More modern forms of feedback control include a model predicting the final form of the output based on a measurement early in the production process. These systems adjust according to the measures obtained. An example might be a chip in a refrigerator that monitors conditions within the enclosed environment and contacts the manufacturer's representative to send a repairperson before damage is done. Actually, this implies feedforward control, because the outcome of the system is predicted before the problem actually occurs.

Computer chips can be placed in items such as refrigerators to monitor conditions and alert users of possible malfunctions.

Systems Communication.   Many systems failures are the result of problems with communications links among system components. These can be missing links, inadequate links, or links that are not used. There is a vicious circle in organizational communication. Information overload describes situations where so much information is provided that no understanding is obtained. A correction for this condition is to filter communications to those bits that have important information content. However, this leads to distortion and omission of some information, some of which may turn out to be important. The reaction to this is more messages, which inevitably leads to information overload.

Each of us has to cope with the potential for information overload. Newspapers contain more information each day than any one individual cares to know. Therefore, newspapers classify articles by content. Some spend their time reading the front page, others the comics, and yet others concentrate on the sports page. If one can filter out the advertising, the newspaper can be used to gain a good picture of the highlights of what is going on in the world. But modern technology provides even more concentrated news. There are television channels that purvey nothing but news, others that show nothing but cartoons, and others that have sports around the clock. With expanded cable coverage, one can specialize even more. There are headline news channels and classic sports networks. The age of information overload has certainly arrived.

Human Aspects of Systems.   Part of understanding the system is to identify the structure of responsibility—who is responsible for what. Another part of the system is the set of organizational codes of behavior—what is appropriate conduct. Some information is communicable, and some is not. For instance, in the nuclear energy field, some information is classified by the government. In any organization, some information may well be considered sacrosanct, not to be broadcast. Understanding a system includes understanding what portions of the system are fixed and unchangeable and what elements are merely there for temporary purposes. For control purposes, understanding the procedure followed to solve problems can be one of the most important system components. Organizational aspects of information systems projects will be discussed in Chapter 8.

Demonstration of the Systems Failure Method

Fortune and Peters used a medical information systems project to demonstrate the systems failure method.[32] Medical records are the primary means that health care professionals have to communicate with each other and facilitate continuity of care. However, there is strong evidence that medical records are often incomplete and inaccurate. Automation would speed care and improve efficiency. Automatic review of medical records would lower error and help control costs. Systematic analysis of medical records offers the ability to better select policies in the future.

Fortune and Peters also presented experience with the electronic patient record, a three-year strategic research and development program for a computer system in the United Kingdom in 1993.[33] The prototyping approach was applied to develop the system. Systems analysis was used to identify tangible and intangible benefits and costs, as well as to understand cultural issues.

The systems failure approach began with review of published accounts of attempts to introduce clinical information systems in hospitals. These accounts were selected on the basis of providing sufficient detail to allow analysis of the systems involved. Each selected account was complex, with wide-ranging consequences. Eight cases were found—six in the United States, one in Canada, and one in the United Kingdom.

One of the eight cases was a 700-bed teaching hospital at an eastern U.S. university. In 1981 consultants had recommended expansion of the use of information technology, which had successfully been applied to financial and accounting applications. The proposed medical information system was expected to provide more than $26 million in savings over five years, with a payback period of less than two years. It was designed to deliver administrative support to activities such as admissions by 1987, be extended to provide dietary and radiology support, and to assist laboratories and the pharmacy by 1991.

The system encountered delays, driving the cost to more than three times the original estimate. Three necessary communication links in the system were not sufficient to system needs. Development of the system placed great strain on the relationships between medical staff and the administration. It was found that implementing a decision subsystem was not possible immediately. The new system turned out to challenge basic institutional assumptions, and it disturbed traditional patterns of conduct. The project builder had no authority, and medical professionals declined to use the system, which would require them to modify their established routines. Not only did the system fail in the sense that it ran over budget, it also failed because it was not used as designed.

A second case was a project to develop an outpatient medical records system for a hospital that would have involved 1,400 terminals for direct entry of information by clinicians. The system was brought online in 1989, using parallel operation with the preexisting (manual) system to ensure continuity of service. However, four years later both systems were still operating in parallel. The new system turned out to require so much printing that it was hard to find space for the printers. It also turned out that data security and privacy were far more important than the project team had originally understood.

Based on study of these eight accounts, a formal system model was constructed. Common themes were identified as follows:

- Links with other systems were commonly deficient.
- There was a low ability to influence the environment.
- Decision making tended to be isolated.
- System expectations were not widely understood.
- Required resources were often lacking.

Major failures occurred when key system participants were not involved. Poor communication was also considered a major critical success factor. User interfaces were too complex, and there were no standard interfaces for communication. Rules of information use were not clearly defined. On the human side, there was a great deal of prejudice between the professional and administrative groups. With respect to the project, there was uncertainty about roles, responsibility, and power that led to anomie. Clinicians and the project staff were unable to form a team for consensus decision making for project implementation. Intended users resented the system since they viewed it as something imposed by management.

The results of the systems failure analysis included a formal systems model for the proposed project at the system level for patient care, at the subsystem level for messages, and at the sub-subsystem level for computers. This led to better understanding of organizational climate. Among the many things that the systems failure analysis provided was consideration of how records would be used, the level of detail required, usage patterns over time, and the need to support different individual styles.

The approach resulted in a recognition of the need for flexible design that practitioners could use for information about specific patients, and researchers could use for information about particular diseases. Standardization of records led to greater consistency. Patient confidentiality was a major concern, placing extra security requirements on the system. The systems failure analysis led to a design in which the client had greater confidence.

Summary

Requirements analysis is important in identifying what a proposed system is to do. Project proposers, whether management or users, are the best source of what the system should provide. Technical requirements to accomplish the project come from the subsequent systems design. Therefore, requirements analysis is focused on the intended use of the system.

Requirements analysis can be conducted by an expert analyst, especially if the analyst has access to the historical performance of similar projects. However, most requirements analysis techniques focus on eliciting ideas from humans.

Group support systems can help generate better ideas, can help reach consensus on what issues are important, and can aid in expediting voting in various forms. They can play a key role in supporting many project-related meetings, and can be especially useful in requirements analysis. Group support systems have been credited with saving a great deal of managerial time. The *nemawashi* approach focuses on the group process—trying to get the group to agree without forcing individuals into taking irretrievable positions from which they cannot back down.

Methods of eliciting ideas include brainstorming and other techniques. The nominal group technique provides a structured implementation that can efficiently lead to better understanding of important issues. The Delphi method also can be useful, but it is often slower and more expensive than the nominal group technique. Brainstorming is subject to social limitations as a result of dominating individuals, but when implemented on group support systems, it can be extremely effective in generating new ideas and identifying needs of proposed information system projects. Brainstorming on group support systems also can be useful in identifying risks by drawing upon the experience of users.

The systems failure method offers a systematic way to apply the principles of the systems approach to the analysis of new project proposals. It is based on a simple idea—learn from the experience of others. While other projects clearly faced different environments, the key is to see the pertinent factors that apply to the project being designed.

Key Terms

brainstorming   67
conceptual design   60
Delphi method   68
Extranet   61
formal specification   61
group support systems (GSSs)   61
Intranet   61
logical design   60

negative disasters   69
nemawashi   64
nominal group technique   68
positive disasters   70
requirements analysis   60
systems failure method   69
validation   60

Exercises

1. Describe the actions of Caterpillar to implement information technology to enhance group communication. What benefits were sought?
2. What types of GSSs are there?
3. Describe the *nemawashi* approach.
4. Discuss positive and negative features of the *nemawashi* system in the context of U.S. decision making.
5. Discuss the risk aspects of the Chunnel project.
6. What are the relative advantages and disadvantages of brainstorming, nominal group technique, and the Delphi method?
7. Describe the conditions that make a negative disaster.
8. Describe the conditions that make a positive disaster.
9. What were the causes given for the Star*Doc disaster?
10. What characteristics were identified by Ingram in successful downsizing projects?
11. Which did Ingram find to be more critical: technical excellence or effective project management?
12. What is the basic idea of the systems failure method?
13. *Field trip:* Visit an organization implementing information systems projects, and interview them about how they conduct requirements analysis.

Microsoft Project Exercise

You can access *Microsoft Project* and open a file for a new project (see the Appendix chapter). When you enter activities, the software will produce a Gantt chart (a graphical display of activity work by time period). The initial activity for which a planning software package can help is entering the project and providing an initial Gantt chart. The initial information required is the list of tasks, those tasks that must be completed before other tasks can begin, and task durations. This information is sufficient to get an initial view of the project.

Requirements for the following software project have been developed, yielding the following worklist. Enter the tasks, predecessors, and durations (days) for the following project. Start the project on July 1, 2000.

Identifier	Activity	Predecessor	Duration
Perform Planning and Scheduling			
A1	Revise overall project plan	None	15
A2	Complete detailed plan for detail design	A1	5
A3	Revise skeleton and generic plan for rest	A1	3
A4	Brief new team members	A2, A3	1
A5	Complete phase estimate	A4	7
A6	Review plan	A5	1

Identifier	Activity	Predecessor	Duration
A7	Revise plan	A6	10
A8	Complete project schedule	A5 start + 3	4
A9	Milestone	A7, A8	0

Prepare Database Design

B1	Document data models to catalog	None	15
B2	Determine file structures for flat files	B1	12
B3	Prepare copylibs for flat file structures	B1	7
B4	Define each process	B2, B3	3
B5	Review process access with database admin.	B4	1
B6	Physical database design	B5	20
B7	Review design	B6	1
B8	Revise design	B7	15
B9	Conduct call pattern reviews	B6	10
B10	Milestone	B8, B9	0

Prepare Physical Design Documents

C1	Prepare process-to-program specifications	B4	13
C2	Determine security specifications	B9, C1	8
C3	Prepare physical system flow	C2	12
C4	Milestone	C3	0
D1	Design programs & write specifications	A8, B9	18
D2	Write data conversion & interface programs	D1	6
D3	Revise documents	D2	30
D4	Milestone	D3	0
E1	Implementation	C3, D3	5
E2	Testing	E1	15
E3	Final acceptance	E2	1
E4	Milestone	E3	0

Work 5 days per week
Holidays
   January 1
   3rd Monday in January
   3rd Monday in February
   July 4
   4th Thursday in November
   December 25

The initial information for the project needs to be entered. When you open the package, you may have a window asking for the project start date (which you can enter as 7/1/2000). If not, you can obtain this window from the sequence:

Project
Project Information

The next thing to do is to identify holidays for the period of time over which you expect the project to be scheduled. To be safe, we might identify holidays for the second half of 2000 and all of 2001 and 2002.

Tools
Change Working Time
Click the radio button for Nonworking Time

The last thing to do is to enter the tasks, durations, and predecessors. Click on the Gantt Chart button, which displays a large working template with room for tasks on the left and a bar graph schedule on the right. All that needs to be done to enter tasks is to type them in. For instance, the tasks for "Perform planning and scheduling" can be entered as shown. The default duration of 1 day is entered for each task. These could be corrected as each task is entered, but it may be faster to enter them all at once. The same is true for predecessors.

Activity	*Duration*
A1 Revise overall plan	1 day
A2 Complete detailed plan for detail design	1 day
A3 Revise skeleton and generic plan for rest	1 day
A4 Brief new team members	1 day
A5 Complete phase estimate	1 day
A6 Review plan	1 day
A7 Revise plan	1 day
A8 Complete project schedule	1 day
A9 Milestone A	1 day

Note that here we have included identifiers as part of the task label. Once all tasks have been entered, durations can be entered. Note that if the default time unit is not what you want, you have to include the letter indicating the time unit. Options are "m" for minutes, "h" for hours, "d" for days, and "w" for weeks.

Activity	*Duration*	*Start*	*Finish*
A1 Revise overall plan	15 days	Mon 7/3/00	Mon 7/24/00
A2 Complete detailed plan for detail design	5 days	Mon 7/3/00	Mon 7/10/00
A3 Revise skeleton and generic plan for rest	3 days	Mon 7/3/00	Thu 7/6/00
A4 Brief new team members	1 day	Mon 7/3/00	Mon 7/3/00
A5 Complete phase estimate	7 days	Mon 7/3/00	Wed 7/12/00
A6 Review plan	1 day	Mon 7/3/00	Mon 7/3/00
A7 Revise plan	10 days	Mon 7/3/00	Mon 7/17/00
A8 Complete project schedule	4 days	Mon 7/3/00	Fri 7/7/00
A9 Milestone A	0 days	Mon 7/3/00	Mon 7/3/00

All that needs to be done to identify a milestone activity is to enter a duration of 0. As indicated, starting dates and inferred completion dates are automatically generated by the software. At this stage, all activities are starting on 7/3/00 (the first working day for the project). The next thing to enter is the predecessor relationships.

Predecessor relationships can be entered as tasks are entered or all at once. All that needs to be entered for the conventional finish-to-start relationship is to list the number of the preceding task in the successor task's predecessor column. There is one task with a complication. Task A8 can start 3 working days after the start of task A5. This relationship can be entered as 5SS+3d. To ensure that the relationship worked, the bar chart can be reviewed. The best view can be obtained by the sequence:

View	Zoom	select Entire Project

This provides a view that clearly shows that task A8 starts three working days after the start of task A5.

Activity	Duration	Start	Finish	Predecessor
Revise overall plan	15 days	Mon 7/3/00	Mon 7/24/00	
Complete detailed plan for detail design	5 days	Tue 7/25/00	Mon 7/31/00	1
Revise skeleton and generic plan for rest	3 days	Tue 7/25/00	Thu 7/27/00	1
Brief new team members	1 day	Tue 8/1/00	Tue 8/1/00	2, 3
Complete phase estimate	7 days	Wed 8/2/00	Thu 8/10/00	4
Review plan	1 day	Fri 8/11/00	Fri 8/11/00	5
Revise plan	10 days	Mon 8/14/00	Fri 8/25/00	6
Complete project schedule	4 days	Mon 8/7/00	Thu 8/10/00	5SS+3d
Milestone A	0 days	Fri 8/25/00	Fri 8/25/00	7, 8

The Gantt chart shows all predecessor relationships by arrows. The latest completion time is 1/12/01, which is the early start schedule for the project, assuming all required resources will be available.

Endnotes

1. T. A. Byrd, K. L. Cossick, and R. W. Zmud, "A Synthesis of Research on Requirements Analysis and Knowledge Acquisition Techniques," *MIS Quarterly* 16, no. 1 (1992), pp. 117–38.
2. R. B. Cooper and E. B. Swanson, Management Information Requirements Assessment: The State of the Art," *Data Base* 10, no. 2 (1979), pp. 5–16; G. B. Davis, "Strategies for Information Requirements Determination," *IBM Systems Journal* 21, no. 1 (1982), pp. 4–30; and M. Telem, "Information Requirements

Specification II: Brainstorming Collective Decision-Making Approach," *Information Processing and Management* 24, no. 5 (1988), pp. 549–57.

3. R. T. Mittermeir, P. Hsia, and R. T. Yeh, "Alternatives to Overcome the Communication Problem of Formal Requirements Analysis," in *Requirements Engineering Environments,* M. Ohno, ed. (Amsterdam, Netherlands: North-Holland, 1982).

4. R. W. Zmud, *Information Systems in Organizations* (Glenview, IL: Scott, Foresman & Co., 1983).

5. P. D. Chatzoglou and L. A. Macaulay, "A Review of Existing Models for Project Planning and Estimation and the Need for a New Approach," *International Journal of Project Management* 14, no. 3 (1996), pp. 173–83.

6. T. Tamai, "Current Practices in Software Processes for System Planning and Requirements Analysis," *Information & Software Technology* 35, nos. 6–7 (1993), pp. 339–44.

7. D. Kirkpatrick, "Here Comes the Payoff from PCs," *Fortune,* March 23, 1992, pp. 93–96.

8. J. F. Nunamaker, Jr., D. Vogel, A. Heminger, B. Martz, R. Grohowski, and C. McGoff, "Experiences at IBM with Group Support Systems: A Field Study," *Decision Support Systems* 5, no. 2 (1989), pp. 183–96.

9. M. S. Poole, M. Holmes, R. Watson, and G. DeSanctis, "Group Support Systems and Group Communication," *Communication Research* 20, no. 2 (1993), pp. 176–213.

10. K. Watabe, C. W. Holsapple, and A. B. Whinston, "Coordinator Support in a *Nemawashi* Decision Process," *Decision Support Systems* 8 (1992), pp. 85–98.

11. H. Barki, S. Rivard, and J. Talbot, "Toward an Assessment of Software Development Risk," *Journal of Management Information Systems* 10, no. 2 (1993), pp. 203–25.

12. R. L. Kliem and I. S. Ludin, *Reducing Project Risk* (Aldershot, England: Gower, 1998).

13. Ibid.

14. C. Chapman, "The Effectiveness of Working Group Risk Identification and Assessment Techniques," *International Journal of Project Management* 16, no. 6 (1998), pp. 333–43.

15. Ibid.

16. C. M. Moore, *Group Techniques for Idea Building,* 2nd ed. (Thousand Oaks, CA: Sage Publications, 1994).

17. C. Chapman, "Project Risk Analysis and Management—PRAM, the Generic Process," *International Journal of Project Management* 15, no. 5 (1997), pp. 273–81.

18. C. Chapman and S. Ward, *Project Risk Management: Processes, Techniques and Insights* (Chichester, England: John Wiley & Sons, 1997).

19. R. Wyatt, "How to Assess Risk," *Systems Management* 23, no. 10 (1995), pp. 80–83.

20. J. Fortune and G. Peters, *Learning from Failure: The Systems Approach* (New York: John Wiley & Sons, 1995).

21. Ibid.

22. P. Thibodeau, "Private Sector to Tackle IRS," *Computerworld,* January 4, 1999, http:///www.computerworld.com.

23. E. Oz, "Information Systems MIS-Development: The Case of Star*Doc," *Journal of Systems Management,* September 1994, pp. 30–34.

24. Ibid.

25. T. Ingram, "Managing Client/Server and Open Systems Projects: A 10-Year Study of 62 Mission-Critical Projects," *Project Management Journal* 25, no. 2 (1994), pp. 26–36.

26. Ibid.

27. P. B. Checkland, *Systems Thinking, Systems Practice* (Chichester, England: John Wiley & Sons, 1981).

28. R. Ormerod, "Putting Soft OR Methods to Work: Information Systems Strategy Development at Sainsbury's," *Journal of the Operational Research Society* 46 (1995), pp. 277–93.

29. _____, "Putting Soft OR Methods to Work: Information Systems Strategy Development at Richards Bay," *Journal of the Operational Research Society* 47 (1996), pp. 1083–97.

30. C. J. Khisty, "Soft-Systems Methodology as Learning and Management Tool," *Journal of Urban Planning and Development* 121, no. 3 (1995), pp. 91–101.

31. Fortune and Peters, *Learning from Failure.*

32. Ibid.

33. Ibid.

System Development

Chapter Outline

Main Ideas Discussed

- Late, over budget, and failed information systems projects
- Methods used to analyze and design information systems
- Standards for software systems development
- Prototyping as a way to develop projects in uncertain environments
- Types of information systems projects
- A project systems life-cycle development approach

There are seemingly unlimited proposals for implementation of computer systems to aid organizations. Every time one of these proposals is adopted, it creates the need for an information systems project—to bring an application online. Project management is one of the most important developing areas in information systems because it is so difficult to bring an information systems project to completion on time, within budget, and meeting specifications.

There are many citations of the scope of this problem. A partner of KPMG Peat Marwick said that, based on a survey of 250 companies, some 30 percent of information systems projects exceeded the original budget and time frame by at least a factor of 2, or did not conform to specifications.[1] A report issued by The Standish Group in 1994 (based on a survey of 365 companies with more than 8,000 development projects) found that only 16 percent came in on time and within budget. For large companies, the success rate was only 9 percent. It was also reported that only 42 percent of planned features and functions end up in the final version of the software.[2] A 1995 report by The Standish Group stated that more than half the software development projects initiated by large companies would cost 189 percent more than originally estimated. American Express Financial Advisors experienced project budget overruns as high as 500 percent.[3] The Standish Group issued yet another report in 1997, reporting that in 1996 73 percent of U.S. software projects had been canceled, were over budget, or were late, but that this was much better than the corresponding 84 percent in 1995.[4] Meta Group Inc. reported in 1997 that poor project planning and management had led to U.S. companies scrapping almost one-third of their new software projects at an annual loss of $80 billion. One out of every two projects ran more than 180 percent over budget for another $59 billion in losses.[5] Yet information systems projects offer great value for companies.

To develop systems efficiently, a methodology needs to be applied. Organizations use a wide variety of methodologies. The purpose of this chapter is to provide an overview of traditional systems development methodologies. It is becoming more and more important to apply continuous improvement standards to the processes used within business. Standards such as ISO 9000 and Software Engineering Institute's Capability Maturity Model focus on improving the processes of software development. Software development organizations are being required by some user organizations to certify compliance with these standards. Compliance is also very beneficial to software production organizations. We review these standards in this chapter. Types of information systems projects and their features are examined, followed by a broad framework of the systems development approach.

Overview of Analysis and Design Methods

There are a number of approaches that traditionally have been used for the analysis and design of information systems projects. **Systems analysis** helps determine the software components required to accomplish certain functions. **Systems**

design is the process by which the software system is set up to accomplish those functions. Boehm[6] reviews some of the older approaches, such as the "code-and-fix" model, where code is written and problems are fixed. This approach resulted in many problems when it came to implementation, and fixing was often expensive. We now discuss several other approaches.

The Waterfall Model

The **waterfall model** recognizes feedback loops between stages of software development stages to minimize rework, as well as incorporating prototyping as a means to more thoroughly understand new applications. The waterfall model (named because each step follows its predecessor in sequence) consists of the stages listed in Table 4–1, each of which can involve reversion to the prior stage if attempts at validation uncover problems. The waterfall model has the advantages of encouraging planning before design, and decomposes system development into subgoals with milestones corresponding to completion of intermediate products. This allows project managers to more accurately track project progress, and provides project structure. The list shown in Table 4–1 is for a software life-cycle product. Variations in the stage labels are used for different types of projects, such as acquisition of software, implementation of a vendor system, or other kinds of projects. Each stage involves a test, either validation or verification. **Validation** is the process of evaluating software to ensure compliance with specification requirements. (Is this the right product?) **Verification** is the process of determining whether the software component functions correctly. (Is the product built right?)

In the original waterfall model, problems accumulated over stages and were not noticed until project completion, resulting in very expensive code. User needs were often not met, resulting in rejection of products after they were built. Therefore, feedback loops were added, along with prototyping to catch problems early. The waterfall model does not allow rapid response to the pervasiveness of change

---

TABLE 4–1   Waterfall Model of Software Life-Cycle Stages

Stage	*Feedback Determinant*
System feasibility	Validation
Software plans and requirements	Validation
Product design	Verification
Detailed design	Verification
Code	Unit test
Integration	Product verification
Implementation	System test
Operations and maintenance	Revalidation

Source: Based on B. Boehm, "A Spiral Model of Software Development and Enhancement," *Computer,* May 1998, p. 27.

in information system projects. The orderly sequence of activities in the waterfall model does not accommodate new developments. Some systems, especially those involving higher levels of uncertainty and with less investment at stake, are often designed and built using more flexible development methods, such as rapid prototyping, object-oriented process, or rapid application development.

Prototyping is the process of developing a small working model of a program component or system with the intent of seeing what it can do. Thus it is a learning device, and it is especially appropriate when users are not absolutely sure what they want in a system. Prototyping can be a valuable part of the waterfall approach.

Prototyping

When dealing with systems, which involve beneficial features that are both difficult to predict and difficult to price, the systems development approach has proven ineffective. What happens is that the hard, clear dollar benefits are rarely sufficient to justify adopting the system.

Keen[7] advocated the use of an evolutionary approach for evaluating systems applied in unstructured environments because users very often do not know what benefits or what features the system will provide until they see it in operation. A prototyping approach involves building a small-scale mockup system, allowing the user to try it out. The user could then ask for modifications based on a better idea of what the system could do. Prototyping is a much less thoroughly planned approach, but it is often appropriate for applications with low investment and low

Prototypes, such as this model of an apartment complex in Beijing, China, allow developers to peer into a project before moving to full-scale implementation.

structure. This can result in much lower development cost and time, especially when there are many uncertainties about what the system should consist of.

Prototyping is very useful and can lead to greater understanding and definition of project requirements. It has also been found to improve design effectiveness because users are directly integrated into the design process in a manner that they clearly understand. However, some problems have been encountered in its implementation. Lantz[8] found that prototyped computer systems had less efficient performance. Alavi[9] found that large-scale projects were difficult to prototype. Iivari and Karjalainen[10] found that prototypes tended to create unrealistic expectations on the part of users. Prototyping isn't appropriate for all types of system development. But for smaller scale systems, prototyping is a very effective means of demonstrating what proposed systems would be able to do.

The Spiral Model

The **spiral model**[11] uses iterative prototypes (see Table 4–2). For each portion of the system, a risk analysis is performed. Starting with a concept of systems operation, a requirements plan is developed. Software requirements are generated and validated, followed by a development plan. Risk analysis is repeated, and a new prototype incorporating the new development plan is generated, followed by software product design, which is validated, verified, integrated, and tested. After another risk analysis, an improved prototype is developed with a more detailed design. Given this more complete information, coding proceeds, along with testing, integration, acceptance testing, and implementation.

Each cycle of the spiral begins with the identification of objectives, alternative means of implementing the particular stage of the product, and consideration of constraints. Each cycle involves risk analysis, an identification of what might

TABLE 4–2   The Spiral Model

Cycle 1	Cycle 2	Cycle 3	Cycle 4
Risk analysis	Risk analysis	Risk analysis	Risk analysis
Prototype	Prototype	Prototype	Operational prototype
	Models	Models	Models
Operation concept	Software requirements	Software product design	Detailed design
Requirements plan	Requirements validation	Design validation and verification	Code Unit test
Life-cycle plan	Development plan	Integration and test plan	Integration and test Acceptance test Implementation

Source: Adapted from B. Boehm, *Software Risk Management* (Washington, DC: IEEE Computer Society Press, 1988), p. 64.

go wrong, and a plan to deal with problems if they occur. Then prototypes are developed to demonstrate what the system can do at this stage. Models, in the form of simulation to determine risk, and benchmarks to test system modules are applied. This is followed in each cycle by design considerations, followed by validation and/or verification, and integration.

Boehm[12] also gave detailed discussion of risk items that need to be considered in software development, along with risk management techniques to deal with each risk (see Table 4–3). This list demonstrates that risk can arise in all aspects of information systems project management. Personnel problems might arise, but they could be dealt with by getting better people if needed or developing the skills of existing people. Project estimates are often problematic. If it appears that budgets will be exhausted, one approach would be to spend more effort on estimation in order to have a better idea of the scope of the problem. Another approach is to build the project in modules and closely monitor cost and time progress. If the budget or time allotted is clearly insufficient, project scope can be reduced.

If there is risk that software may not do what it was intended to do, users can be surveyed to gain better understanding of requirements. Prototyping can reveal more about what software does or does not do. The risk of interface components not performing adequately also can be alleviated by involving users to a greater extent.

If users ask for too many features, prototyping can again reveal the capabilities of software. Less expensive options may perform more than adequately, but users may require demonstration so that they can understand this. Cost/benefit analysis is useful in showing users what more advanced features would cost and what they are expected to save. If strict budget limits exist, designing to budget would provide the best system within a specified budget limit. If many requirements changes are experienced, changes may be postponed until the last minute, with the possibility that the last proposed changes will be superceded.

The risk of external system components failing to perform as specified can be reduced by closely monitoring performance during development. By benchmarking and inspection, problems can be identified early, when corrections will cost less. Use of award-fee contracts provide added incentive for vendors to provide superior products.

Technical performance of the system is often a risk. Modeling can identify expected performance before building systems. Prototyping provides a means of empirically assessing a system.

Many risks exist in information systems projects. The management of these risks is critical to successful delivery of needed information systems support. The spiral model emphasizes risk analysis to yield more consistent system performance.

Rapid Prototyping

Rapid prototyping[13] uses feedback from users on the suitability of requirements. If requirements were not totally understood in the development stage (often a

TABLE 4–3   Software Risk Checklist

Risk Item	Risk Management Responses
Personnel shortages	Staff with best talent
	Teambuilding
	Match individual to jobs
	Training
Budget and schedule problems	Detailed cost and schedule estimates
	Multiple sources
	Design to cost
	Software reuse
	Incremental development
	Requirements scrubbing
Wrong software functions	User surveys
	Early user manuals
	Prototyping
Wrong user interface	Prototyping
	Scenarios
	Task analysis
Excessive features	Requirements scrubbing
	Cost/benefit analysis
	Prototyping
	Design to cost
Continuing requirements changes	High change threshold
	Incremental development (defer changes)
External component problems	Benchmarking
	Reference checking
	Inspections
	Compatibility analysis
External task problems	Reference checking
	Award-fee contracts
	Prototyping
	Pre-award audits
	Competitive design
	Teambuilding
Real-time performance shortfalls	Simulation
	Modeling
	Instrumentation
	Benchmarking
	Prototyping
	Tuning
Technical limits	Technical analysis
	Prototyping
	Cost/benefit analysis
	Reference checking

Source: Adapted from B. Boehm, *Software Risk Management* (Washington, DC: IEEE Computer Society Press, 1988), p. 344.

problem in large-scale projects), user feedback provides greater chance of accurate understanding. The rapid prototyping process consists of:

- Problem analysis.
- Requirements description.
- Requirements specification.
- Prototype design/implementation.
- Prototype evaluation.
- Formal specifications for design of system.

During the requirements phase, a simple prototype system is built and shown to users, who evaluate current system strengths and weaknesses. This feedback is used to identify errors and to revise the requirements description.

Prototyping is often used within a variety of systems development approaches. It can be used within a full-system development. It is often used when new systems are being designed for new purposes. For instance, Britton et al.[14] show prototyping applied to the implementation of multimedia systems.

The Wavefront Model

The requirements process can be decomposed into problem analysis, problem description, prototyping and testing, and validation. Requirements analysis takes general notions of what the user wants as elicited by the requirements analyst and generates a set of system requirements. System requirements are a set of interrelated problem statements in the language of system designers.

In the **wavefront model** (see Table 4–4), problem analysis and problem description are informal. All of the user's needs have to be captured and translated into a formal, structured specification. Prototyping and testing are used to explore the feasibility of user requirements. Validation ensures that the project as implemented reflects what the user expected.

TABLE 4–4   Wavefront Model

Problem analysis
    Errors or inconsistencies? New or changing needs?
Problem description
    Changed technique? Changed view?
Prototyping and testing
    Formal specifications incomplete?
    Programming errors?
Validation
    User concerns? Invalid requirements?

Source: Adapted from M. F. Theofanos and S. L. Pfleeger, "Wavefront: A Goal Driven Requirements Process Model," *Information and Software Technology* 38 (1996), pp. 507–19.

The wavefront model is iterative in that the problem is revisited as insights are gained by either users or the requirements analyst. The activities are also concurrent. As problem analysis proceeds, those aspects of the problem that are well-understood are recorded in the formal specification. Prototyping proceeds along with problem analysis and product description.

Other Options for Systems Development

Many projects are developed from scratch, applying conventional systems development approaches. In addition to prototyping, McLeod and Smith[15] give the following iterative life-cycle approaches where tasks are performed repetitively to more exactly meet their goals:

- *Component assembly projects*—typically object-oriented modules for use in a variety of other applications.
- *Rapid application development*—techniques to compress the life cycle include computer-aided software engineering (CASE) and joint application development (JAD). CASE tools involve a degree of reuse of previously developed systems. To complete projects on an accelerated time scale, project objectives and scope need to be identified early, and joint development of user requirements must be effective. Group systems, as discussed in Chapter 3, may be of use in this type of application. Care must be taken in assigning team members on a full-time basis, and heavy user participation is very important. Rapid application development can lead to reduced development time, lower development cost, greater user and employee satisfaction, and lower ultimate maintenance costs. However, it is appropriate for small projects, not for those involving significant levels of complexity.

Software Development Standards

Quality improvement has been an area of major development in the operations management area. One of the key ideas involved is that of continuous improvement—developing a philosophy of business in which the ways in which work is done (**processes**) are continuously reviewed with the intent of improving them. This emphasis on quality process has been widely implemented in the United States in the annual Baldrige Award competition, as well as the European Quality Award Assessment Model. Two other programs that have had a major effect on the software development industry include ISO 9000 (European standards for production and management processes) and the Software Engineering Institute's capability maturity model.

ISO 9000 is a set of standards that focuses on an organization's processes rather than the quality of products these organizations produce. The philosophy is that if the processes of design, manufacturing, logistics, and other managerial areas are performed correctly, they will yield quality goods. The purpose of ISO 9000

TABLE 4–5   Capability Maturity Model

Level	Features	Key Processes
1. Initial	Chaotic	Survival
2. Repeatable	Individual control	Software configuration management
		Software quality assurance
		Software subcontract management
		Software project tracking and oversight
		Software project planning
		Requirements management
3. Defined	Institutionalized process	Peer reviews
		Intergroup coordination
		Software product engineering
		Integrated software management
		Training program
		Organization process definition
		Organization process focus
4. Managed	Process measured	Quality management
		Process measurement and analysis
5. Optimizing	Feedback for improvement	Process change management
		Technology innovation
		Defect prevention

Source: Adapted from CMU/SEI-93-TR-24, Capability Maturity Model for Software, V1.1 (1993).

standards are to ensure that processes can consistently meet customer expectations. The standards require that processes be defined and documented, that action be taken to ensure that these procedures are followed, that processes be measured and recorded, and that continuous improvement be implemented. In the United States, ISO registration is becoming more and more important as a qualification to doing business, especially with military and other governmental agencies.

The Software Engineering Institute's **capability maturity model** includes five levels of maturity. These are shown in Table 4–5, along with actions generally required to move from one level to another. Organizations that have done nothing to improve their software development methods are assigned to level 1 and are considered to involve high levels of risk and a focus on survival. To move from the initial level 1 to level 2 requires instilling basic discipline into management activities. This is accomplished through adopting software management approaches.

To move from level 2 to level 3 requires that organizations identify the primary competencies required in processes and then take action to make sure that the people assigned to these activities have these competencies. This can be done through training or hiring. Processes are defined and institutionalized in level 3 organizations.

Moving from level 3 to level 4 requires quantitative management of organizational growth in human management capabilities and establishment of competency-based teams. Process measurement and analysis need to be implemented.

TABLE 4–6   Effect of CMM Level on Software Development of Code

Level	Development Cost ($\$ \times 10^6$)	Development Time (months)	Product Quality (defects/thousand)	Lines of Code/Hour
1	33	40	9.0	1
2	15	32	3.0	3
3	7	25	1.0	5
4	3	19	0.3	8
5	1	16	0.1	12

Source: Adapted from S. McConnell, "From Anarchy to Optimizing," *Software Development*, July 1993, pp. 51–55.

Moving to level 5 requires continuous improvement of methods for developing personal and organizational process abilities. In this state, greater technology innovation is expected by some. All expect better defect prevention.

McConnell[16] reviewed projects accomplished by organizations at various levels for a typical 500,000-line software project. The results dramatically indicate the benefits of attaining higher levels of capability maturity (see Table 4–6). It is clear that adopting capability maturity principles pays. Level 1 projects are expected to take far longer (thus costing far more). They also have much inferior quality as measured by defects. Implementing the capability maturity model requires significant investment, effort, and discipline, but it clearly is better than the ad hoc state of doing nothing.

Information Systems Project Types

There is a wide variety of possible information systems projects that can be classified as three basic types:

- Maintenance
- Conversion
- New systems development

McLeod and Smith[17] view projects a bit differently:

- *Systems architecture projects*—projects that are part of the strategic systems plan for the organization, supporting the firm's business strategy.
- *End-user computing*—installing a system for target users, with heavy user involvement in development.
- *Business reengineering projects*—implementing new ways of processing business functions.
- *Technology implementation projects*—installation of technology such as a network or e-mail.

- *Package implementation*—installing a prewritten application, with any required modifications.

Each of these implementation project categories can be found in each of the three categories given earlier (maintenance, conversion, and new systems development), although to varying degrees. Systems architecture projects are the focus of the information system, and most maintenance work would be expected in this project category. Business reengineering can involve maintenance and conversion, but would be expected to involve mostly new work. Conversion work often arises from corporate takeovers, or when new systems architectures are adopted.

Maintenance Projects

Maintenance projects are by far the most common type of information systems project. They can arise from the need to fix errors or to add enhancements to some system, or they can involve major enhancements. The way in which maintenance work is treated depends a great deal on the effect of the system in question on the organization's master plan. If the system being maintained is extremely important, it will *not* be treated as a project. It would have a permanent unit assigned to perform all required maintenance. Some organizations use maintenance work as a training ground for new employees. This is a good way to get exposure to the spectrum of the organization's operations.

Fixing errors involves a clear purpose—to make the system work correctly. The complexity of this type of work depends on the nature of the system, the error, and the personnel affected. The best case is a small system, with easily traced errors. It also is easier if someone who has experience with the system is available to fix it.

Minor enhancements involve such things as adding, modifying, or deleting data or reports from the information system. Sometimes minor enhancements involve a degree of original design work. Usually, however, this type of work is constrained by the original design. Minor enhancements are not typically critical. Therefore, there are likely to be more alternatives that can be considered. Minor enhancements are most likely to be assigned to those with design capabilities and knowledge of the organization.

Major enhancements involve high levels of design and implementation. This type of work can involve wide-scale modification of an existing module or development of a new module. Sometimes a collection of minor enhancements with some common characteristics are packaged together to make a major enhancement. Major enhancement work calls for experienced personnel.

Major enhancements are easiest if the maintenance personnel know the system well and involve straightforward processes. It is obviously easier if a CASE tool was used to develop the original system, because CASE can then be used to make the modification as well. Major enhancements are more trouble when new personnel are assigned to accomplish them, when it is hard to assess the criticality of the system, and when there are no design and implementation standards available.

Conversion Projects

Conversion projects involve changing an existing system. This existing system doesn't necessarily even have to be currently computerized (if you can imagine manual information system components in this day and age, but, remember, every system has to start somewhere!). Most conversion projects consist of moving an application from one computer platform to another. There also are many projects that develop from firm acquisitions in the form of legacy systems. Legacy systems create enormous potential for difficulties in integrating systems based on entirely different platforms.

Converting manual systems is the closest type of maintenance project to pure design and development. The major problems that one should expect in this type of environment are improper specifications and failure to accommodate changes. To successfully perform this type of work, one would need to understand the existing system, what is desired, and the means to move from the first state to the second.

Managing conversion change depends a great deal on senior management support. The affected employees need to be informed about the change, and it is a lot easier if they can be convinced that their working environment will be easier after the conversion. Often conversions change what employees do, and some people have problems with that. In extreme cases, conversions may displace employees, either because different skill levels are required after conversion or because jobs are eliminated. In this case, one hopes that the displaced employees can be retrained for other work.

Conversion of new technology is easiest when there is a great deal of similarity between new and old hardware and new and old operating systems. It also is easier if existing applications are modular and if vendors supply routines for conversion. The worst case is when major changes occur, especially if there is a change from a single-task to multitask environment. It is difficult, for instance, to move from a line-oriented system to an icon-oriented system such as *Windows*.

Language-based conversions are often encountered. This involves translation from one language to another, usually from a third-generation language such as COBOL to a fourth-generation language. In these situations it helps to have experts in both the old and new languages on the project team. It is necessary to consider the effect on data structures and code structure. It is usually wise to take full advantage of the capabilities of the newer language.

Nonprocedural conversions have unique characteristics. Instead of a sequential control, statements written in the form of rules are fired when all conditions are satisfied, as in a rule-based expert system. Object-oriented approaches are becoming more common, where objects have the power to control processing. Again, it is good to have expertise in both the old and new languages. In the case of converting to object-oriented systems, it is possible to take advantage of code reuse.

Hardware conversions can arise from the need to convert to a new platform for marketing purposes, from pulling an outsourced application back in-house, or from purchase of a new computing platform. Most of the effort involved in this type of conversion arises from converting low-level input and output processing routines.

If hardware is obtained from the same vendor that provided the old system, there are fewer problems. For instance, IBM equipment involves 32-bit words with 8-bit bytes, while CDC has 60-bit words with 6-bit bytes. Switching from one to the other is obviously much more difficult. In fact, many codes written on one system, especially if they were written to take advantage of hardware features, will cause problems when attempts are made to run them on another system. Vendors usually supply different codes for the same application, depending on the type of system.

The best case is when vendor-specific input/output is localized in routines supplied by the vendor. Occasionally, however, some adjustments are required.

New Systems

There are many ways in which technology can be used to enhance the information system flow, as well as accomplish needed work. The accompanying box describes some such system examples. New systems development involves different management characteristics by type of system. The types of systems discussed here include the following:

- Transaction processing.
- Management control.
- Decision support systems.
- Data warehousing and data mining.
- Group support systems.
- Executive information systems.
- Enterprise resource planning.
- Internet commerce.

Reengineering Cases Using Information Technology

Kralovec reported on four projects that implemented a new technology. These four examples provide views of the potential of technology to improve business processes.

United Services Automobile Association, one of the largest insurers in the United States, deals directly with more than 2 million customers, and receives 80,000 to 125,000 letters per day. An inexpensive way to maintain huge amounts of informa-

Video teleconferencing can save companies both travel expenses and employee's time. Aided by videophone hook-ups, staff meetings can include team members in remote locations.

tion was required. The use of high-density storage technology (optical storage) eliminated filing space, reduced support costs, and improved productivity.

Picture Tel System introduced video teleconferencing. A high-tech audio and video communications system was installed using video camera and audio hookups at each office using telephone lines. Staff meetings, discussion groups, personal meetings, and educational seminars were teleconferenced, saving travel expenses and employee time.

Cellular Automated Transmission System used portable communications to save costs and improve productivity. A direct portable link between truckers and headquarters was required. Laptop computers, cellular telephones, high-speed modems, and mobile fax machines were installed in truck cabs to facilitate delivery receipts, orders, and bills of lading.

United Parcel Service needed a way to eliminate excessive paperwork, resolve delivery disputes, and increase tracking ability. Pen-based computing was adopted through the Delivery Information Acquisition Device (DIAD). An electronic pen is used to enter commands and data. Customers sign for packages directly on the DIAD. Data can be scanned or keyed in by the driver, saving time, paper, and money. The project was extended to 65,000 UPS drivers nationally.

Source: J. Kralovec, "IS-Directed Engineering," *Information Systems Management,* Winter 1998, pp. 79–81.

Transaction processing is generally focused on efficient operation. The application usually involves high volumes of quantitative data from a variety of input sources. These data are used to generate standard reports as part of the information system. Most of the complexity arises from the volume of computations. Sound systems analysis and design procedures should be followed to thoroughly examine the effects of the new system on everyone involved.

Management control is more specialized than transaction processing. Example applications are monitoring manpower allocations, progress of project activities, production by unit, and sales by region or sales representative. These systems often compare expected performance with actual performance, and if the difference is great enough, some action may be triggered. Clearly this type of system requires more flexibility. Because multiple numbers of people are affected by changes, systems analysis and design processes should be adopted.

Decision support systems (DSSs) by definition are meant to be customized for the specific user. The application of a DSS is to explore decision alternatives. Often data need to be accessed from a variety of sources, including internal and online commercial sources. Each individual decision maker has his or her own preferences for data, computer interface, and model access. The project team installing a DSS must have knowledge of the models to be installed. A complicating factor is that the decision maker may not have much idea of what features are desired until the system is in operation. Therefore, a prototyping approach is usually more appropriate for development of a decision support system.

Data warehousing and data mining are new technologies that expand the concepts of database systems and statistics (as well as artificial intelligence). **Data warehousing** applications allow access to vast quantities of data, including cash register data, that can be searched electronically to gain insights into many marketing and financial environments. Data warehouses provide repositories, where large amounts of data can be stored in a manner that allows rapid recovery. **Data mining** applies electronic technology to try to identify customer clusters that would have a greater payoff in response to marketing campaigns and other statistical analyses of large data sets.

Group support systems (GSSs), discussed previously in Chapter 3, allow multiple decision makers to work on a decision problem. They are very process oriented, in that their primary function is to allow people to communicate, sometimes from different places, sometimes at different times. GSSs usually include features of anonymity, allowing participants to enter comments without attribution. A major function of a GSS is to foster group brainstorming, which works quite well by triggering creative ideas. The system may have the ability to build consensus. Some decision support systems can be purchased almost complete from vendors and be installed like a complete vendor package. A higher proportion of group support systems are obtained from vendors in this form. Group support systems come in a variety of forms, some of which are primarily focused on electronic communication.

Executive information systems are more complex applications. They require access to a variety of types of data, both in-house and external. Some of

Laptop computers and cellular phones can improve communications between truckers and their headquarters.

these data are much more subjective, and may even be qualitative, such as *The Wall Street Journal* or periodic government reports. The interface is critical. A common feature of executive information systems is the ability to search data (drill-down) for details about the summary data that are generally reported to the user. There is an emphasis on graphics and key statistics to quickly give a picture of what is going on in the organization. Exception reporting is therefore important. There can be a great deal of work to build such a system. Many products of this type are sold by vendors, for fairly high prices. A great deal of the purchase price often is for installation support. It is possible to build executive information systems in-house, but while a company may gain the opportunity to custom design the system, it can turn out to be very expensive.

Enterprise resource planning systems are systems designed to comprehensively serve all computing needs of an organization. These systems are usually implemented in modules, but this type of product usually takes over an organization's computing because the intent is to integrate systems. Enterprise resource planning systems are not trivial to implement, but vendors are more than willing to provide assistance (at the normal nominal fee).

Implementing **Internet commerce** involves rethinking the business and its keys processes, developing an appropriate and affordable information technology infrastructure, and constructing specific Internet products and services. There are many kinds of systems that need to be installed, lending variety to the many information systems projects found in business. The following presentation of Academic Business Process Reengineering demonstrates some of the advantages of implementing one of these types of projects.

Academic Business Process Reengineering

Babson College implemented a three-year project to transform its business processes. The primary objective was to improve the quality of service delivery to students for admission, records, registration, advising, financial aid, career services, and field-based learning. The college also sought to reduce administrative costs and redirect these funds to teaching and academic support. Change management teams were formed to reengineer each of the operational areas supported by the system. Critical performance measures were established for each application. The focus was on easy-to-use and effective information systems that students could access themselves.

The pre-existing system was a mainframe system with a dial-up network and text-based applications. The new system was a multitiered client/server infrastructure with 6,000 nodes, more than 50 servers, and 1,500 workstations. Data warehousing was used. The system reduced operating costs about 20 percent, half of the planned 40 percent, because some vendor systems were late.

One of the problems faced by the information technology team was how to organize access for the system to customers or service providers. Initially it was decided that a graphical electronic mail system front end would be used, with applications written as executables within mail system file folders. But this design was not approved by end users because the mail system was not robust or fast enough for the transaction volumes experienced. The Internet proved to be a solution. The Internet provides widespread access. The platform is not as reliable as it needs to be, but it is expected that this will improve with time.

Source: R. M. Kesner, "Building an Internet Commerce Capability: A Case Study," *Information Strategy,* Winter 1998, pp. 27–36.

Systems Development Approach

The **systems development approach** provides a rational way to evaluate information systems projects. The systems development approach is based on a complete life-cycle analysis. Project proposals evaluated by this approach are measured on cost, time, and performance. *Cost* is concerned with resources being spent as expected. Accurate budgets and benefit estimates are needed to accurately evaluate proposals. They also provide valuable control mechanisms during project implementation. *Time* is a critical variable in projects. First, it is highly correlated with cost. Second, delayed benefits are worth much less than early benefits, because of the time value of money. Keeping a project on schedule is a major challenge. *Performance* is a critical third measure. Projects need to perform to specifications and user requirements.

Later, when the project is being implemented, these measures are critically important. Performance needs to be ensured through quality testing. Time is a major means of evaluating how well the project is progressing. We will take a look at Gantt charts later in this chapter as a means of planning the time dimension of projects. Cost budgets are also critically important to control project implementation. Because of the high levels of uncertainty inherent in projects, management must closely monitor project progress and be prepared to shift resources and replan activities as required.

System life cycles consist (in broad terms) of the activities of specification, design, coding, data conversion, testing, and implementation. These activities tend to be serial, although data conversion can proceed in parallel with coding.

Specification

Projects start with somebody's problem. Computer systems are powerful tools that solve many problems. Therefore, there are many times when they offer improved means of doing things.

Once a proposed application is identified, a systems analyst who understands how to build such systems needs to be assigned to plan a solution. The systems analyst needs to start off by talking to the people who proposed the application to find out what they want and to the people who are budgeting the project to find out the constraints in terms of cost that need to be considered. It is best to discuss the proposed project with all groups affected so that something isn't designed that will be counterproductive or create unexpected problems. After these interviews, a clearer statement of the problem should be developed. An effective way to proceed is to identify alternate solutions, and to determine the costs and expected performance features of each so that the budgeting authority can select the best system possible. A **feasibility study** is a clear, concise statement of the problem, followed by a detailed formal description of the current system describing the problem. Adequate qualitative and quantitative information should be provided to determine if the effort should be continued. The elements and components of the proposed system are identified.

The **specification phase** should provide a clear problem statement of what the system is intended to do, with a rudimentary idea of a systems solution. Once the initial authorization is obtained, the system is defined in greater detail. A **statement of work** specifies what is to be done. It should specify new system objectives and provide measures for the acceptability of the system upon completion. Performance objectives should not be constrained by the existing system. One approach that works well is to start with general objectives. Objectives should include subelements that are measurable. This phase of the systems development approach results in a comprehensive list of activities, along with their schedules, costs, and required resources. This includes hardware and software requirements. When presented with the costs of proposed systems, many are rejected. It is in the specification phase that most projects die.

Design

The **design phase** develops how software will meet requirements. One of the classic business analyses is the **make or buy decision.** This decision is very pertinent to computer systems because there are many vendors that produce and sell many useful computer systems. Every organization has the option of buying products from vendors or of building the product themselves. In general, buying products from vendors is much more efficient, but the features that vendors put into the product are not always optimal. Vendors make a living telling clients that their system is exactly what the client needs. In truth, it often isn't. Furthermore, even if it is, vendors may charge more than the product is worth. Building products in-house, however, requires a great deal more risk and time. If required expertise is not available, it may well be worth spending a little more on the vendor. Usually the vendor route is faster, and quite often it is cheaper. The problem usually lies with matching the existing system and doing the job required.

Recently it has become very popular to hire out large portions of information processing, or **outsourcing.** One purpose of outsourcing is downsizing. Unocal, like many other oil companies, pared their staff by 40 percent over a two-year pe-riod, with 130 layoffs in the information systems group.[18] The Illinois Central Railroad outsourced its most important function, railcar management, to the in-formation systems group of competitor Union Pacific.[19] Illinois Central manage-ment stated that outsourcing enabled the railroad to take care of its customers without requiring a sizable investment in new applications and equipment. US Airways outsourced its information technology services and application develop-ment work to Sabre in a multibillion dollar deal. Sabre's work would include Year 2000 fixes for US Airways' legacy systems, as well as reservations systems, air-port check-in, aircraft and crew scheduling, yield management, and electronic ticketing.[20] Swiss Bank Corp. signed with Perot Systems to run major parts of its information technology operations for at least 10 years for $250 million per year. DuPont contracted with Andersen Consulting and Computer Sciences Corpora-tion for more than $4 billion per year for 10 years of service. J. P. Morgan & Co. paid four outsourcers a reported $2 billion to run its computers, manage its net-works, and build new applications for seven years. Ryder System Inc. hired An-dersen and IBM for $1.4 billion to provide computing assistance for 10 years, including a new system for logistics. Ryder expected to save about $160 million over the 10-year contract.

Another recent trend has been to tie payment to vendors based on the value of computing service received. Xerox signed a $3.2 billion contract with EDS in 1994 for 10 years' service as a way to release its reduced information technology staff of 700 to focus on flexible network computing, a key strategic core compe-tency[21] (see the accompanying box).

Xerox Focuses Their Information Technology Efforts

Early in 1994 Xerox Corporation, a very financially sound company, outsourced its information systems operations to Electronic Data Systems Corporation (EDS). While outsourcing often is used by companies needing quick cash, in the case of Xe-rox the firm was quite sound. Xerox had an operating profit of $620 million on sales of $14.6 billion at that time. The aim was to shed noncore business to focus on the strategically more important document business. The stated motivation was to speed the rate at which Xerox could move into new technologies and to free management to focus on strategic information management issues. EDS took over data center operations, worldwide voice and data communications, desktop system support, and legacy software support. EDS was also responsible for new client/server projects. Xerox reduced its information systems staff by 2,000 (many transferring to EDS). The remaining Xerox information technology staff of 700 worked on moving Xerox into flexible network computing (architecture, strategy, and application development) to support Xerox's long-term needs.

Sources: M. Halper, "Xerox Signs Up EDS," *Computerworld,* March 28, 1994, http://www.computerworld.com; and J. W. Verity, "Megadeals March On," *Computerworld,* July 28, 1997, http://www.computerworld.com.

Many functions can be outsourced, including data center management, telecommunications, disaster recovery, and legacy systems maintenance. This avoids the need to waste scarce resources and can gain efficiencies by hiring vendors with expertise. Outsourcing can also be used for company Internet operations. Eastman Kodak, which began outsourcing in 1989, held on to its Internet activities because the environment was too dynamic, and its own plans were too uncertain. If plans are clearer, Internet functions that could be outsourced include connectivity, Web server hosting, firewall security, web site development, and content development. These activities are complex, subject to change, and not particularly relevant to organizational core competencies.[22] Outsourcing makes sense when fast startup is important, internal skills are lacking, and the vendor can provide strong features. Outsourcing for Internet operations is not as worthwhile if such operations are of strategic importance to the business or if requirements are ill-defined. Rarely is outsourcing used for everything involved within a project. For one thing, there will be need for internal training to implement the system and to integrate it with the existing system.

If vendors or outside contractors are being considered, a **request for proposal** is required, including the feasibility study and the plan for project development. The request for proposal states the user requirements in terms of system objectives, project scope, and performance specifications as well as constraints, especially in terms of time. It is necessary to develop a qualified bidders list of those with the ability to accomplish the work required.

The project team needs to be selected at this stage. The project manager should be selected, with characteristics we discuss later. Team members are drawn from functional areas. Functional managers should be sold on the project, so that good team members are obtained.

The output of the design stage is a detailed list of user requirements and system requirements. Tasks are broken down into work packages, and team members are given specific assignments. The project manager is responsible to set up schedules, budgets, and controls. The output of the design stage is a task breakout, with each task scheduled by date. It is necessary to continue close coordination among the systems analyst, the ultimate user of the system, and the budget authority. A project never is completely designed, nor finally adopted, until it is complete. Accurate understanding among analyst, user, and owner is necessary to develop systems that are useful and cost-effective. A Gantt chart is the standard way to display a schedule of project activities over time. A Gantt chart is pictorially described in the Appendix chapter on Microsoft Project. It is a bar chart with time as the horizontal dimension. Each bar shows when an activity is scheduled to be worked on.

Code (or Acquisition)

Options, in-house or vendor, need to be evaluated. If in-house, the conventional **coding phase** to implement the design is applied. If options including purchasing the products or services of a vendor are adopted, the term *acquisition* seems more appropriate.

If outside vendors or contractors are being considered, selection of the bidder to build the project (or project components) involves some options. There are a number of bases for selecting a bidder. If the system quality has been thoroughly defined to the extent that every bidder has the knowledge and if each bidder has been screened to ensure their competence, selection on the basis of low bid is usually used. This has obvious advantages, using the competitive system, to lower costs. However, selecting the low bidder has obvious risks if the bidder is not truly qualified. In fact, in some parts of Europe, the winning bidder is the one closest to the average bid, using the logic that they must know what they were asked to do. Regardless, there are other considerations besides low price:

- Cost—need to ensure that it is within the allowable budget.
- Feasibility—need to ensure that the bidder can actually do the project.
- Experience—look at the bidder's record on similar projects.
- Reputation—bidder's record with respect to quality work.

Oftentimes, if the bid is too high, the user can negotiate with the bidder. There is a degree of ethics involved if an open competitive bidding process was used. Those not selected may not have been treated fairly if the rules are changed after the initial bid. However, in the private sector, this is a legal way to proceed, and the owner and the bidder can work together to negotiate an acceptable agreement for both. Negotiation is especially appropriate when dealing with complex systems when it is attractive to share risks.

In-house systems development begins with the design stage, which involves converting specifications from the definition phase into plans. The proposed system is broken down into subsystems, components, and parts. All elements need to be checked for compatibility as well as for their ability to meet specifications. Prototyping can be used if there is benefit from seeing what the system will look like.

The system is developed and whatever hardware and software is needed is procured. The system is constructed, and any code and interfaces that are needed are programmed. System testing is conducted concurrently with assembly of the system to catch errors as quickly as possible. Development of training materials is often accomplished concurrently as well.

A cost/benefit analysis (see Chapter 2) is often used to evaluate projects. This study is based on a preliminary and high-level estimate of project costs and benefits. If bids are taken, the acquisition cost is pretty well defined. Costs to implement and operate the system need to be considered as well. The cost side of the ratio is usually much easier to accurately measure than are the benefits. System performance standards are often used as the basis for estimating the value of expected benefits. Everything connected with the project needs to be put in dollar (or other) terms to use the cost/benefit ratio, which is nothing more than the net present value of the proposed project. Cost/benefit ratios have the advantage of clearly identifying whether proposals make economic sense. If the net present value of the benefits exceed the net present costs associated with the project, adopting the project should improve the financial position of the organization. If the budget allows for only a limited number of projects, the proposals could be ranked by the cost/benefit ratio. The concept is very good, but it depends on the accuracy of the numbers used in the calculations, which often involve high degrees of uncertainty. Therefore, other selection techniques are sometimes used that consider value functions.

The production of a system follows analysis and design. The production itself can involve a large group of diverse people, including programmers, people building user interfaces, people designing the database interfaces, people dealing with the users to design reports, and people to set up any required networks for multiple users. The project manager must work hard to ensure that people with the right skills are available at the right time, obtain needed facilities in terms of tools and places to work, set up realistic time estimates allowing for the appropriate level of uncertainty, and of course obtain the necessary capital. Quality testing should be accomplished throughout production. It is a good practice to build systems in modules and thoroughly test each component before adoption. If at all possible, it is be best to include the user in this testing.

Data Conversion

When a system is developed, data access and input need to be compatible with the new system. An extreme example of this problem occurs in data mining, where masses of raw data are processed with the intent of obtaining insight into more effective ways of running a business. Data for data mining are almost always stored in data warehouses, capable of storing mammoth quantities of input, such as cash register data. **Data conversion** is important because for data mining to work, data must be in a usable form, it must include having no missing observations, and all data must be in numeric form and readable in the proper format. A major element of data warehousing is cleaning data to obtain this state. Executive information systems and enterprise resource planning systems also require data converted to a compatible form.

Testing

Quality control is very important throughout the system development cycle. In the **testing phase** each module needs to be checked before a block of work is considered complete. Organizations usually have independent testing groups assigned to review system components to ensure that they are capable of dealing with the expected workload.

Implementation

Once the system is satisfactorily built and tested, it is moved from the builder to the user; this is the **implementation phase.** The system must be installed and checked out to ensure that it does what was specified. Training the users with technical support available once the system is turned over to the user wraps up the project cycle. The user evaluates system performance, and if any flaws are detected, the builder fixes them. Sound contractual agreements spelling out procedures before the project is started are very useful at this stage. Builders often provide maintenance support for systems, usually at some nominal fee. The implementation phase includes system improvement.

Summary

Many systems and analysis methods have evolved to support information systems projects. The different methodologies discussed in this chapter all have important roles to play for software projects with specific environmental conditions. Each organization tends to adopt a particular methodology. It is not as important which methodology is adopted as it is that a methodology be adopted. It is also important that software producing organizations adopt process standards. The capability maturity model has proven to be dramatically effective at improving process quality and productivity.

Information systems project management can involve a wide variety of tasks. Typical information systems project types include maintenance work, conversion projects, and new systems implementation. Most projects are maintenance related, involving relatively low levels of change. Maintenance of critical activities is often best managed by assigning a permanent team, passing beyond the project stage to a process operation. Conversion work is often required when firms change computer systems or firms are reorganized. New technology can take a variety of forms, ranging from efficiency-focused transaction processing to software product installation.

Systems development needs to consider cost, time, and performance in addition to specific criteria of importance to a specific project. The activities by system stages were reviewed.

Key Terms

capability maturity model 96
coding (or acquisition) phase 108
data conversion 109
data mining 102
data warehousing 102
decision support system (DSS) 102
design phase 105
enterprise resource planning
  systems 103
executive information systems 102
feasibility study 105
implementation phase 110
Internet commerce 103
ISO 9000 95
make or buy decision 105
management control 102

outsourcing 106
process 95
prototyping 90
rapid prototyping 92
specification phase 105
spiral model 91
statement of work 105
systems analysis 88
systems design 88
systems development approach 104
testing phase 110
transaction processing 102
verification 89
waterfall model 89
wavefront model 94

Exercises

1. Information systems projects usually have budget, time, and quality restraints. Estimates of project time and cost are revised as the project develops. As the project proceeds, would you expect estimates to be more accurate? Under what conditions would you expect the revised estimates to be higher than the original? What biases would you expect in the original estimates, used to obtain project approval?

2. Describe the waterfall method. The original model was a sequence of activities in series, where subsequent steps followed completion of prior steps. Why was that modified to include feedback at each step?

3. Discuss the difference between validation and verification in the context of information systems project design.

4. Prototyping involves developing small-scale models of systems. This provides the ability to learn more about what the system will do. Why is this not adopted for all projects?

5. What is different between the spiral model and the waterfall model including feedback and prototyping?

6. What actions did Boehm recommend to deal with the risk of changes in specified requirements on the part of the user?

7. How does rapid prototyping aid systems analysis and design?

8. Describe the wavefront model. What is different about it relative to the spiral model?

9. Describe the characteristics of maintenance projects.

10. Describe the characteristics of conversion projects. What is different about conversion projects relative to maintenance projects?

11. Describe the characteristics of new systems projects. What is different about new systems projects relative to maintenance and conversion projects?

12. What is a statement of work, and what is it for?

13. *Field Trip:* Visit a local organization producing software, and interview them about the methodology they use (if any). Inquire if they have adopted the capability maturity model. Also ask them about the type of information systems projects they are involved with.

Microsoft Project Exercise

This exercise adds resources to the project entered at the end of Chapter 3. Expanded input information is as follows.

Schedule the following project subject to given resource limits. Start July 1, 2000.

Identifier	Activity	Predecessor	Days	Resource
Perform Planning and Scheduling				
A1	Revise overall project plan	None	15	N, P
A2	Complete detailed plan for detail design	A1	5	P
A3	Revise skeleton and generic plan for rest	A1	3	P
A4	Brief new team members	A2, A3	1	M, N, P
A5	Complete phase estimate	A4	7	O, P
A6	Review plan	A5	1	M, N, O, P
A7	Revise plan	A6	10	O, P
A8	Complete project schedule	A5 start + 3	4	N
A9	Milestone	A7, A8	0	
Prepare Database Design				
B1	Document data models to catalog	None	15	B, P
B2	Determine file structures for flat files	B1	12	B
B3	Prepare copylibs for flat file structures	B1	7	B
B4	Define each process	B2, B3	3	B, P
B5	Review process access with database admin.	B4	1	D, M, N, P
B6	Physical database design	B5	20	B, R
B7	Review design	B6	1	B, D, M, N, P
B8	Revise design	B7	15	B, R
B9	Conduct call pattern reviews	B6	10	B
B10	Milestone	B8, B9	0	
Prepare Physical Design Documents				
C1	Prepare process-to-program specifications	B4	13	P
C2	Determine security specifications	B9, C1	8	B, P
C3	Prepare physical system flow	C2	12	B, P
C4	Milestone	C3	0	

Identifier	Activity	Predecessor	Days	Resource
D1	Design programs and write specifications	A8, B9	18	B, P
D2	Write data conversion & interface programs	D1	6	R (3)
D3	Revise documents	D2	30	R (3)
D4	Milestone	D3	0	
E1	Implementation	C3, D3	5	B, P, R
E2	Testing	E1	15	B, P, R
E3	Final acceptance	E2	1	M, N, D
E4	Milestone	E3	0	

Work 5 days per week
Holidays
  January 1
  3rd Monday in January
  3rd Monday in February
  July 4
  4th Thursday in November
  December 25

Resources	Cost/day	Resources	Cost/day
M Manager	$500 (1)	R Systems programmers	$300 (3)
N Assistant	$150 (1)	R = first, R3 = team	
O Cost estimator	$300 (1)	D Database administrator	$600 (1)
P Systems analysts P1, P2	$450 (2)	B Database designers	$400 (1)

Resources by task can be entered on the Gantt chart, using the initial letter. When the resource sheet is called up, the full names can be entered (the Gantt chart labels will be automatically updated). The initial column on the resource sheet can be revised to reflect the initial input. The standard rate column can be used to enter cost per day. Because the default time unit for costs is per hour, rates are entered "500/d" to reflect $500 per day. The last entries are for multiple resources. Two systems analysts can be identified by increasing the available number of systems analysts to 200 percent. This will allow either systems analyst to be used whenever one systems analyst is required. This reflects what is intended here. The other option is to enter each systems analyst independently, possibly by individual name. This would avoid any problems with *Microsoft Project* taking it upon itself to shorten durations should it assume the "resource-driven" mode. (Under this mode, if 200 percent of a resource is available, it assumes it can cut durations in half if this resource is not being used elsewhere.)

There is one resource that causes a minor problem. Activities B6 and B8 require one programmer representative to participate in project design. Activities D2 and D3 require the same three programmers as a team. The way this is treated here is to identify these as two different resources.

Resource	Initial	Available	Standard Cost
Assistant	N	100%	$150.00/d
Systems analyst	P	200	450.00/d
Manager	M	100	500.00/d
Cost estimator	O	100	300.00/d
Database designer	B	100	400.00/d
Database administrator	D	100	600.00/d
System programmer	R	200	300.00/d
Programming team	R(3)	100	600.00/d (always pair with R)

The availability of resources can be checked by reviewing the Resource Graph. The Assistant resource shows up first. To view the entire project, use the sequence:

View	Zoom	Entire Project

The Assistant resource is not overscheduled. Time periods of work are indicated in blue. The next resource can be viewed by hitting the page down key. Systems Analysts turn out to be overscheduled in July 2000, when 300 percent are required, but only 200 percent are available (overscheduled resources are shown in red, available resources scheduled in blue). Database designers also turn out to be overscheduled at various times.

One of *Microsoft Project*'s most valuable features is to level project schedules to stay within available resources. All that needs to be done is to activate the sequence:

Tools	Resource Leveling	
	Don't check	Level within available slack
	Don't check	Leveling can adjust individual assignments on a task
	Do check	Leveling can create splits in remaining work
Level Now		

This generates a new project schedule to stay within available resources. The new project completion date is 1/24/2001, two weeks later than the unleveled completion time of 1/12/2001.

Save the project with a baseline.

Endnotes

1. E. Booker, "No Silver Bullets for IS Projects," *Computerworld,* July 11, 1994, http://www.computerworld.com.
2. R. Cafasso, "Few IS Projects Come In on Time, on Budget," *Computerworld,* December 12, 1994, http://www.computerworld.com.
3. J. King, " 'Tough Love' Reins in IS Projects," *Computerworld,* June 19, 1995, http://www.computerworld.com.
4. _____, "IS Reins in Runaway Projects," *Computerworld,* February 24, 1997, http://www.computerworld.com.
5. _____, "Project Management Ills Cost Businesses Plenty," *Computerworld,* September 22, 1997, http://www.computerworld.com.
6. B. Boehm, A Spiral Model of Software Development and Enhancement," *Computer,* May 1988, pp. 61–72.
7. P. G. W. Keen, "Adaptive Design for Decision Support Systems," *Database* 12, nos. 1–2 (1980), pp. 15–25.
8. K. E. Lantz, *The Prototyping Methodology* (Englewood Cliffs, NJ: Prentice-Hall, 1988).
9. M. Alavi, "An Assessment of the Prototyping Approach to Information Systems Development," *Communications of the ACM* 27, no. 6 (1984), pp. 556–63.
10. J. Iivari and M. Karjalainen, "Impact of Prototyping on User Information Satisfaction during the IS Specification Phase," *Information & Management* 17 (1989), pp. 31–45.
11. B. Boehm, *Software Risk Management* (Washington, DC: IEEE Computer Society Press, 1989) and "A Spiral Model of Software Development and Enhancement."
12. _____, *Software Risk Management.*
13. _____, "Rapid Prototyping, Risk Management, 2167, and the Ada Process Model," *IEEE Software,* 1989, pp. 47–52.
14. C. Britton, S. Jones, M. Myers, and M. Sharif, "A Survey of Current Practice in the Development of Multimedia Systems," *Information and Software Technology* 39 (1997), pp. 695–705.
15. G. McLeod and D. Smith, *Managing Information Technology Projects* (Cambridge, MA: Course Technology, 1996).
16. S. McConnell, "From Anarchy to Optimizing," *Software Development,* July 1993, pp. 51–55.
17. McLeod and Smith, *Managing Information Technology Projects.*
18. S. Moore, "Unoval's Outsourcing Decision Stirs Up Networking Operations," *Computerworld,* November 14, 1994, http://www.computerworld.com.
19. S. Alexander, "Make or Buy?" *Computerworld,* October 9, 1995, http://www.computerworld.com.
20. J. Vijayan, "Sabre Lands US Airways Outsourcing," *Computerworld,* December 19, 1997, http://www.computerworld.com.
21. J. W. Verity, "Megadeals March On," *Computerworld,* July 28, 1997, http://www.computerworld.com.
22. G. H. Anthes, "Net Outsourcing a Risky Proposition," *Computerworld,* April 7, 1997, http://www.computerworld.com.

<table>
<tr><td>CHAPTER
5</td><td># Estimation</td></tr>
</table>

Chapter Outline

Main Ideas Discussed

- The project planning process
- Productivity factors applicable to software estimation
- Standard information system project estimation methods
- The uncertainty inherent in large projects
- Means of coping with project uncertainty

Once a system is developed, more detailed estimating is required. At the strategic level, macro-estimates were used to evaluate the project for approval. As the project moves to requirements analysis and determination of feasibility, more accurate estimates are possible as more detailed planning is conducted. During the planning process, detailed tasks and milestones (completed project module elements, resulting in a completed, functioning system component) are identified. This chapter discusses the planning process, as well as factors important in information system project estimation. Several quantitative methods of software project estimation are explained.

Planning Process

Information systems projects have high levels of uncertainty. The size of the project is usually not well understood until systems analysis has been completed. Most of the unexpected delay in these projects occurs during the latter stages of testing, late in the project. Brooks[1] contended that systems builders tend to report projects as on time and budget targets until the last stages of testing. But at this point, most projects are found to require additional work, often substantial in scope.

McLeod and Smith[2] cited unique factors of information systems projects that lead to high variability in project durations, including variances in productivity across people for specific work and in the technology used. Resources available are often not known at the beginning of a project. Many specific resources may be planned for use on a project during the planning stages, but months later other events may arise that make it impossible to use the best people on a project.

The **planning process** consists of a number of steps, including:

- Determining requirements.
- Identifying specific work to be done.
- Planning project organization.
- Scheduling.
- Budgeting resources.
- Establishing control mechanisms.

Set Objectives and Requirements

The first step is to determine requirements. Project objectives are set in the early stages of project proposals. Once these objectives are identified, the measures of accomplishment needed to identify successful completion of the project have to be established. These are the standards for each element of the project. In building a bridge, this would be the carrying capacity of the structure. In terms of information systems projects, this would be a statement of what the final project is ultimately supposed to do.

A statement of work can be viewed as a contract between the information systems development team and project end users (see Figure 5–1). The statement of work can contain product descriptions, discussion of project constraints, schedule requirements, budget limits, and an explanation of the roles and responsibilities of project participants.[3]

Constraints under which the system must be developed should be identified early in the project. These include time parameters such as deadlines. The project may have to be accomplished within existing skill levels. Levels of project complexity can be specified. Budgets are an important resource limitation. Technol-

FIGURE 5-1

Statement of work

Statement of Work for: Installation of Decision Support System for Purchasing Manager

This system is to provide the Purchasing Manager support in considering vendors for any external material purchased by Acme Distilleries.

The system is to consist of:

a. the necessary hardware for a personal computer station, including central processing unit, monitor, speakers, and printer, in addition to linkage to the management local area network. This system is to have the following technical specifications:

    750 megahertz or higher INTEL 64-bit processor

    15 gigabyte secondary storage

    64–128 megabyte RAM memory

    DVD/CD-ROM reader and writer

    USB bus

    High-speed modem-network interface

b. standard operating software, to include latest Microsoft operating system;

c. specialty software to include a database for Acme specifications by material, as well as room for vendor price quotations;

d. a backup drive.

The system is to be installed no later than October 4, 2001.

The base system cost is not to exceed $15,000.

Any proposed changes will be priced by the system builder and presented to the user, who will decide if the proposed changes should be adopted. The user will fund these changes at the stated price.

---

ogy might be imposed, such as using CASE tools. Interoperability opportunities, such as the availability of proprietary or open systems, may be specified.

Specify Work Activities

A **work breakdown structure** is a top-down hierarchical chart of tasks and subtasks required to complete the project (see Figure 5–2). The work breakdown structure can be focused on a product, a function, or anything describing what needs to be accomplished. The work breakdown structure is hierarchical in that different levels of detail can be described. The overall project consists of a set of major activities or major project subelements. The schedule consists of a set of tasks, usually denoting work done by a specific worker or work group. This is usually the lowest level of project activity that is used for planning. In Figure 5–2, task "System Design" is a major task with four subelements at two levels. Subactivity "Design Software System to Support Work Process" consists of three unique subactivities. Task "Installation" consists of only one level of five activities. For large projects, quite a few levels in the work breakdown structure hierarchy may be required.

A **detailed task list** is a listing of unique work packages, briefly describing work to be done. The detailed task list also includes the assignment of responsibilities by job title and predecessor relationships. Predecessor relationships identify the conditions required for tasks to begin. Resources required, deliver-

FIGURE 5–2

*Work breakdown
structure*

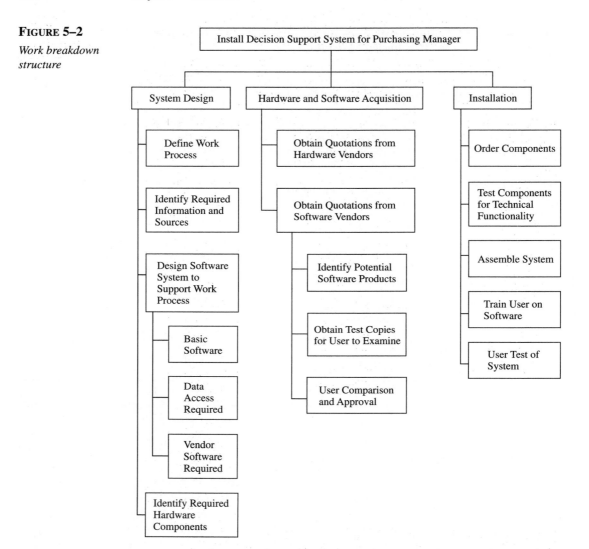

ables, and estimated durations are also provided. Figure 5–3 demonstrates a detailed task list for an example project. This information makes it possible to schedule and plan the project.

The work packages for tasks can include a summary of work to be done, predecessors (activities that must be completed before this task can be started), who is responsible, specifications for output, resources required, and deliverables. In Figure 5–3, predecessors and durations are provided for those tasks that are not subdivided. Specifications or required output could be provided as needed.

This detailed task list is the basis for estimating, scheduling, and allocating resources. The time required to accomplish each task, as well as the resources required by task, are included. Identifying these numbers is the task of estimation at this stage. Accurate estimation is a very difficult task. The best way to increase

FIGURE 5–3

Detailed task list

Project: Installation of Decision Support System for Purchasing Manager

Tasks	Subtasks	Responsible Parties	Predecessors
A	System Design		
A1	Define work process	system engineer, user	none
A2	Identify required information and sources	system engineer, user	A1
A3	Design software system to support work process		
A31	Basic software	system engineer	A2
A32	Data access required	system engineer, user	A2
A33	Vendor software required	system engineer, user	A2
A4	Identify required hardware components	system engineer, user	A31, A32, A33
A0	System Design Milestone		A4
B	Hardware and Software Acquisition		
B1	Obtain quotations from hardware vendors	hardware acquisition	A0
B2	Obtain quotations from software vendors		
B21	Identify potential software products	software acquisition	A0
B22	Obtain test copies for user to examine	software acquisition	B21
B23	User comparison and approval	system engineer, user	B22
B0	Hardware and Software Acquisition Milestone		B1, B23
C	Installation		
C1	Order components	software acquisition	B0
C2	Test components for technical functionality	system engineer	C1
C3	Assemble system	system engineer	C2
C4	Train user on software	trainer, user	C3
C5	User test of system	system engineer, user	C4
C0	Installation Milestone		C5

Task	Resources Required	Deliverable	Estimated Duration
A1	system engineer, user	document describing work process	2 days
A2	system engineer, user	list of required information sources	1 day
A31	system engineer	document describing system	3 days
A32	system engineer, user	list of data access required	1 day
A33	system engineer, user	list of software required	1 day
A4	system engineer, user	document formally identifying components	2 days
B1	hardware acquisition	list of specifications with prices	2 days
B21	software acquisition	list of software available with prices	4 days
B22	software acquisition	examination copies	10 days
B23	system engineer, user	user approval	5 days
C1	software acquisition	purchase orders	3 days
C2	system engineer	letters of certification	2 days
C3	system engineer	functioning system	1 day
C4	trainer, user	trainer certification	2 days
C5	system engineer, user	user signed approval	3 days

accuracy is to rely on experience supplemented by careful study and record keeping. McLeod and Smith[4] suggest building a database of norms based on past experiences for reference in estimating future projects. Any project environment involves difficulty in estimating, because by their nature, projects involve dealing with new activities. This is especially true in the field of information systems, because of the phenomenal rate of change in technology.

Goldratt[5] noted a natural human tendency to "pad" estimates of the time required to do things. If your professor should ask you how long it will take you to write a 10-page paper, would you respond with the fastest time you have ever written such a paper? You would not even respond with the average time you have taken to write such a paper. You would most likely respond with an estimate that you felt was safe. If you ask a programmer how long it will take to write a specific piece of code, you will probably receive an estimate that the programmer expects to beat 80 or 90 percent of the time. The programmer's supervisor will in turn probably add an inflationary factor to allow for contingencies, such as having to use a slower programmer. This continues up the chain of command until the final estimate is made. Everyone, even management, realizes that the estimate is padded. Management then adjusts for this padding by cutting the estimate drastically. What results is a wild guess that may or may not have much relationship to reality. Goldratt further notes that statement of a due date becomes a self-fulfilling prophecy. If an activity actually takes less time than the due date, work is usually slowed until the due date becomes accurate. Due dates thus can have a negative impact on project performance.

Goldratt[6] also suggests that better estimates will result from a systematic change in this process. Those doing the work need to be convinced that accurate estimates are in their best interest (the ability of the firm to accurately estimate what is required to do work so that they can submit competitive yet realistic prices for project work). Goldratt suggests elimination of due dates, which become reasons to delay. The focus should rather be on the *chain of critical activities* and those activities that might become critical. (The critical chain consists of those activities that cannot be delayed without delaying the project completion time.) This is accomplished by close management attention to make sure adequate resources are provided to critical activities and by frequent reporting of the need to finish this critical work to those who are doing it.

It is very easy for estimators to be overly optimistic. At the beginning of a project, it is natural to assume that everything will work as planned. But because of the need to accomplish a wide variety of tasks—and their interrelationships—projects rarely proceed as scheduled. Rarely will things go faster than planned. This is because of the need to obtain approval of end users and the need for delivery of materials and other components.

Plan Project Organization

Organizing refers to identifying the roles in the project organization. A **responsibility matrix** is a way to allocate tasks to individuals by responsibility (see Figure 5–4). Such a matrix can be invaluable in complex projects, enabling management to quickly identify who is responsible for each activity. This matrix can also be used when forming the project team, enabling identification of what needs to be done for comparison with the capabilities of candidates.

An **organization chart** shows the reporting relationships of all involved in the project. Figure 5–5 shows the organization for the project we have been demonstrating. The organization chart outlines the communication network and

FIGURE 5–4

*Responsibility
matrix*

Project: **Installation of Decision Support System for Purchasing Manager**

Tasks	Subtasks	SE	HA	SA	TR	User
A	System Design					
A1	Define work process	x				x
A2	Identify required information and sources	x				x
A3	Design software system to support work process					
A31	Basic software	x				
A32	Data access required	x				x
A33	Vendor software required	x				x
A4	Identify required hardware components	x				x
A0	System Design Milestone	x				x
B	Hardware and Software Acquisition					
B1	Obtain quotations from hardware vendors		x			
B2	Obtain quotations from software vendors			x		
B21	Identify potential software products			x		
B22	Obtain test copies for user to examine			x		
B23	User comparison and approval	x				x
B0	Hardware and Software Acquisition Milestone	x				x
C	Installation					
C1	Order components			x		
C2	Test components for technical functionality	x				
C3	Assemble system	x				
C4	Train user on software				x	x
C5	User test of system	x				x
C0	Installation Milestone	x				x

Key: SE Systems engineer personnel
      HA Hardware acquisition
      SA Software acquisition
      TR Trainer

coordination patterns required within the project as well. Within matrix organizational forms, this organization chart should show both primary and secondary reporting relationships. This can include not only those temporarily assigned from functional elements to the project, but also external relationships, such as the project owner and vendors.

Develop the Schedule

Schedules consist of the sequence of tasks from the work breakdown structure, along with their start and completion dates and relationships to other tasks (see Figure 5–6). Schedules include not only time estimates but also resource requirements. *Microsoft Project* allows display of resources to the right of the bar representing the planned activity schedule. Schedules give everyone an understandable plan and impose structure on the project and should, therefore, be widely distributed among members of the project team.

Schedules are the basis for resource allocation and estimated cost for monitoring and control purposes. The focus is on identifying when activities (tasks) are completed so that work can proceed on following activities.

FIGURE 5–5

Organization chart

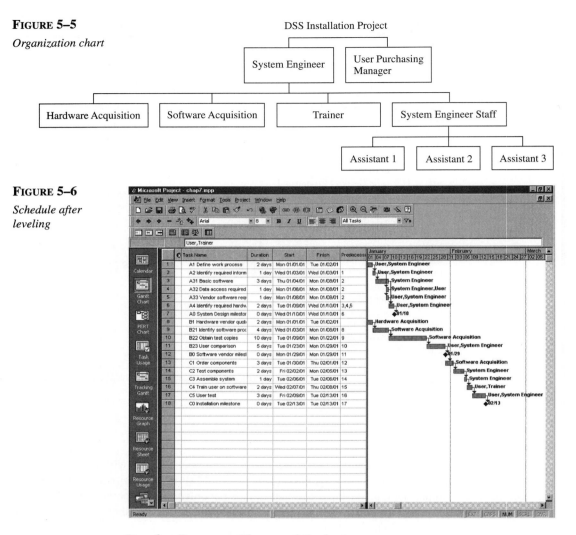

FIGURE 5–6

Schedule after leveling

Develop Resource Plans and Budget

Once schedules are developed that identify the estimated durations and sequencing of activities, a resource plan can be developed (see Figure 5–7). Many activities may compete for the same resources. This may guide hiring by identifying the number of people of a specific skill to obtain in reference to time needed. If resources are scarce, some activities may have to be rescheduled to stay within stipulated resource levels.

The **critical path method** provides a basis for identifying the criticality of specific activities, which can help determine which among competing activities can be delayed to stay within resource levels. A **critical activity** is an activity that must be completed on schedule or project completion time will be delayed. There-

FIGURE 5-7

Resource plan for system engineer and staff

Days

Activity	1	2	3	4	5	6	7	8	9	10	11	12	13	14	15	16	17	18	19	20	21	22	23	24	25	26	27	28	29	30	31	32	33	34	35	36	37	38
A1	E	E																																				
A2			E																																			
A31				«	«	«																																
A32				/																																		
A33				'																																		
A4							E	E																														
B1																																						
B21																																						
B22																																						
B23																							E	E	E	E	E											
C1																																						
C2																															«	«						
C3																																	«					
C4																																						
C5																																			E	E	E	E

E – System Engineer
« – Assistant 1
/ – Assistant 2
' – Assistant 3

fore, critical activities are said to have no **slack,** or spare time to complete. A **critical path** is the chain of critical activities from the beginning of the project to project completion. If a project has no overall slack between the time it is to be completed and the minimum time to complete based on duration estimates, there will be at least one critical path for the project. However, there may be multiple critical paths or more than one sequence of activities related by predecessor/follower relationships that have zero slack. Chapter 6 will more completely describe this useful project management tool.

Once the final planned time schedule is developed, it can be used to estimate costs, such as expenditures for human resources, materials, overhead, and so forth. The time resources are required is a major component of estimated cost. Also important are materials used, as well as vendor-delivered products. Overhead expenses can be estimated independently of work volume. Obviously, since time is a major element in estimating budgets, one of the major reasons projects run over budget is because they take more time than expected.

Control Points

Control points include milestones, checkpoint reviews, status review meetings, and staff meetings. When planning the project, control mechanisms should also be included. Because of the existence of interrelated activities, **milestone** events are often used at the end of particular phases, or groupings of activities resulting in the completion of project subcomponents. Meetings are an important control device, providing a way to keep each element of the organization informed of what is going on. In Figure 5–6, activities 7 (system design milestone), 12 (hardware and software acquisition milestone), and 18 (installation milestone) are milestone activities.

Kliem[7] listed three types of meetings that are needed in information systems projects. **Checkpoint reviews** are held at the conclusion of each phase to determine whether or not to proceed with the rest of the project. In information systems projects, this is the appropriate time to test the performance of the completed component. If its performance is less than planned, it may be necessary to change the rest of the project—and possibly even cancel it. **Status review meetings** are used to gather cost, quality, and schedule information. These give project management the measures needed to control the project. Finally, staff meetings are regularly held to maintain communication.

The primary purpose of budgets is to give management control over expenditures. A key activity is tracking actual expenditures relative to the budget. Variance reports are often used to focus on those project elements that are in the greatest amount of difficulty. When such problems are encountered, plans need to be developed to adjust to the new circumstances.

Resource usage can be measured by time period. Figure 5–8 demonstrates the schedule for the user representative before leveling, as displayed by *Microsoft Project.* The week beginning January 7 has a problem, with the user representative assigned to two activities at once (A32 and A33). In the plan shown in Figure 5–6, the project completion was delayed one day to allow the user representative to participate in both activities. Most, if not all, project management software provides similar tools to flag when available resources are overscheduled.

The planning process is key to accurate cost estimation, which, in turn, is required for sound managerial decision making about project adoption. This is especially true for consulting organizations, which price bids to potential customers. In a competitive environment, bidding too high results in no work. Bidding too low is even worse because it leads to undertaking projects at a loss, and ultimately it can lead to bankruptcy. To accurately know what the cost of delivering a project will be, you need to know the resources required. In a complex project, the duration for which these resources are needed is very difficult to estimate without a good database of the time similar activities took in the past and without analysis and understanding of special conditions that could affect these durations.

Software Estimation

Brooks[8] published his first edition of his book *The Mythical Man-Month* in 1975. The book presents many concepts, including a scale of project size. According to Brooks, a **program** is computer code usable by its author. A **programming**

FIGURE 5–8

Original resource histogram for user (before leveling)

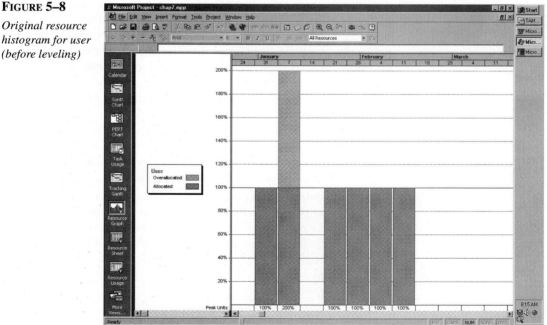

system is a code usable by anyone. All of you who have written a computer program understand the difference. Using someone else's code is very difficult. True professional coders develop the ability to not only make computers do things, but do things in a way that others can understand. A **programming product** is a code that is tested, documented, and maintained; something that a company would not be afraid to market. Brooks said that a programming product took three times the effort of a similar sized program. Finally, there are **programming system products** that involve continued efforts of development teams over time. Continued development of the *Microsoft Office Suite* is a very large programming system product, undergoing continuous improvement. *Microsoft Project* is a smaller programming system product, but it also undergoes continuous improvement leading to new releases every year or so to better serve product users.

Brooks cited lack of calendar time as the most common reason for information system project failure. This implies that more software projects are late than are over budget or fail to meet specifications. This is because, of the three project metrics, usually time is less critical than budget or quality. Other common reasons for project failure include poor estimating technique, poor monitoring of progress, and the assumption that effort equals progress. One of the great myths is that more people assigned to a project will result in a proportional increase in progress. This is sometimes true in other fields. However, in information systems project development it can be catastrophic.

Brooks, based on a career of study, saw three types of projects:

1. *Partitionable* projects consist of activities that can be accomplished independently. In this type of project, adding more people will help, but not at a proportional rate. There is a deterioration in the volume of work per hour or day that is significant. This can be in great part due to the "learning curve concept." People take much more time the first time they do something, and the amount of time per unit continues to decline with experience. New people added to a project must work through the initial inefficient phase.

2. A *nonpartitionable* project is one in which activities are interrelated and need to be coordinated. This is true of most information system development projects. In this type of environment, Brooks found that no benefit was obtained from adding people to a late project.

3. Projects involving *complex interactions* are more adversely affected by the addition of people. Each task must be separately coordinated with all others. Adding people to this type of project starts off with a small beneficial gain that declines as additional people are added. After some number of people are added, the project actually begins to slow down. This is the basis of Brooks' Law:

Adding manpower to a late project makes it later.

Brooks related that in his experience, one-third of the time used in typical projects was required for the planning phase, and coding typically consisted of one-sixth of the project. Coding is the most predictable portion of the project, even more predictable now because of automated code development tools. The last half of the project was testing—one-quarter for component testing and one-quarter for system testing. The activity most difficult to predict was testing. Most projects Brooks observed were on time until testing, but were not on time after the testing phase was complete.

Programmer Productivity

There is a wide variation in productivity between good and fair programmers. Of a 200-person project, Brooks assumed that the best 25 people were the managers. His suggestion was to fire the 175 personnel who were not managers and to use the 25 managers as programmers. This would vastly reduce payroll, while assigning programming work to those he assumed were better programmers. This argument is based on the concept that skilled work accomplished is not a function of the number of hours worked but rather on the productivity of expert workers. In creative work (such as program development), 10 unskilled workers may well be less productive than 1 expert worker. The concept of **surgical team** was proposed. These teams, assigned to specific system tasks, shouldn't have more than 10 people assigned. The OS/360 was a classic software development project yielding a major IBM computer system. This project suffered cost overruns, as do most major projects (computer related or not). The OS/360 project had 1,000 people working on it, for a total of 5,000 man-years. Surgical teams could be applied even to projects of this scale. The concept of leaner project management has also been found to be successful in building and construction project management.[9]

A surgical team is a unit with specific roles assigned for systems development. The analogy runs as follows:

Surgeon	Chief programmer
Copilot	Share thinking and evaluation
Administrator	Deal with boring details
Editor	Take care of references and documentation
Secretaries (2)	
Program clerk	Deal with technical records
Toolsmith	Editing, debugging, expertise with tools
Tester	Develop test cases
Language lawyer	Expert on language

With the advent of more sophisticated development tools, the language lawyer might help the toolsmith, or the size of the surgical team could be reduced. But the same general principles apply.

The primary benefit of this surgical team is that **conceptual integrity** of the product is more easily maintained. On this surgical team there are 10 people, but they have roles supporting 1 person's basic ideas. The OS/360 project's architect manager once told Brooks that his 10-person team could write specifications for the project in 10 months, which would have been 3 months late. The control program manager offered his 150-person group as an alternative that could complete this task in 7 months. This control program group was idle at that time. The architect manager responded that the control program people would take 10 months and would do a poor job. Brooks gave the job to the control program group. They took 10 months to complete the task, but it took another year to debug their output. This led Brooks to a strong bias toward surgical teams. It is better to reflect one set of design ideas than to add independent and uncoordinated features and improvements. Integrity can be gained by having a small team that works together very closely with well-defined roles. The purpose of a programming system is to make the computer easy to use. Conceptual integrity enables attainment of simplicity and straightforward operations.

Software Estimation Methods

Software estimation is a very difficult task. The most commonly used approaches are based on source **lines of code** (SLOC, or LOC). The number of lines of code seems to be of less and less importance as productivity tools are developed and more productive languages are used. One attempt to base estimation on more relevant project features is function point analysis, which focuses on the functions the proposed system needs to accomplish. However, most research[10] has not found any improvement in estimation through use of function point analysis in practice. SLOC is still widely used and is the basis of the COCOMO system covered later in this chapter. While these systems have noted flaws, estimating methods significantly better have not been widely reported.

The software production cycle can be described in many ways. A simple view consists of the following major elements: design and development, production, testing, installation, and maintenance. According to Symons,[11] production is usually relatively predictable. The other elements are highly variable.

The size of the system has been found to be an important variable in the cost and time required to develop software. Size can be measured on a number of dimensions. The most commonly used are the amount of information processed, technical requirements, and performance drivers (cost, time, and quality).

The amount of time required to develop a set of code is a function of its size. The following demonstration of the source lines of code (SLOC, or LOC) and function point (FP) methods are based primarily on McLeod and Smith[12] and Pressman.[13]

Lines of Code

Both LOC and FP methods begin with the scientifically sound approach of gathering historical records of experiences of past projects. This historical data is the basis for identifying the relationship between key measures of importance (such as the person-months of effort and dollars expended) and other factors of importance (such as the pages of documentation generated, errors encountered, system defects, and people assigned). An implementation of the LOC approach uses the key measures per line of code illustrated in Table 5–1.

When a new project is encountered, an estimate is made of the lines of code that the project will require. For instance, if a new project is estimated to involve 10,000 lines of code, estimates of these measures would be

Effort	1.606 × 10,000 LOC = 16 person-months
Budget	15.673 × 10,000 LOC = $157,000
Documentation	58.122 × 10,000 LOC = 581 pages
Errors	9.784 × 10,000 LOC = 98
Defects	2.531 × 10,000 LOC = 25
People	0.195 × 10,000 LOC = 2 people

This approach is admittedly rough, but it provides a very easy to implement estimation method. While gathering the data is time consuming, once it is obtained, it is very quick. It will be more accurate the more appropriate the data are, of course. Ideally, firms could build their database in categories by type of work, as averaging radically different projects together will lead to obvious inaccuracies. Another limitation is that it takes time to generate a database of historical project results. As with any statistical approach, the more data the greater the confidence. However, the older the data, the less likely they are appropriate to current operations. Additionally, the model as demonstrated is totally linear, while project size may have different effects at different size levels. More refined methods have been developed.[14]

Function Point Analysis

Albrecht's **function point analysis method**[15] supplements these project size bases of estimation. The aims of this approach are a consistent measure meaningful to the end user with rules that are easy to apply. The method can be used to estimate cost and time based on requirements specifications, and it is independent of the technology used. Symons[16] criticized the Albrecht method because alternative counting practices are used, weights are questionable, and large systems are underweighted. In 1985 Xerox noted a rapid drop in productivity for information

---

TABLE 5–1   Lines of Code Operation

Averages of past projects:			*Effort*	*$(000)*	*pp. Doc.*	*Errors*	*Defects*	*People*
LOC	20,543		33 mos.	361	1,194	201	52	4
average per KLOC			1.606	15.673	58.122	9.784	2.531	0.195

SLOC: estimate lines of code, multiply

system projects with increasing system size. Symons also thought the range of points used by Albrecht was much too narrow. However, Symons contended that the Albrecht method was much better than the lines of code method.

The function point method works in a manner very similar to lines of code, except that the basis for estimation is function points (reflecting in essence work to do). McLeod and Smith's and Pressman's presentation of the original function point method involved counts of the number of activities in five categories (user inputs, user outputs, user inquiries, files accessed, and external interfaces).[17] The number of functions are counted by complexity level for each factor, and multiplied as shown in Table 5–2. The count total is the sum of the product column. Table 5–3 demonstrates a hypothetical software proposal.

The next step is to find F_1, which is calculated by adding the ratings over the 14 factors listed in Table 5–4 on a 0 to 5 scale, with 0 representing no effect, 1 incidental, 2 moderate, 3 average, 4 significant, and 5 essential effect. The calculation, with a hypothetical set of effects, is given in the table. Function points are then calculated by the formula shown at the top of page 133.

TABLE 5–2   Count-Total Calculations

Measurement Parameter	Complexity Weighting			
	Low	Average	High	Product
Number of user inputs	_____ × 3 +	_____ × 4 +	_____ × 6 =	_____
Number of user outputs	_____ × 4 +	_____ × 5 +	_____ × 7 =	_____
Number of user inquiries	_____ × 3 +	_____ × 4 +	_____ × 6 =	_____
Number of files	_____ × 7 +	_____ × 10 +	_____ × 15 =	_____
Number of external interfaces	_____ × 5 +	_____ × 7 +	_____ × 10 =	_____

TABLE 5–3   Demonstration of Count-Total Calculation

Software: A bank account record system involving:

36 user inputs	Classified as simple in complexity
5 user outputs	Classified as average in complexity
20 possible user inquiries	Classified as simple in complexity
40 files accessed	Classified as simple in complexity
3 external interfaces	Classified as average in complexity

Measurement Parameter	Count	Simple	Average	Complex	Product
Number of user inputs	36	× 3			108
Number of user outputs	5		× 5		25
Number of user inquiries	20	× 3			60
Number of files	40	× 7			280
Number of external interfaces	3		× 7		21
				Total	494

$$FP = \text{Count total} \times [0.65 + 0.01 \times \Sigma F_i]$$

In the hypothetical example, estimation of effort would be:

$$FP = 494 \times [0.65 + 0.01 \times 32] = 479.18$$

Table 5–5 summarizes the results.

Symons[18] developed a modification of the Albrecht method. The same technical complexity adjustment was used, but the number of general application characteristics was increased, and weights were adjusted. Table 5–6 gives Symons's comparison of these methods.

TABLE 5–4   Function Calculation Demonstration

			1–5 scale
F1	Does the system require reliable backup and recovery?	Significant	(4)
F2	Are data communications required?	Moderate	(2)
F3	Are there distributed processing functions?	Significant	(4)
F4	Is performance critical?	Average	(3)
F5	Will the system run in an existing, heavily utilized operational environment?	Essential	(5)
F6	Does the system require online data entry?	Essential	(5)
F7	Does the online data entry require the input transaction on multiple screens or operations?	Incidental	(1)
F8	Are the master files updated online?	No influence	(0)
F9	Are the inputs, outputs, files, or inquiries complex?	Incidental	(1)
F10	Is the internal processing complex?	Incidental	(1)
F11	Is the code designed to be reusable?	Average	(3)
F12	Are conversion and installation included in the design?	Average	(3)
F13	Is the system designed for multiple installations in different organizations?	No influence	(0)
F14	Is the application designed to facilitate change and ease of use by the user?	No influence	(0)
		Total F	32

TABLE 5–5   Function Point Estimation

Averages of past projects:		*Effort*	*$(000)*	*pp. Doc.*	*Errors*	*Defects*	*People*
FP	623	33 mos.	361	1,194	201	52	4
average per FP		0.05297	0.57945	1.91653	0.32263	0.08347	0.00642

Function points: Calculate FP, multiply averages by 479.18

	Effort	*$(000)*	*pp. Doc*	*Errors*	*Defects*	*People*
479.18 ×	0.05297	0.57945	1.91653	0.32263	0.08347	0.00642
Yields **estimates**	**25.4**	**278**	**918**	**155**	**40**	**3**

TABLE 5–6   **Comparison of Methods**

	SLOC	Albrecht	Mk II FPA (Symons)
Accepted standard	No	Yes	Yes
Clarity	Potentially	Some subjective	Objective
Structured	No	No	Yes
Easy to use	Yes	No	No
Automatable	Yes	No	Yes
Usable for estimating	Sometimes	Yes	Yes

While lines of code have proven useful, and while the function point method is also useful and widely used, estimation of software project effort continues to be a difficult task. Mukhodpadhyay, Vicinanza, and Prietula[19] found that experts, as well as a CASE-based method, outperformed both LOC and FP in their experiments. Improvements to the function point approach continue to be generated. Jeffery, Low, and Barnes[20] compared different function point methods. Abran and Robillard[21] compared seven versions of function point analysis. Heiat and Heiat[22] compared lines of code and function point estimation, finding that they were roughly equal in accuracy. Verner and Tate[23] presented a bottom-up approach, identifying factors of importance and using historical data as the basis for generating a more accurate estimate. Many other approaches continue to be generated. In part, new developments are needed because the software project environment is changing, with far less reliance on actual coding (which Boehm pointed out was the most predictable part of a software project[24]).

The next model applies logarithmic regression on past data to more accurately reflect the time required to accomplish code development. The constructive cost model (COCOMO) reflects the effect of learning, in that as the project progresses, programmers and developers are expected to gain in the rate of productivity.

Constructive Cost Model

Boehm[25] presented a series of **constructive cost models** (COCOMO) for estimating the effort required for developing software. The basic COCOMO model computes software development effort based on program size. An intermediate model also considers a set of cost drivers reflecting specific product, hardware, personnel, and project characteristics. The advanced model breaks out cost driver effect on each step of the software engineering process.

For relatively small, simple software projects built by small teams with good experience, COCOMO formulas for person-months of effort and development time in chronological months are as follows:

$$\text{Person-months} = 2.4 \times \text{KLOC}^{1.05} = E \text{ for effort}$$

$$\text{Duration (months)} = 2.5 \times E^{0.38},$$

where KLOC means thousand lines of code. Thus, for a job of this type involving 50,000 lines of code,

$$\text{Person-months} = 2.4 \times 50^{1.05} = 145.925 \text{ months}$$
$$\text{Duration} = 2.5 \times 145.925^{0.38} = 16.6 \text{ months}$$

For software projects of intermediate size and complexity, built by teams with mixed experience and facing more rigid than average requirements, the formulas are as follows:

$$\text{Person-months} = 3.0 \times \text{KLOC}^{1.12}$$
$$\text{Duration (months)} = 2.5 \times E^{0.35}$$

Therefore, a job of this type involving 50,000 lines of code would have the following estimates:

$$\text{Person-months} = 3.0 \times 50^{1.12} = 239.865 \text{ months}$$
$$\text{Duration} = 2.5 \times 239.865^{0.35} = 17.0 \text{ months}$$

Finally, for a software project built under rigid conditions, the formulas are as follows:

$$\text{Person-months} = 3.6 \times \text{KLOC}^{1.2}$$
$$\text{Duration (months)} = 2.5 \times E^{0.32}$$

A job involving 50,000 lines of code under these conditions would be estimated as

$$\text{Person-months} = 3.6 \times 50^{1.2} = 393.610 \text{ months}$$
$$\text{Duration} = 2.5 \times 393.610^{0.32} = 16.9 \text{ months}$$

There are variations in COCOMO under development. Companies could generate their own using regression on their productivity data. Pressman[26] contends that the COCOMO approach is not perfectly accurate in many conditions, but provides a good starting basis for projects oriented around work than can be described in terms of lines of code generated.

There are many causes of productivity loss. For one thing, the amount of time applied by humans to actual coding is only about 20 hours per week because of machine downtime, emergency diversion, meetings, paperwork, sick time, and many other factors. A great deal of this waste is recovered by using automated tools, except for machine downtime.

Interactions are coordinations with others. The greater the number of interactions, the less the productivity. High-level languages increase productivity by almost eliminating the programming component, but the more unpredictable activities still have to be accomplished by the surgical team.

Planning for Change

As we stated at the outset of the previous section, software estimation methods have been found wanting. LOC would seem to be irrelevant to contemporary system development environments, but function point analysis does not appear to be much better. As we also said, these methods appear to be about as good as anything at estimating software projects. Therefore, systems developers can expect high levels of change in project development duration.

Given the pace of technological business change, systems should be developed while anticipating change. The prototyping approach, where a working version of the system is built before final design, is appropriate for some projects, where the idea is to design the product's final details *after* seeing a mockup in action. Development principles that make sense in this environment include modularization, subroutining, documentation of interfaces, and high-level languages.

There are a number of implementations of risk analysis in software development. Buffer approaches are discussed in Chapter 6. Statistical approaches are addressed in Chapter 7. Another approach is to identify threats to project completion with respect to time, budget, and quality and development of contingency plans to be implemented should these threats materialize. One obvious contingency plan is to cancel the project should it encounter too many unexpected delays and budget overruns. Other contingency alternatives are to pull internal experts off other projects to get the project back on track. Outsourcing can also be used, retaining external experts from the consulting field.

Scheduling

In Brooks's experience, people estimated that coding was 90 percent finished for about half of the time it was in process.[27] Debugging was estimated to be 99 percent complete most of the time it was under way. You probably have written a computer code, and should understand this very well. Humans are optimistic. The time required for computer tasks are very difficult to estimate accurately.

In studies of government projects, where estimates were carefully updated every two weeks, there was very little change in estimated duration until the activity actually started. While the activity was under way, those activities that actually took less time than the estimate dropped, to reflect the new knowledge. On the other hand, when things were clearly going to take longer than estimated, the estimates were rarely changed until deep into the activity.

As mentioned earlier, milestones are scheduling tools very useful in coordinating interrelated projects. Milestones are concrete events denoting the completion of a project phase. When a phase of project activity (a set of related tasks, such as completion of all system design tasks in Figure 5–3) is finished, including successful component testing, a milestone is completed. Milestones are scheduled as activities with zero duration, reflecting completion of a block of work.

Critical path models, discussed earlier and to be elaborated on in Chapter 6, are network descriptions of project activities that identify activity start times and completion times. Brooks found preparation of critical path models to be their most valuable aspect.[28] Dependencies are clearly identified, and there is value in estimating activity durations. Critical path models were meant to aid project control by allowing comparison of actual performance with planned performance. However, as a control device, model elements such as task completion status are often not updated until too late, at which time the system change is dramatic.

When delay is first noticed, the tendency is not to report it. Project management systems provide status information that gives the latest reported picture of what is going on. The key to successful management is determining when something needs to be done to correct what is going on.

Summary

Estimation of activity duration and cost is key to sound scheduling and budgeting. It is a very difficult task because project activities are so variable in these terms.

A great deal of effort has been given to accurately estimate software development projects. Specific measures of project size include source lines of code (SLOC or LOC), the most commonly used measurement. This method is based on a concrete measure, which is attractive. But it is deficient in that it is often difficult to specify the specific lines in question. Different languages can require very different approaches for different tasks. In former times, when FORTRAN was the standard language for numerical computation and when COBOL was the standard for data processing, estimates of lines of code were quite consistent. Now, however, with the many productivity tools available and a much greater variety of languages used, lines of code is not as useful a measure. Function points focus more on what software is intended to do. COCOMO reflects learning aspects of software productivity. While all of these methods provide some insight into the time an information systems project might take, each has limitations.

A sound estimating procedure would identify the work to be done (the work breakdown structure), estimated the time required by resource, and estimate the money required to pay the required people or hire the required consultants or equipment. To that, time-independent items such as materials or external purchases can be added. Overhead can then be allocated following company policies.

Uncertainty is a major factor with respect to the time project activities will take. Cost is often correlated with time. Most delays are incurred in the testing phase, late in the project. It is rare for a project to take less time than originally estimated. This in great part is due to the human factor of rechecking work if it is completed early, or sometimes stalling. Projects have on occasion been completed ahead of schedule, but not very often.

Key Terms

Exercises

1. Describe the differences among a program, a programming system, and a programming system product.
2. State Brooks's Law. What kind of project does Brooks's Law apply to?
3. What is a surgical team intended to do?
4. What is a milestone?
5. What is a statement of work?
6. What is a work breakdown structure?
7. What factors have affected estimation of software development projects?
8. Compare the estimates of effort, expenditure, documentation, and errors for the following three projects obtained from the SLOC approach and the function point approach.

Averages of past projects:		*Effort*	*$(000)*	*pp. Doc.*	*Errors*
LOC	18,794	28 mos.	189	688	84
FP	821				

Project 1: Install a data mining package with links, 2,600 lines of code

F1	Backup and recovery	Average	(3)
F2	Data communications	Significant	(4)
F3	Distributed processing	Incidental	(1)
F4	Performance critical?	Average	(3)
F5	Run on existing, heavily used environment?	No influence	(0)
F6	Online data entry?	Incidental	(1)
F7	Online data entry on multiple screens?	Average	(3)
F8	Master files updated online?	Incidental	(1)
F9	Inputs, outputs, files complex?	Incidental	(1)
F10	Internal processing complex?	Essential	(5)
F11	Code reusable?	Significant	(4)
F12	Conversion and installation?	Significant	(4)
F13	Multiple installations across organizations?	No influence	(0)
F14	Facilitate change and user ease of use?	Average	(3)

12 user inputs	Classified as complex
6 user outputs	Classified as simple
2 possible user inquiries	Classified as complex
2 files accessed	Classified as complex
0 external interfaces	

Project 2: Develop a report generator for a monthly management report, 8,000 LOC

F1	Backup and recovery	Significant	(4)
F2	Data communications	Significant	(4)
F3	Distributed processing	Significant	(4)
F4	Performance critical?	Essential	(5)
F5	Run on existing, heavily used environment?	Average	(3)
F6	Online data entry?	Incidental	(1)
F7	Online data entry on multiple screens?	Incidental	(1)
F8	Master files updated online?	Moderate	(2)
F9	Inputs, outputs, files complex?	Incidental	(1)
F10	Internal processing complex?	Moderate	(2)
F11	Code reusable?	Average	(3)
F12	Conversion and installation?	Significant	(4)
F13	Multiple installations across organizations?	Significant	(4)
F14	Facilitate change and user ease of use?	Significant	(4)

22 user inputs	Classified as simple
1 user output	Classified as simple
0 possible user inquiries	
16 files accessed	Classified as complex
4 external interfaces	Classified as complex

Project 3: Develop an online system to update customer records, 17,000 LOC

F1	Backup and recovery	Average	(3)
F2	Data communications	Essential	(5)
F3	Distributed processing	No Influence	(0)
F4	Performance critical?	Average	(3)
F5	Run on existing, heavily used environment?	Average	(3)
F6	Online data entry?	Essential	(5)
F7	Online data entry on multiple screens?	Essential	(5)
F8	Master files updated online?	Essential	(5)
F9	Inputs, outputs, files complex?	Incidental	(1)
F10	Internal processing complex?	Moderate	(2)
F11	Code reusable?	Average	(3)
F12	Conversion and installation?	Moderate	(2)
F13	Multiple installations across organizations?	No Influence	(0)
F14	Facilitate change and user ease of use?	Significant	(4)

36 user inputs	Classified as average
5 user outputs	Classified as simple
48 possible user inquiries	Classified as average
28 files accessed	Classified as average
3 external interfaces	Classified as complex

9. Use the basic, intermediate, and advanced COCOMO models to estimate the expected number of person-months of work and the project duration for a project involving 2,600 lines of code.

10. Use the basic, intermediate, and advanced COCOMO models to estimate the expected number of person-months of work and the project duration for a project involving 8,000 lines of code.

11. Use the basic, intermediate, and advanced COCOMO models to estimate the expected number of person-months of work and the project duration for a project involving 17,000 lines of code.

12. *Field trip:* Visit a local firm doing software development. What estimation methods do they use? How accurate do they find these methods?
    (The responses obtained are expected to be subjective and thus require thoughtful interpretation.)

Endnotes

1. F. P. Brooks, Jr., *The Mythical Man-Month: Essays on Software Engineering,* anniversary edition (Reading, MA: Addison-Wesley, 1995).

2. G. McLeod and D. Smith, *Managing Information Technology Projects* (Cambridge, MA: Course Technology, 1996).

3. R. I. Kliem, "Using Project Management to Put Client/Server Projects Back on Track," *Information Strategy,* Winter 1997, pp. 29–35.

4. McLeod and Smith, *Managing Information Technology Projects.*

5. E. M. Goldratt, *Critical Chain* (Great Barrington, MA: The North River Press, 1997).

6. Ibid.

7. Kliem, "Using Project Management to Put Client/Server Projects Back on Track."

8. The following discussion is based on Brooks, *The Mythical Man-Month.*

9. E. Gabriel, "The Lean Approach to Project Management," *International Journal of Project Management* 15, no. 4 (1997), pp. 131–38.

10. C. F. Kemerer, "An Empirical Validation of Software Cost Estimation Models," *Communications of the ACM* 30, no. 3 (1987), pp. 416–29; and F. Bergeron and J.-Y. St-Arnaud, "Estimation of Information Systems Development Effort: A Pilot Study," *Information and Management* 22 (1992), pp. 239–54.

11. C. R. Symons, *Software Sizing and Estimating: Mk II FPA* (New York: Wiley, 1991).

12. McLeod and Smith, *Managing Information Technology Projects.*

13. R. S. Pressman, *Software Engineering: A Practitioner's Approach,* 4th ed. (New York: McGraw-Hill, 1997).

14. B. W. Boehm, "Software Engineering Economics," *IEEE Transactions on Software Engineering* SE-10, no. 1 (1984), pp. 4–21 and "Understanding and Controlling Software Costs," *IEEE Transactions on Software Engineering* SE-14, no. 10 (1988), pp. 1462–75.

15. J. B. Dreger, *Function Point Analysis* (Englewood Cliffs, NJ: Prentice-Hall, 1989); and Pressman, *Software Engineering.*

16. C. R. Symons, "Function Point Analysis: Difficulties and Improvements," *IEEE Transactions on Software Engineering* 14, no. 1 (1988), pp. 2–11 and *Software Sizing and Estimating: Mk II FPA.*

17. McLeod and Smith, *Managing Information Technology Projects;* and Pressman, *Software Engineering.*

18. Symons, *Software Sizing and Estimating.*

19. T. Mukhodpadhyay, S. S. Vicinanza, and M. J. Prietula, "Examining the Feasibility of a Case-Based Reasoning Model for Software Effort Estimation," *MIS Quarterly* 16, no. 2 (1992), pp. 155–71.

20. D. R. Jeffery, G. C. Low, and M. Barnes, "A Comparison of Function Point Counting Techniques," *IEEE Transactions on Software Engineering* SE-19, no. 5 (1993), pp. 529–32.
21. A. Abran and P. N. Robillard, "Function Points Analysis: An Empirical Study of Its Measurement Processes," *IEEE Transactions on Software Engineering* SE-22, no. 12 (1996), pp. 895–910.
22. A. Heiat and N. Heiat, "A Model for Estimating Efforts Required for Developing Small-Scale Business Applications," *Journal of Systems Software* 39 (1997), pp. 7–14.
23. J. Verner and G. Tate, "A Software Size Model," *IEEE Transactions on Software Engineering* SE-18, no. 4 (1992), pp. 265–78.
24. B. W. Boehm, "Understanding and Controlling Software Costs," *IEEE Transactions on Software Engineering* SE-14, no. 10 (1988), pp. 1462–75.
25. B. W. Boehm, *Software Engineering Economics* (Englewood Cliffs, NJ: Prentice-Hall, 1981).
26. Pressman, *Software Engineering.*
27. Brooks, *The Mythical Man-Month.*
28. Ibid.

APPENDIX 5A

LEARNING CURVES

Learning curves are mathematical models of the time required to perform a task under conditions of improvement with a constant rate of experience. Learning curves reflect the ability of humans to learn, to do something faster the second time than the first time, with improvement for each additional unit of experience.

Eden, Williams, and Ackermann[1] cite Wright's Law (1936) as an early application of learning curves to the estimation of production time required during a manufacturing process. This law stated that for any repeated operation, the mean time for the operation will decrease by a fixed fraction as the number of repetitions double. The general mathematical expression for T_n, the time required to do the nth task, is

$$T_n = an^b,$$

where a is a constant for a particular organization ($a > 1$), b is a negative constant for a particular organization and product type, T_n is the number of time units required for the nth unit, a is the number of time units required for the first unit, n is the number of units for which an estimate is desired, and b is the exponent of the curve corresponding to the learning rate, which is equal to the natural logarithm of the learning rate divided by the natural logarithm of 2.[2] The natural logarithm of 2 is 0.693, so b is ln(Learning rate)/0.693. A learning rate of 80 percent would mean that each time production doubled, the time required to produce a unit would be 80 percent of what it initially was.

For instance, if the time required to write a well-defined module of work, such as creating a web site (given concrete and complete input requirements), was initially eight hours, and given a learning rate of 80 percent, the time required for subsequent work of the same type and complexity would be:

$$T_n = 8n^{\ln(.8)/0693)} = 8 \times n^{(-0.223)/0.693)}$$

The learning curve for this set of values (with item representing *n*) is shown in Figure 5A–1. The tabular values for this curve over 20 observations is given in Table 5A–1 along with the cumulative time (in hours) required to produce *n* items. Note that this formula is expected to provide a rough estimate of the mean time required to perform the given task. There are many factors that can cause the for-

FIGURE 5A–1

Time to produce nth unit at 80 percent learning rate

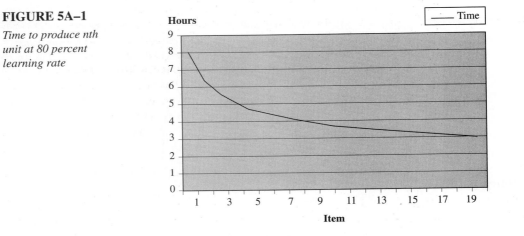

TABLE 5A–1   **Tabular Values**

Item	Time	Cumulative
1	8	8
2	6.4	14.4
3	5.61683	20.01683
4	5.12	25.13683
5	4.765099	29.90193
6	4.493464	34.39539
7	4.275916	38.67131
8	4.096	42.76731
9	3.943597	46.71091
10	3.812079	50.52298
11	3.696889	54.21987
12	3.594771	57.81464
13	3.503324	61.31797
14	3.420733	64.7387
15	3.345593	68.08429
16	3.2768	71.36109
17	3.213467	74.57456
18	3.154878	77.72944
19	3.10044	80.82988
20	3.049663	83.87954

mula to be wrong, including natural variance of human performance, breaks between tasks (requiring relearning), and, in projects, the naturally expected circumstance that no two activities are quite the same. The concept of learning curves is very useful in estimation. Trusting the precise numbers calls for more heroic management.

Endnotes

1. C. Eden, T. Williams, and F. Ackermann, "Dismantling the Learning Curve: The Role of Disruptions on the Planning of Development Projects," *International Journal of Project Management* 16, no. 3 (1998), pp. 131–38.
2. J. R. Meredith and S. M. Shafer, *Operations Management for MBAs* (New York: John Wiley & Sons, 1999).

## CHAPTER 6

Quantitative Project Scheduling Methods

Chapter Outline

Main Ideas Discussed

- The critical path method
- The use of buffers in critical path scheduling
- How critical path schedules can be crashed
- Trade-off analysis of crashed schedules
- Resource leveling adjustment of schedules
- The effect of critical path model assumptions

The Critical Path Method

The critical path method provides a way to easily identify the fastest a project can be completed, given that the estimated durations of activities are accurate. Even though estimated durations are usually at variance with actual outcomes, the critical path method provides a useful analysis of which activities are time bottlenecks. The input to the critical path method is a list of each activity, its expected duration, and those activities that immediately precede this activity. "Immediately precede" in this case means that predecessor activities must be completed before the subject activity can begin, and there are no other activities between the predecessor and the activity in question.

To demonstrate, consider the very simple project, consisting of five activities, given in Table 6–1. This is all of the information required to develop a critical path model. The critical path algorithm is quite straightforward.

TABLE 6–1   Simple Project Example

Activity		Duration	Predecessors
A	Estimate cost to complete project	12 weeks	None
B	Bid job and complete contract	1 week	A
C	Build system	40 weeks	B
D	Develop training	20 weeks	B
E	Implement system	5 weeks	C, D

		w	e	e	k	s						10									20	...	30	...	50									58
Activity	Duration																																	
A	12 w	x	x	x	x	x	x	x	x	x	x	x	x	x																				
B	1 w													x																				
C	40 w														x	x	x	x	x	x	x	x	...	x	...	x	x	x	x					
D	20 w														x	x	x	x	x	x	x	x	...	x		s	s	s	s	s				
E	5 w																														x	x	x	x	x

Early Start Schedule

First an **early start schedule** is developed. For every activity that has no un-scheduled predecessors, schedule the activity to start as soon as possible (either the project start time or the maximum early finish of all predecessors). The critical path schedules are optimal with respect to time. This process continues until all activities are scheduled. The early finish is the sum of the early start time plus the duration (see Table 6–2).

The project *early completion time* is the maximum early finish. In this case the project early completion time is 58 weeks.

Networks

Quite often a **network** is displayed, which graphically displays the relationship between activities (Figure 6–1). Networks are not really needed for development of early start schedules, but they are very useful in sorting out the relationships for late start schedules. Networks also provide a valuable visual aid for managers to identify relationships among activities.

Late Start Schedule

The next phase of the critical path analysis is the **late start schedule**. The late start schedule is the latest an activity can be scheduled without delaying project completion time. The final ending time for the project can be some contract dead-line, which may be different from the early finish schedule, or the early finish project completion time can be used. If the deadline is earlier than the project early finish time, the project is unfeasible (cannot be completed on time with

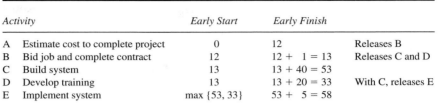

TABLE 6–2   Early Start Schedule

Activity		Early Start	Early Finish	
A	Estimate cost to complete project	0	12	Releases B
B	Bid job and complete contract	12	12 + 1 = 13	Releases C and D
C	Build system	13	13 + 40 = 53	
D	Develop training	13	13 + 20 = 33	With C, releases E
E	Implement system	max {53, 33}	53 + 5 = 58	

FIGURE 6–1

Network

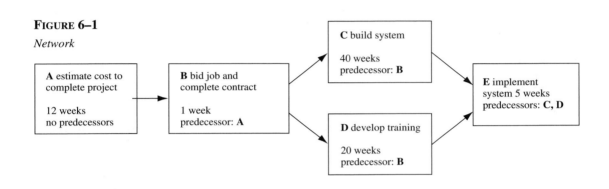

given durations). If the deadline is later than the project early finish time, all activities in the project will have slack, or spare time. If the deadline coincides with the project early finish time, there will be at least one critical path, connecting activities in a chain with zero slack.

The late start schedule is calculated in reverse. Begin with the end time (deadline or early finish time). All activities that do not appear on the list of predecessors for unscheduled activities can be scheduled. The late finish time will be either the project end time, or the minimum of the late start times for all following activities (see Table 6–3).

Slack

Slack is the difference between the late start and early start schedules (it doesn't matter which is used, because in both cases the difference between them is the duration). Those activities with zero slack are critical (see Table 6–4). If they are delayed, the project completion time will be delayed. There can be more than one critical path for a project, and the project network presented in Figure 6–1 can be useful in assuring identification of each critical path.

Slack in the case in Table 6–4 exists for only one activity, D. More complex projects will include slack for multiple activities, such as in the project described in Table 6–5.

TABLE 6–3   Late Start Schedule

Activity		Late Finish	Late Start	
E	Implement system	58	$58 - 5 = 53$	Releases C and D
D	Develop training	53	$53 - 20 = 33$	
C	Build system	53	$53 - 40 = 13$	With D, releases B
B	Bid job and complete contract	min {13, 33}	$13 - 1 = 12$	Releases A
A	Estimate cost to complete project	12	$12 - 12 = 0$	

TABLE 6–4   Slack

Activity		Early Start	Early Finish	Late Start	Late Finish	Slack	
A	Estimate cost to complete project	0	12	0	12	0	Critical
B	Bid job and complete contract	12	13	12	13	0	Critical
C	Build system	13	53	13	53	0	Critical
D	Develop training	13	33	33	53	20	
E	Implement system	53	58	53	58	0	Critical

TABLE 6–5   Slack for Multiple Activities

Activity		Duration	Predecessors
A	Rough design of advertising plan	1 week	None
B	Convince product manager to adopt plan	3 weeks	A
C	Develop marketing plan with staff	3 weeks	B
D	Identify media alternatives	2 weeks	B
E	Print materials	1 week	C
F	Brief sales force	2 weeks	B
G	Select media	1 week	D

This project has the slacks given in Table 6–6. In this case, activities D, G, and F all have slack. Looking at the Gantt chart for this project, it is clear that activity F is independent of D and G, so that if a week is lost in briefing the sales force, it interferes with nothing else. This case is **independent slack.** On the other hand, if identifying media alternatives should take an extra week, the slack of one week is shared with that of activity G, which would become critical if the slack on activity D were used up. This case is **shared slack.**

Project management software includes the ability to have a number of precedence relationships. The default is generally Predecessor finish = Follower start. Other options include Predecessor start = Follower start, or Predecessor start = Follower start plus some lag time.

TABLE 6–6   Slacks for Multiple Activities Project

Activity		Early Start	Early Finish	Late Start	Late Finish	Slack	
A	Rough design of advertising plan	0	1	0	1	0	Critical
B	Convince product manager to adopt	1	4	1	4	0	Critical
C	Develop marketing plan with staff	4	7	4	7	0	Critical
D	Identify media alternatives	4	6	5	7	1	
E	Print materials	7	8	7	8	0	Critical
F	Brief sales force	4	6	6	8	2	
G	Select media	6	7	7	8	1	

---

			w	e	e	k	s			
Activity	Duration	1	2	3	4	5	6	7	8
A rough design of advertising plan	1 week	x							
B convince product manager to adopt	3 weeks		x	x	x				
C develop marketing plan with staff	3 weeks					x	x	x	
D identify media alternatives	2 weeks					x	x	s	
E print materials	1 week								x
F brief sales force	2 weeks					x	x	s	s
G select media	1 week							x	s
	Scheduled	x							
	Slack	s							
	Critical	x							

Another graphical output of the critical path method is a **Gantt chart**, which displays the early start schedule versus time (Figure 6–2). In this case, it is clear that there is only one critical path, consisting of the chain of activities A–B–C–E. Activity D has slack.

The critical path method provides a useful means of identifying the earliest a project can be completed, as well as identifying those activities that are critical. Critical activities need to be managed more closely than slack activities. This is because if any delay is experienced on a critical activity, the project completion time will be delayed. On the other hand, if things are delayed for activity D in our first example, it doesn't really matter until 20 spare days are wasted. However, one should be careful, because once all of an activity's slack is exhausted, it also becomes critical.

There is a bias in projects, in that activity delays accumulate, while gains from finishing early do not.[1] This is because when an activity is late, those that must wait for it to be completed start later than scheduled. On the other hand, if an activity should be finished before it was scheduled to finish, the advantage rarely can be used, because in complicated projects different crews and materials have to be gathered, and many different people need to be coordinated. The early finish

FIGURE 6–2

Gantt chart of project

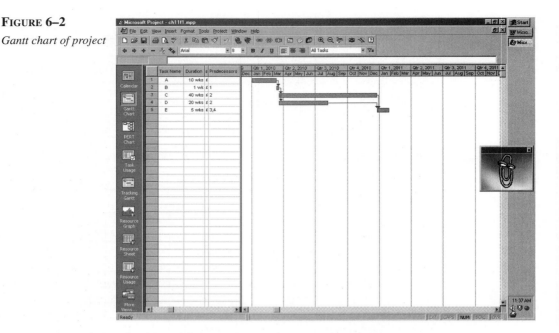

time is not usually known much prior to the activity's completion. Therefore, it is very difficult to gather all of the following activities' resources together in time to start early.

Schonberger[2] recommended focusing on scheduling the critical chain of activities closely to make sure that they have the resources needed to proceed as scheduled. Goldratt[3] adopted the same view. The critical chain of activities includes those activities that are critical (as long as managerial control can influence their duration), but is not limited to these activities. Activities with very little slack can become problems if they are delayed up to or beyond their slack. Therefore, the slack of noncritical activities should also be monitored to make sure that new critical activities are identified.

Buffers

The primary means to ensure that critical activities are completed on time is to use buffers.[4] A **buffer** is time that is included in the schedule to protect against unanticipated delays and to allow early starts. Buffers are viewed by Goldratt and Newbold as different than slack. Slack is spare time. Buffers are time blocks that are not expected to be used for work time (the same as slack), but they are dedicated to cover most likely contingencies, and are closely watched so that if they are not needed, subsequent activities can proceed at the earliest time possible. **Project buffers** are used after the final task of a project to protect project completion time from delays. **Feeding buffers** are placed at each point where a noncritical activity is related to a critical path activity. Feeding buffers protect the critical activities from tasks that precede them and allow for early starts of critical

TABLE 6–7   Advertising Schedule with Buffers and Slack

Activity	Duration	w 1	e 2	e 3	k 4	s 5	6	7	8
A rough design of advertising plan	1 week	x						b	s
B convince product manager to adopt	1 week		x					b	s
C develop marketing plan with staff	3 weeks			x	x	x		b	s
D identify media alternatives	2 weeks			x	x	s		b	s
E print materials	1 week						x	b	s
F brief sales force	2 weeks			x	x	s	s	b	s
G select media	1 week					x	s	b	s
	Scheduled	x							
	Slack	s							
	Critical	x							
	BUFFER	b							

activities. **Resource buffers** are placed before resources that are scheduled to work on critical activities to ensure that resources will be available and that their shortage will not delay critical activities. Resource buffers can be implemented by either warning notices to those managing the resource ahead of the required time, or a time can be scheduled to mobilize the resource as a predecessor to the critical activity using it. In multiple-project environments, **strategic resource buffers** can be used to ensure that key resources are available for critical activities.

To demonstrate the use of buffers, consider the advertising schedule presented in this section. If the campaign had to be completed in eight weeks, there is currently no room for a project buffer because the chain of critical activities (activities A–B–C–E) have a planned duration of eight weeks, equal to the available time. However, there may be ways to accomplish specific tasks at the cost of some extra effort or expenditure. For instance, it may be possible to obtain the product manager's approval in one week rather than the planned three weeks. This is an attractive activity to shorten because it occurs early in the project, and if approval is not obtained, effort on later activities will not be wasted. The product manager may require a thorough analysis. If this thorough analysis is accomplished by working late hours during the week and working weekends, it may be possible to develop the required analysis within a week. This would allow shortening the project by two weeks, as shown in the schedule given in Table 6–7.

There now are two weeks available before the project needs to be completed. One of these weeks can be used as a project buffer, insulating the work that needs to be done from the project deadline. (This leaves one additional week of slack for each activity, making no activities critical at this point.) Project buffer is not planned to be used, but it is available should something go wrong with critical activities or with noncritical activities beyond their available slack.

Feeding buffers can be used as pseudo-activities to marshal required resources, making sure that they are available in time and that critical activities are not delayed. For instance, activity E, printing materials, is crucial. The marketing plan must be completed before printing can begin, because the marketing plan is the essence of what is to be produced. The project manager can plan on using week 6 as a buffer to ensure that all materials needed by the printer are available (see Table 6–8).

Now the critical activities reappear. Critical activities are activities without slack. All seven activities have a week of project buffer in week 8. Activity E has a week of feeding buffer in week 6, when materials are gathered to ensure that the critical printing activity will proceed as planned. There is now no slack for the chain A–B–C–E. An equivalent way to model this schedule would be as shown in Table 6–9.

TABLE 6–8   Advertising Schedule Critical Path

Activity	Duration	w 1	e 2	e 3	k 4	s 5	6	7	8
A rough design of advertising plan	1 week	x							b
B convince product manager to adopt	1 week		x						b
C develop marketing plan with staff	3 weeks			x	x	x			b
D identify media alternatives	2 weeks			x	x	s			b
E print materials	1 week						b	x	b
F brief sales force	2 weeks			x	x	s	s	s	b
G select media	1 week					x	s	s	b
	Scheduled	x							
	Slack	s							
	Critical	x							
	BUFFER	b							

TABLE 6–9   Equivalent Model Using Feeding Buffer

Activity	Duration	w 1	e 2	e 3	k 4	s 5	6	7	8
A rough design of advertising plan	1 week	x							b
B convince product manager to adopt	1 week		x						b
C develop marketing plan with staff	3 weeks			x	x	x			b
D identify media alternatives	2 weeks			x	x	s			b
CE feeding buffer	1 week						b		
E print materials	1 week							x	b
F brief sales force	2 weeks			x	x	s	s	s	b
G select media	1 week					x	s	s	b
	Slack	s							
	Critical	x							
	BUFFER	b							

The critical path would now be A–B–C–CE–E. It is important that if the buffer is not needed, subsequent activities should proceed to work early. For instance, if the feeding buffer between activities C and E is not required, and all required material is ready at the beginning of week 6, printing should go ahead in week 6. If the duration of activity E is the planned one week, the project would then be completed by the end of week 6. If the feeding buffer CE turns out to be needed, and printing requires extra time, there is project buffer available in week 8. This buffer, like all other buffers, should not be used unless necessary in light of sound management principles.

Resource buffers could be used if a key resource, such as the team that develops the advertising plan, were heavily scheduled on other activities. A resource buffer in that case would be time allocated to ensure that the key resource had time to gear up for this particular project. In construction, an obvious resource buffer could exist if there were a key piece of equipment, such as a large crane, that was very expensive and valuable for many other projects. (In this case, it would be a strategic resource buffer.) The key resource might be needed elsewhere or might be found to be across the country working on a prior project. A strategic resource buffer would then be included in the schedule to ensure that time was available to transport it, to replace it if necessary (and possible), or in case of mechanical difficulties, to repair it. The resource buffer, like all four forms of buffer, represents planning ahead for reasonable contingencies.

Project Crashing

Another possibility is that extra resources can be acquired to complete critical activities more quickly. This creates a problem for management, trading off quicker completion time with higher cost. If the savings from faster completion time are known, then the problem is simply one of minimizing cost. Often, however, it is a matter of risk, in that you know some activities are subject to delay, and earlier planned finishing times are far safer than those plans that push things to some deadline.

To demonstrate **crashing,** consider the problem of importing some critical piece of software from Australia, which you have contracted to install for a client. Figure 6–3 gives a network for this project. You have agreed to get the system

FIGURE 6–3

Network for delivery from Australia

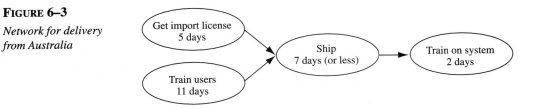

TABLE 6–10   **Importing Software from Australia**

Activity		Duration	Predecessors	Early Start	Early Finish	Late Start	Late Finish	Slack
A	Get import license	5 days	None	0	5	0	5	0
B	Ship	7 days	A	5	12	5	12	0
C	Train users	11 days	None	0	11	1	12	1
D	Train on system	2 days	B, C	12	14	12	14	0

		d	a	y	s										
Activity	Duration	1	2	3	4	5	6	7	8	9	10	11	12	13	14
A license	5 days	x	x	x	x	x									
B slow boat	7 days						x	x	x	x	x	x	x		
C users	11 days	x	x	x	x	x	x	x	x	x	x	x	s		
D system	2 days													x	x
	Scheduled	x													
	Slack	s													
	Critical	x													

running in 12 days. If you are late, you will pay a penalty of $500 per day for each day beyond the contracted 12 days (see Table 6–10).

The critical path, which takes 14 days, is A–B–D. Activity C has one day of slack. But this plan involves a penalty of $1,000 because it is two days late. The options available for activity B are given in Table 6–11. The current plan is based on the least cost method, the slow boat. However, it incurs penalties of $1,000. Clearly it would be cost-effective to adopt a faster delivery method. Crashing analyzes this cost trade-off.

The crashing procedure identifies the least cost method of reducing duration of activities on the critical path one time unit at a time. The critical path here is A–B–D. Actually, in this problem, there is only one activity that can be accomplished faster than the original schedule—activity B. The next least cost method is a fast boat, which costs $300 rather than the slow boat cost of $100, for a marginal added cost of $200. This would reduce the duration of activity B to 6, resulting in the critical path schedule given in Table 6–12.

This new schedule saves $500 in penalties, at an added cost of $200, for a net savings of $300. This clearly is superior to the original schedule. The difference between this schedule and the original schedule is that activity B has been crashed one day. Another result is that now all four activities are critical (all have zero slack). From looking at the network, we can see that there are now two critical paths: A–B–D and C–D. This means that if we want to reduce the project completion time, we have to shorten both critical paths in parallel. While it is possible to reduce the original critical path A–B–D by adopting the bush airplane option, this will do nothing to reduce the new critical path, C–D. Therefore, there are no savings in penalties, while there is an added cost of $100 by moving from the fast

TABLE 6–11   Options Available for Activity B

Slow boat	7 days	$100	(The current option)
Fast boat	6 days	$300	
Bush airplane	5 days	$400	
Normal airplane	3 days	$500	
Chartered plane	1 day	$900	

TABLE 6–12   Fast Boat Critical Path Schedule

Activity		Duration	Predecessors	Early Start	Early Finish	Late Start	Late Finish	Slack
A	Get import license	5 days	None	0	5	0	5	0
B	Ship	6 days	A	5	11	5	11	0
C	Train users	11 days	None	0	11	0	11	0
D	Train on system	2 days	B, C	11	13	11	13	0

		days												
activity	duration	1	2	3	4	5	6	7	8	9	10	11	12	13
A license	5 d	x	x	x	x	x								
B fast boat	6 d						x	x	x	x	x	x		
C users	11 d	x	x	x	x	x	x	x	x	x	x	x		
D system	2 d												x	x

FIGURE 6–4

Network for line project

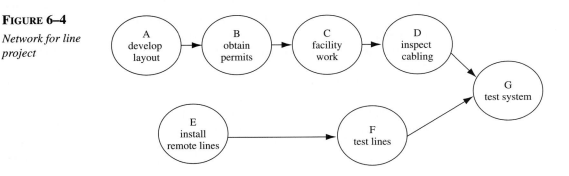

boat to the bush plane. Thus, we would not be interested in further crashing the project, but we would adopt the fast boat shipping option.

Crashing also can be applied to identify a cost/time trade-off. Table 6–13 demonstrates this concept, while the network is diagrammed in Figure 6–4.

The original critical path model requires 58 days to complete. This is with no extra costs for crashing.

TABLE 6–13   Cost/Time Trade-Off

Activity	Duration	Predecessors	Early Start	Early Finish	Late Start	Late Finish	Slack	Crash
A Develop layout	19 days	None	0	19	0	19	0	
B Obtain permits	5 days	A	19	24	19	24	0	10,000/day 1 day max
C Facility work	30 days	B	24	54	24	54	0	3,000/day 2 days max
D Inspect cabling	2 days	C	54	56	54	56	0	
E Install remote lines	53 days	None	0	53	1	54	1	5,000/day 12 days max
F Test lines	2 days	E	53	55	54	56	1	
G Test system	2 days	D, F	56	58	56	58	0	

Activity	Duration	d	a	y	s		10		19	20		24	25		30		40		50		53	54	55	56	57	58
		1	2	3	4	...	10	...	19	20	...	24	25	...	30	...	40	...	50	...	53	54	55	56	57	58
A	19 days	x	x	x	x	...	x	...	x																	
B	5 days									x	...	x														
C	29 days											x	...	x	...	x	...	x	...	x	x				
D	2 days																							x	x		
E	53 days	x	x	x	x	...	x	...	x	x	...	x	x	...	x	...	x	...	x	...	x	s				
F	2 days																						x	x	s		
G	2 days																									x	x
	Scheduled	x																								
	Slack	s																								
	Critical	x																								

The next step is to identify critical activities that can be crashed. If more than one critical path exists, all critical paths must be reduced by the same amount of time. In our case, there is one critical path: A–B–C–D–G. Of these critical activities, B and C can be crashed. The least expensive would be selected. In this case, it is activity C (at $3,000/day as opposed to $10,000/day for B).

By crashing C one day at a cost of $3,000, we can complete the project in 57 days (see Table 6–14).

Now there are two critical paths: A–B–C–D–G and E–F–G. On the first path, our choices for crashing are B and C, with C still the least cost option at $3,000/day. On the second critical path, the only activity that can be crashed is E, at a cost of $5,000/day. If G had been crashable, it would have served for both critical paths, because it is an element of both. But if G is not available (and it is not), we must crash two activities, in this case C and E at a total cost of $8,000. This yields a solution of completing the project in 56 days at an added cumulative cost of $11,000 (including the $3,000 spent to get to 57 days) (see Table 6–15).

We have now trimmed both critical paths. All activities remain critical, and there are two critical paths: A–B–C–D–G and E–F–G. We have exhausted the days we can crash on activity C, so our only option is now to reduce activity B to 4 days by spending another $10,000, at the same time that we reduce activity E to 51 days at an added cost of $5,000. This would reduce the project duration to 55 days, at a cumulative cost of $26,000 (see Table 6–16).

TABLE 6–14   Crash Activity C

Activity		Duration	Predecessors	Early Start	Early Finish	Late Start	Late Finish	Slack	Crash	
A	Develop layout	19 days	None	0	19	0	19	0		
B	Obtain permits	5 days	A	19	24	19	24	0	10,000/day	1 day max
C	Facility work	29 days	B	24	53	24	53	0	3,000/day	1 day max
D	Inspect cabling	2 days	C	53	55	53	55	0		
E	Install remote lines	53 days	None	0	53	0	53	0	5,000/day	12 days max
F	Test lines	2 days	E	53	55	53	55	0		
G	Test system	2 days	D, F	55	57	55	57	0		

Activity	Duration	d 1	a 2	y 3	s 4	...10	19	20	...24	25	...30	...40	...50	...53	54	55	56	57
A	19 days	x	x	x	x	... x	... x											
B	5 days							x	... x									
C	29 days								x	... x	... x	... x	... x	x				
D	2 days														x	x		
E	53 days	x	x	x	x	... x	... x	x	... x	x	... x	... x	... x	x				
F	2 days														x	x		
G	2 days																x	x

TABLE 6–15   Project Completion in 56 Days

Activity		Duration	Predecessors	Early Start	Early Finish	Late Start	Late Finish	Slack	Crash
A	Develop layout	19 days	None	0	19	0	19	0	
B	Obtain permits	5 days	A	19	24	19	24	0	10,000/day 1 day max
C	Facility work	28 days	B	24	52	24	52	0	
D	Inspect cabling	2 days	C	52	54	52	54	0	
E	Install remote lines	52 days	None	0	52	0	52	0	5,000/day 11 days max
F	Test lines	2 days	E	52	54	52	54	0	
G	Test system	2 days	D, F	54	56	54	56	0	

TABLE 6–16   Project Completion in 55 Days

Activity		Duration	Predecessors	Early Start	Early Finish	Late Start	Late Finish	Slack	Crash
A	Develop layout	19 days	None	0	19	0	19	0	
B	Obtain permits	4 days	A	19	23	19	23	0	
C	Facility work	28 days	B	23	51	23	51	0	
D	Inspect cabling	2 days	C	51	53	51	53	0	
E	Install remote lines	52 days	None	0	51	0	51	0	5,000/day 10 days max
F	Test lines	2 days	E	51	53	51	53	0	
G	Test system	2 days	D, F	53	55	53	55	0	

At this stage, we can no longer reduce the duration of the critical path chain A–B–C–D–G, so we must stop. The trade-offs resulting from our analysis are given in Table 6–17. In this case, we do not have a benefit given for saving a day of project time. This often is the case. Managers are provided with the expected cost for a given project duration. Managers seeking the lowest expected cost would risk the 58-day plan. More cautious managers may want to spend the extra money to save time or to increase the cushion for project completion.

Resource Leveling

The critical path model we have considered so far has assumed unlimited resources. **Resource leveling** is the process of spreading out the early start schedule so that the maximum number of a particular resource required can be reduced. For instance, if a particular specialist is needed to accomplish more than one activity, and these activities happen to be scheduled during common periods of time, something would have to give. One or the other of the activities sharing the common resource would have to be delayed (or additional resources acquired).

To demonstrate, consider a project (network in Figure 6–5) with the data given in Table 6–18. If the same specialist was required for both activities B and C, they could not be accomplished concurrently. This means that the original critical path model is infeasible. Either B or C must be delayed. The decision of what to delay is a difficult question if you are after the guaranteed best answer. For small projects, you might as well check all of the possibilities. For instance, in this case there are only two activities to delay. If B is delayed, it cannot start until week 10, when both activity A is completed and the specialist is through with activity C (see Table 6–19).

In this case, nothing is slack, because delaying any activity will delay the end of the project. We can see this, although the method of using only predecessors

---

TABLE 6–17   Trade-Offs

Original schedule	58 days	No extra expenditure
Crash C 1 day	57 days	$3,000 extra cost
Crash C 2 days, E 1 day	56 days	$11,000 extra cost
Crash B 1 day, C 2 days, E 2 days	55 days	$26,000 extra cost

FIGURE 6–5

*Network for
leveling project*

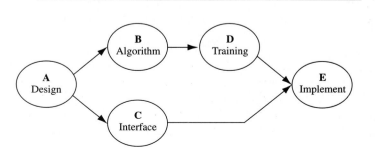

TABLE 6–18   Leveling Project

Activity		Duration	Predecessors	Early Start	Early Finish	Late Start	Late Finish	Slack	Resource
A	Design	3 weeks	None	0	3	0	3	0	
B	Algorithm	5	A	3	8	3	8	0	Specialist
C	Interface	6	A	3	9	6	12	3	Specialist
D	Training	4	B	8	12	8	12	0	
E	Implement	3	C, D	12	15	12	15	0	

Activity	Duration	w	e	e	k	s										
		1	2	3	4	5	6	7	8	9	10	11	12	13	14	15
A design	3 weeks	x	x	x												
B algorithm	5 weeks				x	x	x	x	x							
C interface	6 weeks				x	x	x	x	x	x	s	s	s			
D training	4 weeks									x	x	x	x			
E implement	3 weeks													x	x	x
	Scheduled	x														
	Slack	s														
	Critical	x														

TABLE 6–19   Delay of Activity B

Activity		Duration	Predecessors	Start	Finish	Slack	Resource
A	Design	3 weeks	None	0	3	0	
B	Algorithm	5	A	9	14	0	Specialist
C	Interface	6	A	3	9	0	Specialist
D	Training	4	B	14	18	0	
E	Implement	3	C, D	18	21	0	

Activity	Duration	w	e	e	k	s															
		1	2	3	4	5	6	7	8	9	10	11	12	13	14	15	16	17	18	19	20	21
A design	3 weeks	x	x	x																		
B algorithm	5 weeks										x	x	x	x	x							
C interface	6 weeks				x	x	x	x	x	x												
D training	4 weeks															x	x	x	x			
E implement	3 weeks																			x	x	x
	Specialist	x																				

will not yield that result because of the need to consider the limitation on the number of specialists.

The alternative is to delay activity C. This yields the information in Table 6–20. In this case, activity D will have a slack of 2. The total project is completed

TABLE 6–20   Delay of Activity C

Activity	Duration	Predecessors	Start	Finish	Slack	Resource
A Design	3 weeks	None	0	3	0	
B Algorithm	5	A	3	8	0	Specialist
C Interface	6	A	8	14	0	Specialist
D Training	4	B	8	12	2	
E Implement	3	C, D	14	17	0	

Activity	Duration	w 1	e 2	e 3	k 4	s 5	6	7	8	9	10	11	12	13	14	15	16	17
A design	3 weeks	x	x	x														
B algorithm	5 weeks				x	x	x	x	x									
C interface	6 weeks									x	x	x	x	x	x			
D training	4 weeks									x	x	x	x	s	s			
E implement	3 weeks															x	x	x
	Specialist	x																

in 17 weeks instead of the 21 weeks obtained by delaying activity B. This is still a significant delay, as the original critical path schedule required only 15 weeks.

While there is no guaranteed best way of deciding which activity to delay when sharing scarce resources, it usually works well to use a priority system. A good choice would be to schedule critical activities first, and if more than one critical activity shares the scarce resource, a second priority that is often used is to schedule the longest activity among those selected by the first priority. If multiple resources are limited, an alternative priority could be given to scheduling the resource with the greatest number of limited resources. Project management software usually levels projects for you. They vary in what priority rules they use.

Resource Smoothing

Resource leveling focuses on extending schedules so that particular resources are not overscheduled. **Resource smoothing** focuses on adjusting schedules to obtain a level amount of work for a given resource. This includes possible extension (or compression) of activities to make work volume more even. It also can include identifying gaps in the work schedule that management might be able to fill by finding extra work.

Consider a multiple-project operation in the information technology industry (Figure 6–6). Four resources are involved: crews for design, production, testing, and installation of information technology products. For simplification, assume that these four activities are accomplished in sequence in the order given. The firm currently has three projects, all with a deadline of being completed by the end of week 20 (see Table 6–21). The Gantt chart for this schedule is given in Table 6–22.

FIGURE 6–6

Network for smoothing projects

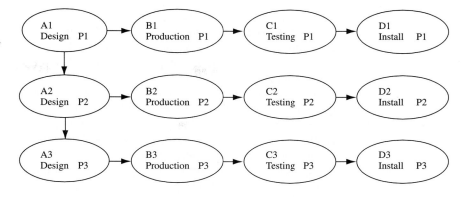

TABLE 6–21   Multiple-Project Operation

Activity		Duration	Predecessors	Start	Finish	Resource
A1	Design P1	2 weeks	None	0	2	Design crew
B1	Production P1	4 weeks	A1	2	6	Production crew
C1	Testing P1	2 weeks	B1	6	8	Testing crew
D1	Install P1	1 week	C1	8	9	Installation crew
A2	Design P2	2 weeks	A1	2	4	Design crew
B2	Production P2	5 weeks	A2	4	9	Production crew
C2	Testing P2	3 weeks	B2	9	12	Testing crew
D2	Install P2	1 week	C2	12	13	Installation crew
A3	Design P3	4 weeks	A2	4	8	Design crew
B3	Production P3	6 weeks	A3	8	14	Production crew
C3	Testing P3	3 weeks	B3	14	17	Testing crew
D3	Install P3	1 week	C3	17	18	Installation crew

TABLE 6–22   Gantt Chart for Multiple-Project Operation

	w	e	e	k	s															
	1	2	3	4	5	6	7	8	9	10	11	12	13	14	15	16	17	18	19	20
A1 design P1	x	x																		
B1 production P1			x	x	x	x														
C1 testing P1							x	x												
D1 install P1									x											
A2 design P2			x	x																
B2 production P2					x	x	x	x	x											
C2 testing P2										x	x	x								
D2 install P2													x							
A3 design P3					x	x	x	x												
B3 production P3									x	x	x	x	x	x						
C3 testing P3															x	x	x			
D3 install P3																		x		

Usages for each resource are given in Table 6–23, with an x indicating the total count of each resource required by week. For instance, one design crew is required in weeks 1 through 8 and none thereafter. One production crew is needed in weeks 3 and 4, and two production crews are needed in weeks 5 and 6.

A smooth schedule is one in which a resource is working the same level of activity each time period. These resource usage charts indicate that there are two types of smoothing that might be useful: gaps in work to do and excess work to do. When there is no work to do, a valley (no activity) is encountered. When there is too much work scheduled for a period, a peak occurs. There are valleys for the testing and installation crews. The only peaks occur for the production crew.

For all four crews, slack resources exist in that there are periods where no work is currently scheduled. This is because greater resource capacity exists than work required. Some spare resources are required to cover the inevitable uncertainty in projects. Efficiency, on the other hand, seeks to utilize all resources at their capacity at all times. Being careful to ensure that important project activities are not delayed for lack of resource, management may be able to increase efficiency by finding useful activities for resources during their unscheduled periods (or laying off crews when no work is scheduled). One approach is investment in

TABLE 6–23   Resource Usage

Design	w	e	e	k	s															
	1	2	3	4	5	6	7	8	9	10	11	12	13	14	15	16	17	18	19	20
# crews needed:																				
Two																				
One	x	x	x	x	x	x	x	x												

Production	w	e	e	k	s															
	1	2	3	4	5	6	7	8	9	10	11	12	13	14	15	16	17	18	19	20
# crews needed:																				
Two					x	x			x											
One			x	x	x	x	x	x	x	x	x	x	x	x						

Testing	w	e	e	k	s															
	1	2	3	4	5	6	7	8	9	10	11	12	13	14	15	16	17	18	19	20
# crews needed:																				
Two																				
One							x	x		x	x	x				x	x	x		

Install	w	e	e	k	s															
	1	2	3	4	5	6	7	8	9	10	11	12	13	14	15	16	17	18	19	20
# crews needed:																				
Two																				
One									x				x					x		

training and development activities. Another approach is to find more work. However, it is apparent here that there is also an imbalance across resources. If management were to obtain more work similar to what they have, the production crew would fall further and further behind because their work per project is always longest. The gaps for the testing crew, and especially for the installation crew, would get wider and wider. Sound management practice here calls for balancing, through hiring additional production crews. If a great deal of similar work is obtained, more analysis crews might be called for as well. As a simple fix to this operation's problem, a second production crew is added to accomplish production work on the second project in Table 6–24. The schedules for each of the production crews now are smoothed in the sense that they are not overscheduled (see Table 6–25). However, there is obviously more waste time that management needs to fill.

TABLE 6–24   Addition of Second Production Crew

	w	e	e	k	s															
	1	2	3	4	5	6	7	8	9	10	11	12	13	14	15	16	17	18	19	20
A1 design P1	x	x																		
B1 production 1			x	x	x	x														
C1 testing P1							x	x												
D1 install P1									x											
A2 design P2			x	x																
B2 production 2					y	y	y	y	y											
C2 testing P2										x	x	x								
D2 install P2													x							
A3 design P3					x	x	x	x												
B3 production 1									x	x	x	x	x	x						
C3 testing P3															x	x	x			
D3 install P3																		x		

TABLE 6–25   Smoothed Production Schedules

Production 1	w	e	e	k	s															
	1	2	3	4	5	6	7	8	9	10	11	12	13	14	15	16	17	18	19	20
# crews needed:																				
Two																				
One			x	x	x	x			x	x	x	x	x	x						

Production 2	w	e	e	k	s															
	1	2	3	4	5	6	7	8	9	10	11	12	13	14	15	16	17	18	19	20
# crews needed:																					
Two																					
One				y	y	y	y	y												

TABLE 6–26   Second Smoothing Condition

	w	e	e	k	s															
	1	2	3	4	5	6	7	8	9	10	11	12	13	14	15	16	17	18	19	20
A1 design P1	x	x																		
B1 production 1			x	x	x	x														
C1 testing P1							x	x												
D1 install P1									x											
A2 design P2			x	x																
B2 production 2							x	x	x	x	x									
C2 testing P2												x	x	x						
D2 install P2															x					
A3 design P3					x	x	x	x												
B3 production 1												x	x	x	x	x	x			
C3 testing P3																		x	x	x
D3 install P3																				

The second smoothing condition is to lower the peak workloads. This requires either delaying the schedule, or hiring additional resources (demonstrated in the last section). Delaying the schedule (returning to the case using one production crew) can eliminate the excess workload (see Table 6–26). However, eliminating the overscheduling entirely using existing resources would require extending the last project into week 21. The resource usages would now be as given in Table 6–27.

Smoothing is a managerial decision. The ideal would involve balancing crew capacities so that each crew could work the same amount each time period. That is what assembly-line operations do. It requires a highly predictable environment, which simply does not exist in projects. Projects will inevitably experience gaps in work, along with some periods of critical resource shortage. The quality of project management can be measured on a scale of efficiency by the proportion of waste time encountered. However, priority should be given to ensuring that critical activities have the resources they need, even if it involves some waste. It is more important to get the job done right, on time, and within budget, than to obtain a perfectly smooth schedule.

Critical Path Criticisms

Like any model, the critical path approach makes a number of assumptions. Usually, the more convenient the assumptions are for mathematical solution, the less realistic the assumptions are relative to the real decision. The critical path model as demonstrated in this chapter is very useful in identifying the fastest one can expect to complete a project. But we have seen in prior chapters that things rarely

TABLE 6–27   **Update Resource Usage**

Design	w	e	e	k	s															
	1	2	3	4	5	6	7	8	9	10	11	12	13	14	15	16	17	18	19	20
# crews needed:																				
Two																				
One	x	x	x	x	x	x	x	x												

Production	w	e	e	k	s															
	1	2	3	4	5	6	7	8	9	10	11	12	13	14	15	16	17	18	19	20
# crews needed:																				
Two																				
One			x	x	x	x	x	x	x	x	x	x	x	x	x	x				

Testing	w	e	e	k	s															
	1	2	3	4	5	6	7	8	9	10	11	12	13	14	15	16	17	18	19	20
# crews needed:																				
Two																				
One						x	x			x	x	x						x	x	x

Install	w	e	e	k	s															
	1	2	3	4	5	6	7	8	9	10	11	12	13	14	15	16	17	...	20	21
# crews needed:																				
Two																				
One							x						x					...		x

proceed as planned, and in practice the original critical path plan usually requires significant modification as the project proceeds and more accurate activity durations are obtained. There is usually significant variance in possible durations of activities, with options available to speed selected activities. Crashing provides one means of obtaining greater understanding for these situations. One approach to uncertainty is to focus on scheduling milestones.[6] Uncertainty in activity durations will also be addressed in Chapter 7. Another key idea is that the critical path includes those activities that should be most closely managed. Critical activities are important to monitor closely. But as Goldratt[7] emphasized, those activities with apparent slack can become critical, and should not be ignored. Again, material in Chapter 7 includes models that consider the aspect of activity duration uncertainty.

The critical path model assumes unlimited resources. We have discussed leveling as a means of analyzing the effects of limited resources. An additional extension of this concept is smoothing. Projects typically involve highly variable work loads, with employment starting at a very low volume, jumping to high levels in the middle of the project, and then in general declining. This overall trend masks even greater variations for the workload of specific skill sets, which can be highly erratic. Smoothing seeks to level the workload of the project, sacrificing minimum time for a more even workload. In information systems projects this is less important because the usual condition is many projects going on at once, with more than enough work for individuals on other projects as soon as their work on this project is completed. The matrix form of organization, discussed in Chapter 8, is highly appropriate for this environment, allowing individuals to be shuffled into a particular project to perform their specialty, and then moving on to the next project requiring their services.

Shtub[8] noted that the critical path model assumes that activities can be addressed as entities, with clear beginning and ending points. In reality, the content of complex projects changes over time. As new events unfold, project progress may require a change in direction. An obvious effect relative to information systems projects is the outcome of testing. According to plan, testing will find that everything was successfully built as scheduled. In reality, the outcome of testing is highly uncertain. There is a possibility that testing will find that the system components do perform as designed. If they do not, however, new activities will be required to identify the cause of the problem, decide how to revise the system, and quite possibly build new system components.

Project activity-sequence relationships can be specified and described by a network. However, in some projects sequence relationships cannot always be specified in the planning stage but are conditional on the outcome of previous activities. In the prior example, the original plan would logically be based on the assumption that testing would find a functioning system. Installation is logically scheduled to occur after testing is completed in the original plan. The actual outcome may encounter some problems in testing for some components, but indications may be that a particular subsystem was successfully developed. In this case, installation of that subsystem might proceed after management affirms that this component is worthwhile, even if the functionality of the overall system is suspect. An extra activity of managerial approval appeared, and decomposing the original testing/installation activities can lead to a revised network. Shtub's solution to this critical path modeling problem is to divide activities into smaller components. This idea is supported by Keane's contention that information system project activities should include work that can be accomplished in no more than 80 hours.[9] The negative feature of dividing all activities into their smallest components is that it overcomplicates the critical path model for a project and loses the clarity provided by simplicity. However, when complications arise, those components that need to be subdivided to reflect new conditions could be remodeled to more accurately reflect the current situation.

Summary

The critical path method provides project managers with valuable information. The criticality of project activities can be identified, and those activities that are critical can be managed more closely. The critical path method provides an estimate of how long the project will take if everything takes no longer than estimated. The critical path method displays what can happen because of predecessor relationships. Crashing provides a means of comparing the trade-off in cost and time in project scheduling. However, the critical path method assumes unlimited resources, which may not be realistic.

There are some things managers can do when facing resource limits. Buffers provide a way to better manage the chain of critical activities. Most project management software systems allow managers to level resources, generally following a priority system as outlined in the chapter. While not guaranteed to give the best solution, this ability of software packages to level resources is extremely useful.

Projects can also be leveled to stay within available resources and even smoothed to more efficiently schedule resources. Project management software is very good at accomplishing the task of leveling project activities to stay within prescribed resource levels. The solutions provided are not necessarily the best possible, but they are usually very good. The activity of smoothing is not as critical in project management because efficiency is not as important as dealing with the high levels of uncertainty present in projects. Smoothing in uncertain environments is usually not effective.

Key Terms

buffers   150
crashing   153
early start schedule   146
feeding buffers   150
Gantt chart   149
independent slack   148
late start schedule   146
network   146

project buffers   150
resource buffers   151
resource leveling   158
resource smoothing   160
shared slack   148
slack   147
strategic resource buffers   151

Exercises

1. If no project completion time is given or stated, what is conventionally used as the project completion time for calculation of slack activities?
2. A network is not needed to calculate the critical path start times and finish times. What value does a network have?
3. What is slack?
4. What is a critical path?
5. Identify the early start, early finish, late start, late finish, and slack for each activity, and the critical path for the following project:

Activity		Duration	Predecessor	ES	EF	LS	LF	Slack
A	Initial analysis	3 weeks	None					
B	Final analysis	3 weeks	A					
C	Production	8 weeks	A					
D	Test	4 weeks	B, C					
E	Install	2 weeks	D					

6. Identify the critical path(s) of the following project.

Activity	Duration	Predecessors
A	5	None
B	4	None
C	4	A
D	5	A, B
E	6	B

7. Goldratt pointed out that the critical chain of activities (which should be managed closely to do all that can be done to keep on schedule) will not necessarily coincide with the critical path. Why might other activities also be important to manage?

8. Describe the difference between slack and buffers.

9. Four kinds of buffers were discussed. Compare project buffers, feeding buffers, resource buffers, and strategic resource buffers.

10. The following project is scheduled in years. There is a penalty of $5 million for each year over 9 years to completion. Identify the least cost schedule.

Activity		Duration	Predecessors
A	Economic feasibility study	7 years	None
B	Environmental impact study	6 years	None
C	Budget approval	3 years	A, B
D	Perform work	1 year	C

Costs for reducing times:
Activity A can be reduced from 7 years to 6 years at a cost of $3 million.
Reducing activity A from 6 years to 5 years costs an additional $4 million.
Activity B can be reduced from 6 years to 5 years for an additional $2 million.
Activity C can be reduced from 3 years to 2 years at a cost of $7 million.

11. Level the following project.

Activity	Duration	Predecessors	Resource
A	5	None	Henry
B	4	None	Mark
C	4	A	Louise
D	5	A, B	Daniel
E	6	B	Daniel

12. You work for a company providing small business information systems consulting. Your department is working on a proposal to put the company's marketing plan on the Internet. As an initial step, you have identified the following work packages, durations, and precedence relationships.

Activity		Duration	Predecessors
A	Obtain your boss's approval of your plan	8 days	None
B	Obtain budget approval	12 days	None
C	Obtain systems development approval	10 days	D
D	Develop user specifications	1 days	A
E	Obtain a marketing program from in-house marketing	120 days	A, B
F	Obtain a marketing program from an external consultant	60 days	A, B
G	Review and select marketing program	5 days	E, F
H	Perform systems development of module contents	80 days	C
I	Design system interface	50 days	C, G
J	Review and approve systems development	5 days	H, I
K	Test prototype	10 days	J
L	Revision and final systems development	20 days	K

Identify:
Early starts and finishes for each activity
Late starts and finishes for each activity
Slack by activity
Critical path activities

13. You work for a company implementing a new online communication systems network. Cabling and facility work will be performed by a civil engineering contractor. The hardware installation will be performed by the hardware vendor's local representative. The conversion and systems testing will be performed by your company's information systems staff. It is important to coordinate all of the separate activities to get work done within a required 85-day period. You have a penalty of $7,000 per day (in lost revenues) for every day the job takes over 85 days. Costs per day are given for those activities that can be shortened, along with the maximum number of days that could be squeezed out at the premium price.

Work Packages	Duration (days)	Predecessors	Cost/Day	Max
A Review current layout	5	None		
B Develop new layout	14	A		
C Obtain permits	5	B	$10,000/day	4 days
D Facility work	30	C	$3,000/day	5 days
E Inspect cabling	2	D		
F Install remote lines	53	None	$5,000/day	12 days
G Test lines	2	F		
H Test cabling	2	E, G		
I Install hardware	12	None	$8,000/day	2 days
J Test hardware	4	H, I		
K Develop operations/network procedures	10	None		
L Develop user procedures/training materials	20	None	$2,000/day	10 days
M Test procedures	2	K, L		
N Test network and systems	5	J, M		
O Convert and test software	21	N	$1,000/day	1 day
P Implement systems	4	O		

Give the original critical path solution (early start, early finish, slack) as well as the final economically optimal schedule. Explain why you don't suggest a shorter time schedule.

14. Level the following multi-project operation.

Work Packages	Duration (weeks)	Predecessors	Resources
A1 Analysis and design—Project 1	4	None	SAD
B1 Production—Project 1	7	A1	PROD
C1 Testing—Project 1	3	B1	TEST
D1 Install—Project 1	2	C1	INST
A2 Analysis and design—Project 2	4	A1	SAD
B2 Production—Project 2	5	A2	PROD
C2 Testing—Project 2	3	B2	TEST
D2 Install—Project 2	1	C2	INST
A3 Analysis and design—Project 3	8	A2	SAD
B3 Production—Project 3	12	A3	PROD
C3 Testing—Project 3	5	B3	TEST
D3 Install—Project 3	3	C3	INST
A4 Analysis and design—Project 4	8	A3	SAD
B4 Production—Project 4	10	A4	PROD
C4 Testing—Project 4	4	B4	TEST
D4 Install—Project 4	2	C4	INST

If all work was to be done by the deadline of the end of week 20, what resources are causing delay?

15. Identify resource usage for each of the four resources in Problem 14. What would be needed to smooth work for each of the four resources?

Microsoft Project **Exercise**

Use *Microsoft Project* to generate Gantt charts and networks for Problems 5, 6, 10, 12, 13, and 14.

For Problem 5, the task list is:

		Duration	Start	Finish	Predecessor
A	Initial analysis	3w	Mon 1/3/00	Fri 1/21/00	
B	Final analysis	3w	Mon 1/24/00	Fri 2/11/00	1
C	Production	8w	Mon 1/24/00	Fri 3/17/00	1
D	Test	4w	Mon 3/20/00	Fri 4/14/00	"2, 3"
E	Install	2w	Mon 4/17/00	Fri 4/28/00	4

The PERT chart view is:

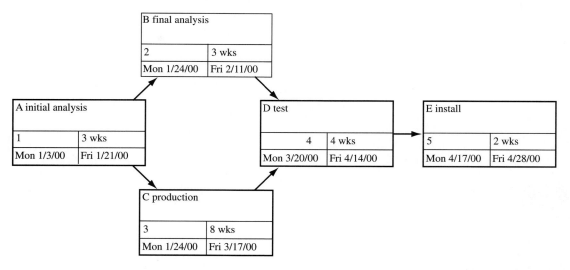

Endnotes

1. E. M. Goldratt, *Critical Chain* (Great Barrington, MA: The North River Press, 1997).
2. R. J. Schonberger, "Why Projects Are 'Always' Late: A Rationale Based on Manual Simulation of a PERT/CPM Network," *Interfaces* 11, no. 5 (1981), pp. 66–70.
3. Goldratt, *Critical Chain.*

4. Ibid.
5. R. C. Newbold, *Project Management in the Fast Lane: Applying the Theory of Constraints* (Boca Raton, FL: The St. Lucie Press, 1998).
6. E. S. Andersen, "Warning: Activity Planning Is Hazardous to Your Project's Health," *International Journal of Project Management* 14, no. 2 (1996), pp. 89–94.
7. Goldratt, *Critical Chain.*
8. A. Shtub, "Project Segmentation—A Tool for Project Management," *International Journal of Project Management* 15, no. 1 (1997), pp. 15–19.
9. D. H. Plummer, *Productivity Management: Keane's Project Management Approach for Systems Development,* 2nd ed. (Boston: Keane Inc., 1995).

## Chapter 7

Probabilistic Scheduling Models

Main Ideas Discussed

- Time uncertainty in projects
- The PERT method and its limitations
- How simulation can accurately model time uncertainty
- Generating random numbers from the appropriate distribution
- Generating output for statistical interpretation

In Chapter 6, critical path models were discussed. The critical path method has been useful in project management planning and control. But it is widely recognized that the assumed durations of activities very often turn out to be different from those assumed in the planning stage. In this chapter we look at two types of project scheduling models that consider some of the uncertainty involved in project management. The *program evaluation and review technique (PERT)* assumes a beta distribution for project durations, which in itself is not necessarily realistic. PERT can easily be implemented on a spreadsheet. *Simulation* can be used to model projects with uncertain durations on a spreadsheet. Any realistic distribution can be modeled using simulation. While more flexible than PERT, simulation analysis of projects involves more complications than PERT.

PERT

The **program evaluation and review technique (PERT)** method is a modification of the critical path method, where uncertainty in activity durations can be considered. Three estimates of activity durations are required: minimum, most likely, and maximum. The most likely estimate is relatively easy. The minimum duration of an activity also might be fairly easy to identify—the length of time the activity would take if everything went right. The third estimate, the maximum duration, is often difficult for estimators. The longest any activity can take is infinity, never finishing. However, the method won't work with that. What is meant by maximum is the activity duration if everything went wrong, but the activity was completed regardless. When PERT is used, clear definitions of what is meant by minimum and maximum duration need to be specified. Many different variants are used.

Consider a problem to install a new software for an element of an institution. The activities and expected times are given in Table 7–1. Figure 7–1 gives the network for this project. The early start schedule would be as given in Table 7–2.

The critical path in this case is the chain of activities A–B–E–F, a unique path, with an **expected duration** of 16 months. The PERT model is the same, except that three duration estimates are used instead of one. Given these three estimates, the expected duration is given by the formula:

$$\text{Expected duration} = \frac{a + 4m + b}{6}$$

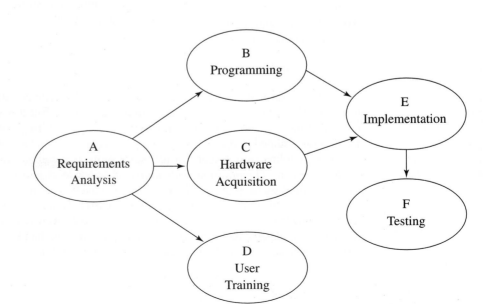

FIGURE 7–1

where a is the minimum estimated duration, m is the most likely duration, and b is the maximum estimated duration. The variance of the duration of any activity is also a function of these estimates:

$$\text{Variance} = \left(\frac{b - a}{6}\right)^2$$

Table 7–3 tabulates these data.

The variance of an activity with no uncertainty, such as for activity C, is 0. The expected duration is used as the duration in a critical path analysis (see Table 7–4). The variance of the project can be calculated as the sum of the variances of

TABLE 7–1   Activities and Expected Durations

Activity	Duration	Predecessors
A Requirements analysis	3 months	None
B Programming	7 months	A
C Hardware acquisition	3 months	A
D User training	12 months	A
E Implementation	5 months	B, C
F Testing	1 month	E

TABLE 7–2   Early Start Schedule

Activity	Early Start	Early Finish	Late Finish	Late Start	Slack
A	0	3	3	0	0*
B	3	10	10	3	0*
C	3	6	10	7	4
D	3	15	16	4	1
E	10	15	15	10	0*
F	15	16	16	15	0*

TABLE 7–3   Variance of the Duration

Activity	Minimum	Likely	Maximum	Expected Duration	Activity Variance
A Requirements analysis	2	3	4	3	4/36
B Programming	6	7	9	7.17	9/36
C Hardware acquisition	3	3	3	3	0
D Train users	12	12	12	12	0
E Implementation	3	5	7	5	16/36
F Testing	1	1	2	1.17	1/36

TABLE 7–4 Critical Path Schedule Using Expected Duration

Activity	Expected Duration	Predecessors	Early Start	Early Finish	Late Start	Late Finish	Slack
A	3	None	0	3	0	3	0*
B	7.17	A	3	10.17	3	10.17	0*
C	3	A	3	6	7.17	10.17	4.17
D	12	A	3	15	4.33	16.33	1.33
E	5	B, C	10.17	15.17	10.17	15.17	0*
F	1.17	E	15.17	16.33	15.17	16.33	0*

TABLE 7–5 Project Variance Calculation

Activity	Maximum	Minimum	Variance
A	4	2	0.111
B	9	6	0.25
E	7	3	0.444
F	2	1	0.028
	Project variance		0.833

TABLE 7–6 Project Completion Probabilities

Duration	z	Probability
15	(15 − 16.33)/0.913 = −1.461	0.072
16	(16 − 16.33)/0.913 = −0.365	0.357
17	(17 − 16.33)/0.913 = 0.730	0.767
18	(18 − 16.33)/0.913 = 1.826	0.966
19	(19 − 16.33)/0.913 = 2.921	0.998
20	(20 − 16.33)/0.913 = 4.017	0.999+

the chain of critical activities (see Table 7–5). This yields a project standard deviation (square root of the variance) of 0.913. Because the durations were beta distributed, the project duration is assumed to be normally distributed. The probability of completing the project on or before any particular target time can be calculated using the Z formula:

$$z = \frac{x - \mu}{s}$$

To calculate the probability of finishing in *x* months, $z = (x - 16.333)/0.913$. The probability can be obtained by referring to a normal **distribution,** or by using the NORMSINV(z) function in *Excel*. Table 7–6 gives the probabilities of completing the project on or before the given duration. In these calculations, the variance of activities C and D were disregarded because they had slack. If activities C or D were to experience delay, while the other activities were closer to their expected durations, this could also delay the project. If activity D were to be delayed more than two months, for instance, it would most likely delay the overall project completion. However, this possibility is disregarded with PERT. Here, activities C and D are estimated as constants, with no expected delay. They still could become critical if activities A or B were early for some reason.

Criticisms of PERT

PERT was developed in the 1950s for the U.S. Navy.[1] It is theoretically attractive in that it addresses an obvious limitation of the critical path method. However, it is not widely used in practice, and when it is, the minimum durations are often casual estimates, such as one-half of the expected duration, and the maximum duration is stated as twice the expected duration. When this type of input is entered, there is obvious degradation of the quality of the analysis, with no thought given to specific activity variance. *Microsoft Project* uses the term "PERT" as a label for their network diagram. (*Microsoft Project* does provide support to apply PERT analysis, although not on its featured menu.)

Schonberger[2] demonstrated that PERT was biased to give overly optimistic schedule estimates because of a failure to consider time delays due to interaction of noncritical activities with critical activities. Webb[3] found that the beta distribution used in the PERT method was appropriate in only three sets of conditions (the symmetric case with the most likely time the exact mean of the minimum and maximum times, when the most likely time is about 40 percent of the distance from the minimum to the maximum, and when the most likely time is about 60 percent of the distance from the minimum to the maximum). For all other cases of the beta distribution, Webb found some error in the PERT duration calculation. Webb gave the formula:

$$\text{Expected duration} = \frac{a + 3m + 2b}{6}$$

as a more accurate duration calculation based on observed cases.

Webb also cited the very real problem of obtaining multiple estimates of durations. Projects are one-time affairs, and there are not a lot of data upon which duration estimates can be based. Estimators have a great deal of trouble developing the most likely duration estimate and quite often resort to quick-and-dirty estimates for the minimum and most likely estimates (such as the minimum = one-half of the most likely, and the maximum = twice the most likely).

The PERT method is also based on independence of activity durations. However, this is not true in projects. If one activity is late, there is a tendency for management to rush following activities to compensate. This would result in a case of negative correlation between durations. There also can be similar underlying causes of lateness that might be positively correlated, such as skill shortages.

Ragsdale[4] considered **Monte Carlo simulation** as an alternative means of analysis. Monte Carlo simulation is a sampling experiment whose purpose is to estimate the distribution of an outcome variable that depends on several probabilistic input variables. Schonberger[5] considered simulation too expensive, as well as yielding output too complex for lay people to understand. However, simulation software has advanced a great deal since 1981, and is widely available in all spreadsheet software, and is even found in some project management software. Simulation is far superior to PERT in that whatever distribution is appropriate can be included in the analysis for each activity.[6]

Simulation for Project Scheduling

Simulation is a very valuable tool for analyzing models involving elements described by probability distributions. Projects involve interrelated activities, many of which are probabilistic. This class of problem is very easily modeled on spreadsheets, such as *Excel*.

Excel *Simulation Model*

The software installation example scheduled earlier involved six activities, A through F. Assume the durations of some of these activities, for instance A, B, E, and F, involve some uncertainty. The best way to proceed is to gather statistics on past projects (if possible) so that sound data can be used to estimate the expected durations and probability distribution for specific activities. For purposes of demonstration, assume that the data for these four activities were found to be normally distributed (a possibility, although certainly not the only possible appropriate distribution).

The *Excel* critical path method model is used as the basis for a simulation of this problem. We use column A of a spreadsheet to list the six activities. Following the critical path spreadsheet model form from Chapter 6, we use column B for start times for each activity, and column E for finish times. We reserve two columns (C and D) to generate simulated durations. We use the first of these columns (C) to generate a normally distributed random number and use column D to convert the random numbers in column C to the appropriate outcomes reflecting simulated durations in column D.

In column B, the early start for any activities without predecessors is assigned the value of time 0. In this model, only activity A has no predecessor. Other cells in column B give maximum finish times values (column E) for all predecessors. Uncertain events are generated using **random numbers** in *Excel*. There are a number of ways to generate random numbers in *Excel*. The function: =**RAND()** returns a uniform random number between zero and one, which changes every time an action is executed in *Excel*. This uniform random number can be transformed into other distributions, but this operation requires more advanced study.[7] A second way to generate random numbers within *Excel* is through the Data Analysis Toolpak on the **Tools** menu of the *Excel* command ribbon. From the Data Analysis Toolpak menu, select **Random Number Generator**. The window given in Figure 7–2 is obtained.

In the following example, data was normally distributed in the four random durations modeled in cells **C2**, **C3**, **C6**, and **C7**. The Random Number Generator procedure in *Excel* requires the following information:

Number of variables	The number of columns of random numbers requested
Number of random numbers	The number of rows of random numbers requested
Distribution	From the menu, select **Normal**
Mean	Enter the random variable mean
Standard Deviation	Enter the standard deviation of the random variable
Seed?	You can set a seed that will return the same sequence of random numbers

In this example, random numbers were generated one-by-one. For each random number, the number of variables was set to 1, and the number of random numbers was set to 1. A seed was not used in the example in Table 7–7, but seeds can be very useful in controlling experiments, making it possible to replicate the sequence

FIGURE 7–2

Excel random number generation window

TABLE 7–7   Excel Formulation of Schedule Using Random Numbers

	A	B	C	D	E
1		Start	Random	Duration	Finish
2	Requirements analysis	0	Toolpak	=IF(C2>0,C2,1)	=B2+D2
3	Programming	=E2	Toolpak	=IF(C3>0,C3,1)	=B3+D3
4	Hardware acquisition	=E2	3	=IF(C4>0,C4,1)	=B4+D4
5	User training	=E2	12	=IF(C5>0,C5,1)	=B5+D5
6	Implementation	=MAX(E3,E4)	Toolpak	=IF(C6>0,C6,1)	=B6+D6
7	Testing	=E6	Toolpak	=IF(C7>0,C7,1)	=B7+D7

of random numbers to make comparison simulation experiments easier to analyze. Specifying seeds is shown in Figure 7.2.

The durations in column C are generated from the analysis toolpak, using the following distributions.

Duration	cell C2 = normal(3,.5)	from Analysis Toolpak
	cell C3 = normal(7,1)	from Analysis Toolpak
	cell C6 = normal(5,1)	from Analysis Toolpak
	cell C7 = normal(1,.5)	from Analysis Toolpak

Column D is used to ensure that durations less than one time period are not included. Any minimum could be used for any activity. The formulation yields Table 7–8. Column D could also be used to convert durations to integer values if that would be more appropriate. Cell D2, for instance, could be:

$$=INT(IF(C2>1,C2,1)+0.5)$$

The 0.5 is added to round the value generated by *Excel*. This yields the data in Table 7–9. This provides more realistic scheduling simulations if complete time units are more appropriate.

Generating Multiple-Simulation Runs

The benefit of simulation is that the experiment can be repeated many times so that patterns can be identified from the set of possible outcomes generated by the

TABLE 7–8   Schedule with Random Numbers

	A	B	C	D	E
1		Start	Random	Duration	Finish
2	Requirements analysis	0	3.47987	3.47987	3.47987
3	Programming	3.47987	6.9808	6.9808	10.46067
4	Hardware acquisition	3.47987	3	3	6.47987
5	User training	3.47987	12	12	15.47987
6	Implementation	10.46067	5.06744	5.06744	15.52811
7	Testing	15.52811	1.36085	1.36085	16.88896

TABLE 7–9   Schedule with Integer Random Numbers

	A	B	C	D	E
1		Start	Random	Duration	Finish
2	Requirements analysis	0	3.47987	3	3
3	Programming	3	6.9808	7	10
4	Hardware acquisition	3	3	3	6
5	User training	3	12	12	15
6	Implementation	10	5.06744	5	15
7	Testing	15	1.36085	1	16

simulation. Multiple-simulation runs can be obtained in a number of ways.[8] We discuss four. The hard way (1) is to generate results one-by-one. The easy way (2) is to use simulation add-ins, such as @RISK or CRYSTAL BALL. Within *Excel*, multiple simulations, each with different results, can be obtained using random numbers generated by the Data Analysis Toolpak (3), but this requires use of VISUAL BASIC. The final procedure (4) works using the RAND() function, although random numbers cannot be controlled with this method. Methods (3) and (4) are demonstrated in Appendix 7A.

In the short example just demonstrated, based on 100 runs the mean project completion time was 16.85 months, with a minimum of 10.15 months and a maximum of 29.86 months. The distributions used in this case were all normal. The sum of critical variances is 3.0, so there was more dispersion than there was in the PERT model. There may be even more variance (depending on the probability distributions used), because occasionally noncritical activities will become critical in the simulation. The standard deviation of the simulated project completion time was 4.04 months. Activity D, which had slack in the critical path and PERT models, was critical more than 25 percent of the time in the simulated runs, and thus delayed project completion time in those cases.

The percentile values for expected project completion time appeared to be symmetric, so we can apply the normal distribution, obtaining the probabilities of project completion by the times given in Table 7–10. The corresponding PERT probabilities are given for comparison. The simulation has much more dispersion as a result of the higher variances of inputs used.

The simulation output implies a much more distinct possibility that the project could take longer than does the PERT output. We can see that there is a 0.416 probability of completing the project within 16 months, but the 95th percentile was just over 24 months (obtained by identifying the 95th longest simulated time). With PERT's assumptions, the 95th percentile was below 18 months.

PERT addresses the widely recognized uncertainty involved in project management activities, but it makes a rigid assumption about the distribution of durations, and the calculation of probability of completion by a specified time disregards noncritical activities. Simulation provides a flexible means to evaluate the probability of projects being completed by specific times. Any distribution of

TABLE 7–10   **Probabilities of Project Completion**

Months	*z*	*Cumulative Probability*	*PERT Probability*
15	$(15 - 16.853)/4.045 = -0.458$	0.324	0.073
16	$(16 - 16.853)/4.045 = -0.211$	0.416	0.359
17	$(17 - 16.853)/4.045 = 0.036$	0.514	0.768
18	$(18 - 16.853)/4.045 = 0.284$	0.613	0.966
19	$(19 - 16.853)/4.045 = 0.531$	0.702	0.998
20	$(20 - 16.853)/4.045 = 0.778$	0.782	0.999+

duration can be assumed. The distribution used should be based on empirical data if possible. All activity paths are considered in the simple spreadsheet network. For instance, observed data may not be symmetric. The triangular distribution might provide a better fit to such data than does the normal distribution.

Scheduling Example

A firm is implementing a new information technology project to support production operations. This project requires coordination of delivery of materials and equipment as well as development of a new personnel team. A simple critical path model of the operation consists of the activities, predecessor relationships, and durations listed in Table 7–11. Some of these activity durations involve uncertainty. The best guess of management (based on experience and judgment) includes triangularly distributed data for these uncertain events, measured in weeks. The network for this model is given in Figure 7–3.

An *Excel* model is given in Table 7–12. Those durations that are not constant are drawn from the triangular distribution. The full formula is given in cell F2. The formula looks imposing, but it is simply a contingent formula based on two abutting triangles. This same formula is needed in cells F3, F4, and F7, differing only in that the row reference changes (in our table, the full formulation for these cells is not included). The final duration of the project appears in cell H8, which is the concluding activity of the project. Columns G and H implement the network model. Column G assigns the start times, equal to the maximum finish time of all predecessor activities. Column H calculates activity finish time by adding the

FIGURE 7–3

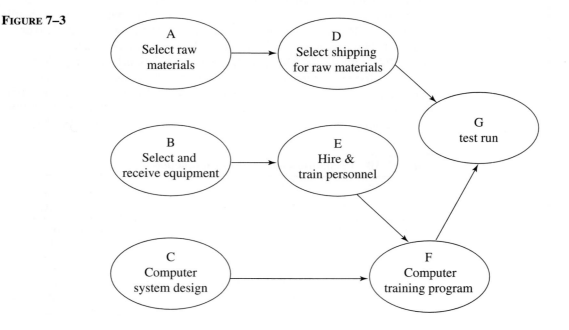

duration to the start time. Because the particular observation for each simulation run is determined by the random numbers drawn in column E, each simulation run is liable to have a different critical path.

This model can be used to estimate the probability of project completion by any given time, and the distribution of project completion times can be estimated as well. Table 7–13 is a run of the model. The duration in this particular simulation run was 11.961, or almost 12 weeks. Note that in this case, fractional weeks are modeled. If desired, integer values can be obtained as demonstrated earlier.

TABLE 7–11   Information Technology Project Data

Activity		Predecessors	Durations (min, mode, max)
A	Select raw materials (by bid)	None	(3,3,5)
B	Select and receive equipment (fob plant)	None	(4,5,8)
C	Computer system design	None	(5,7,10)
D	Select shipping for raw materials	A	1
E	Hire and train personnel	B	2
F	Computer training program	C,E	(3,3,4)
G	Test run	D,F	1

TABLE 7–12   *Excel* Formulations for Information Technology Project

	A	B	C	D	E	F	G	H
		Min	Mode	Max	Random	Duration	Start	Finish
1	Activity							
2	A select raw materials	3	3	5	=RAND()	=IF(E2<=(C2−B2)/(D2 −B2), B2+SQRT((C2−B2)^8(D2−B2)* E2),D2−SQRT((D2−C2)* (D2−B2)*)(1−E2)))	0	=G2+F2
3	B select & receive equipment	4	5	8	=RAND()	Triangular function (3)	0	=G3+F3
4	C computer system design	5	7	10	=RAND()	Triangular function (4)	0	=G4+F4
5	D select shipping for raw materials		1			=D6	=H2	=G5+F5
6	E hire & train personnel		2			=D7	=H3	=G6+F6
7	F computer training program	3	3	4	=RAND()	Triangular function (7)	=MAX(H4,H6)	=G7+F7
8	G test run		1			=D9	=MAX(H5,H7)	=G8+F8

TABLE 7–13

	A	B	C	D	E	F	G	H
1	Activity	Min	Mode	Max	Random	Duration	Start	Finish
2	A select raw materials (by bid)	3	3	5	0.728	3.956	0	3.956
3	B select & receive equipment (fob plant)	4	5	8	0.447	5.423	0	5.423
4	C computer system design	5	7	10	0.583	7.498	0	7.498
5	D select shipping for raw materials		1			1	3.956	4.956
6	E hire & train personnel		2			2	5.423	7.423
7	F computer training program	3	3	4	0.711	3.463	7.498	10.961
8	G test run		1			1	10.961	11.961

TABLE 7–14   Results for 100 Repetitions

Range	Occurrences	Probability	PERT Probability
Below 10 weeks	0	0.00	0.03
Between 10 and 10.5 weeks	2	0.02	0.06
Between 10.5 and 11 weeks	2	0.02	0.14
Between 11 and 11.5 weeks	10	0.10	0.27
Between 11.5 and 12 weeks	18	0.18	0.27
Between 12 and 12.5 weeks	21	0.21	0.16
Between 12.5 and 13 weeks	17	0.17	0.06
Between 13 and 13.5 weeks	17	0.17	0.01
Between 13.5 and 14 weeks	12	0.12	0.00
Over 14 weeks (< 14.5)	1	0.01	0.00

For instance, in column F, duration can be defined as =INT(IF(. . .)+.99), which would round fractional durations up.

The results of multiple repetitions of the simulation model can be used to define a distribution of project completion times. The calculation of probability is very simple. If 100 repetitions are generated, divide the number of observed occurrences by the total number of simulation runs. The 100 results in tabular form yielded the probabilities in Table 7–14, which are compared with the probabilities obtained from PERT for the critical path BEFG, which had a mean time of 11.5 weeks and a standard deviation of 0.6872 weeks. In this case, specific probabilities for each range as given in the table are reported, as opposed to cumulative probabilities used earlier.

We can see that the expected project duration is almost certain to exceed 10 weeks (with a 0.96 probability of exceeding 11 weeks) and will very likely be completed within 14 weeks. But there is a lot of variance between these limits. There is a 0.28 probability that the project will take between 11 and 12 weeks, a 0.38 probability that it will take between 12 and 13 weeks, and a 0.30 probability that it will take more than 13 weeks. These results demonstrate the theoretical bias of PERT to be below the true values. Simulation provides output that enables interpretation of probability for any particular duration or range. Relying on sampling theory, the degree of accuracy of these estimates is a matter of the number of samples (runs) taken.

Summary

Project management techniques have proven very useful in the planning and control of interrelated activities, but the durations of projects are notoriously variable. The critical path model and PERT are very useful in analyzing the interrelationships among activities, but the critical path model assumes constant durations, and though PERT allows a specific type of duration distribution, this particular distribution is not always appropriate; PERT also includes other inaccuracies.

Simulation of project management problems is much more flexible. Whatever distributions of expected times are appropriate can be entered into a simulation model. Simulation analysis is very flexible as well. Analysis in much greater detail is possible with simulation than is possible with PERT, although simulation requires more in the way of statistical analysis to interpret output. The mean values of simulation output provide the same information as critical path methods, and a more complete probabilistic output is obtained with simulation than is available from PERT.

Key Terms

distribution   176

expected duration   174

Monte Carlo simulation   177

program evaluation and review
  technique (PERT)   174

random number   178

simulation   173

Exercises

1. Describe the difference between the critical path model and PERT.

For Problems 2, 3, and 4:

Activity	Minimum	Most Likely	Maximum	Predecessor
A	15 years	15 years	15 years	None
B	18 years	19 years	21 years	A
C	19 years	21 years	23 years	B

2. Calculate the expected value for activities A, B, and C.
3. Calculate the variance for the project.
4. What is the probability that the project will be completed in 55 years?

For Problems 5, 6, and 7:

Activity	Minimum	Most Likely	Maximum	Predecessor
A	9 days	10 days	13 days	None
B	5 days	8 days	11 days	None
C	3 days	4 days	7 days	B

5. Calculate the expected value for activities A, B, and C.
6. Calculate the variance for the project.
7. What is the probability that the project will be completed in 13 days?
8. You have the following project (six activities). Identify the critical path and the probability that the project will be completed by the end of 40 days.

Duration Estimates (days)

Activity		Minimum	Most Likely	Maximum	Predecessors
A	Get equipment	3	5	7	None
B	Hire people	4	4	4	None
C	Develop system	12	15	24	A, B
D	Develop training program	3	3	9	C
E	Documentation	4	6	14	C
F	Install system	6	9	18	D, E

9. Develop an *Excel* spreadsheet model to simulate the following set of activities, all of which are normally distributed.

Activity		Duration Mean	Standard	Predecessors
A	Economic feasibility study	7 years	1	None
B	Environmental impact study	6 years	3	None
C	Budget approval	3 years	1	A, B
D	Perform work	1 year	0.1	C

10. You have the following simulation output (ordered by duration) measuring the duration of a simulated project:

Run	Days		
1	8		
2	10	Average	12.4
3	11	Standard Deviation	2.8
4	11		
5	12		
6	12		
7	13		
8	14		
9	15		
10	18		

What is the probability the project will be completed in no more than 16 days?

11. You are charged with presenting a training program to a client who has bought a software package from your firm. This software package applies the critical path method, with a lot of colorful and attractive screens. Users have to know and understand the critical path method, as well as Visual Basic and Windows 95 to make the product work. You have the following activities with duration estimates and predecessor relationships:

Activity		Optimistic	Most Likely	Pessimistic	Predecessors
A	Identify teaching goals for CPM	3 days	5 days	6 days	None
B	Identify teaching goals for Visual Basic	7 days	8 days	12 days	None
C	Identify teaching goals for Windows 95	2 days	3 days	4 days	None
D	Develop lesson plans for CPM	7 days	10 days	15 days	A
E	Develop lesson plans for Visual Basic	20 days	25 days	35 days	B
F	Develop lesson plans for Windows 95	1 day	3 days	5 days	C
G	Generate teaching aids for CPM	20 days	30 days	50 days	D
H	Generate teaching aids for Visual Basic	50 days	70 days	100 days	E
I	Generate teaching aids for Windows 95	2 days	4 days	8 days	F
J	Hire teachers	15 days	20 days	30 days	None
K	Schedule teaching program with client	1 day	3 days	6 days	D,E,F
L	Obtain facilities	1 day	5 days	20 days	K
M	Obtain equipment	3 days	5 days	7 days	L
N	Develop exercises	20 days	30 days	50 days	D,E,F
O	Develop tests	5 days	7 days	10 days	D,E,F
P	Train teachers	30 days	35 days	45 days	G,H,I,J
Q	Rehearse teachers	5 days	5 days	5 days	P

a. Identify expected durations for each activity, as well as early start, late start, early finish, and late finish using these expected durations.

b. Identify the critical path.

c. The contract calls for this program to begin in 150 days (working days, the unit used in durations). What is the probability that you can begin this training? (You're not supposed to begin training until teachers are rehearsed.)

12. A consulting firm has been hired to assist you in the evaluation of software to replace existing legacy systems. As manager of the information systems department, you are responsible for coordinating all of the activities involving the consultants and your company's resources. You have identified the following work packages, and have identified minimum (*a*), most likely (*b*), and maximum (*c*) times for each. Assume a triangular distribution. (Constant activities have only the most likely estimate given.) This can be modeled in *Excel* with the following function (n is the row number; random is a uniformly distributed random number between 0 and 1).

=INT(IF(random<=(bn−an)/(cn−an),an+SQRT((bn−an)*(cn−an)*random),cn−SQRT((cn−bn)*(cn−an)*
(1−random)))+.99)

(Type the formula into the first cell of the column, then copy down. Where there are constant values, replace the formula with the value (such as 15 for activity A below).

Activity		Predecessor	Minimum	Most Likely	Maximum
A	Select steering committee	None	15	15	15
B	Develop requirements list	None	40	45	60
C	Develop system size estimates	None	10	14	30
D	Determine prospective vendors	None	2	2	5
E	Form evaluation team	A	5	7	9
F	Issue request for proposal	B,C,D,E	4	5	8
G	Bidders conference	F	1	1	1
H	Review submissions	G	25	30	50
I	Select vendor short list	H	3	5	10
J	Check vendor references	I	3	3	10
K	Vendor demonstrations	I	20	30	45
L	User site visit	I	3	3	5
M	Select vendor	J,K,L	3	3	3
N	Volume sensitive test	M	10	13	20
O	Negotiate contracts	M	10	14	28
P	Cost/benefit analysis	N,O	2	2	2
Q	Obtain board of directors approval	P	5	5	5

Analyze the probability of completing this work in 150 days. Base your probability estimate on 50 observations (count the cases where it took less than 150 days, and divide this count by 50).

TO GET MULTIPLE SIMULATION RUNS: (requires using RAND() function, which changes the random number every time you enter a value)
build your simulation model of the critical path problem
IN A SPARE COLUMN RIGHT OF YOUR WORK:
1st row
   EDIT
      FILL
         SERIES
            COLUMN circle
               STOP cell = **50**
this causes EXCEL to do the simulation 50 times
IN THE NEXT SPARE COLUMN TO THE RIGHT
copy the project completion cell value to the **1st** row of this column
block off both columns, rows 1 through 50
   DATA
      TABLE
         COLUMN
            Fill Column input column (the first cell of the EDIT FILL series above)

Microsoft Project Exercise

Use the PA_PERT views on *Microsoft Project* for Problem 8. (Use time durations of days instead of years.)

Microsoft Project allows you to enter pessimistic, expected, and optimistic estimates on the PA_PERT view, one of the "More Views" available at the lower left of the window. Page down and select PA_PERT Entry Sheet. The optimistic, expected, and pessimistic estimates can easily be entered. These are not used following the PERT procedure outlined in the chapter, but any of the three sets of estimates can be made active. Select the PA_Optimistic, PA_Expected, or PA_Pessimistic charts under "More Views" to activate the selected set of estimates. Returning to the Gantt chart, you can see the effect of each set of estimates in turn.

To calculate PERT values by formula, you need the PERT toolbar, which can be obtained under "View" and "Toolbar," selecting "PERT." PERT calculations default to the weighting system discussed in the chapter. You can change these weights by pressing the button with the scales on it.

Endnotes

1. P. G. W. Wright, *The Management of Projects* (London: Thomas Telfors House, 1994), Chapter 4.
2. R. J. Schonberger, "Why Projects are 'Always' Late: A Rationale Based on Manual Simulation of a PERT/CPM Network," *Interfaces* 11, no. 5 (1981), pp. 66–70.
3. A. Webb, "Comment: One Hump or Two?" *International Journal of Project Management* 14, no. 2 (1996), pp. 121–23.
4. C. Ragsdale, "The Current State of Network Simulation in Project Management Theory and Practice," *Omega: International Journal of Management Science* 17, no. 1 (1989), pp. 21–25.
5. Schonberger, "Why Projects are 'Always' Late."
6. M. A. Badri, A. Mortagy, D. Davis, and D. Davis, "Effective Analysis and Planning of R&D Stages: A Simulation Approach," *International Journal of Project Management* 15, no. 5 (1997), pp. 351–58.
7. See J. R. Evans and D. L. Olson, *Introduction to Simulation and Risk Analysis* (Englewood Cliffs, NJ: Prentice-Hall, 1998).
8. See ibid.

APPENDIX 7A

GENERATING MULTIPLE-SIMULATION RUNS

This appendix demonstrates how sample output from a simulation model can be obtained. It is an advanced topic presented for use should the need to obtain multiple observations of output arise. It is not a necessary part of the introduction to project management.

Method (3): Using Data Analysis Toolpak Random Number Generator and Visual Basic

To generate simulation runs using random numbers generated with Data Analysis Toolpak, you need to develop a Visual Basic macro. In the model demonstrated, four random numbers are required. The basic macro is very easy to generate. Select TOOLS, MACRO, and GENERATE NEW MACRO. This provides an icon with a RECORD button, which needs to be selected. Then walk through one simulation on the spreadsheet. Here we generate four random numbers for the example problem in the chapter, using a unique random number seed for each of the four normally distributed activities. The macro will record these steps in Visual Basic code. The code generated by Visual Basic is shown in Figure 7A–1.

FIGURE 7A–1

Visual Basic Macro

```
Sub Macro1()
'
' Macro1 Macro
'
Range("C2").Select
Selection.Clear
Range("C3").Select
Selection.Clear
Range("C6").Select
Selection.Clear
Range("C7").Select
Selection.Clear
    Application.Run "ATPVBAEN.XLA!Random",
        ActiveSheet.Range("$C$2"), 1, 1, 2 _, 1234, 3, 0.5
    Application.Run "ATPVBAEN.XLA!Random",
        ActiveSheet.Range("$C$3"), 1, 1, 2 _, 2345, 7, 1
    Application.Run "ATPVBAEN.XLA!Random",
        ActiveSheet.Range("$C$6"), 1, 1, 2 _, 3456, 5, 1
    Application.Run "ATPVBAEN.XLA!Random",
        ActiveSheet.Range("$C$7"), 1, 1, 2 _, 4567, 1, 0.5
    Range("G2").Select
    ActiveCell.FormulaR1C1 = "1"
    Range("H2").Select
    Selection.PasteSpecial Paste: =xlValues, Operation: =xlNone,
        SkipBlanks:=False, Transpose:=False
End Sub
```

Figure 7A–1 generated one simulation run, generating four normally distributed numbers from the distributions with the parameters given. To obtain multiple runs, the macro code needs to be edited and a loop placed around the run. These edited additions are indicated in bold in Figure 7A–2.

FIGURE 7A–2

```vba
Sub Macro1()
'
' Macro1 Macro
'
rn1 = 1234
rn2 = 2345
rn3 = 3456
rn4 = 4567
For i = 1 To 100
Range("C2").Select
Selection.Clear
Range("C3").Select
Selection.Clear
Range("C6").Select
Selection.Clear
Range("C7").Select
Selection.Clear
rn1 = rn1 + 10
rn2 = rn2 + 10
rn3 = rn3 + 10
rn4 = rn4 + 10
    Application.Run "ATPVBAEN.XLA!Random",
        ActiveSheet.Range("$C$2"), 1, 1, 2, rn1, 3, 0.5
    Application.Run "ATPVBAEN.XLA!Random",
        ActiveSheet.Range("$C$3"), 1, 1, 2, rn2, 7, 1
    Application.Run "ATPVBAEN.XLA!Random",
        ActiveSheet.Range("$C$6"), 1, 1, 2, rn3, 5, 1
    Application.Run "ATPVBAEN.XLA!Random",
        ActiveSheet.Range("$C$7"), 1, 1, 2, rn4, 1, 0.5
Range("E7").Select
Selection.Copy
Cells(i + 1, 7).Select
    Selection.PasteSpecial Paste:=xlValues, Operation:=xlNone,
        SkipBlanks:=False, Transpose:=False
Next i
End Sub
```

Method (4): Using RAND() Function

In your spreadsheet, in a place where you have room for the outputs you want (two columns with 100 rows for the 100 project completion times), in the second row click on:

> **EDIT** on the ribbon at the top of the *Excel* worksheet
> **FILL**
> **SERIES**
> Click on the **COLUMN** radio button
> Enter **100** in the **STOP** cell.

This will generate 100 results, which *Excel* will place in a table you are about to create. Copy the project completion cell value to the first row of the column just to the right of the one you performed the previous operation on. Block off (highlight) both columns, rows 1 through 100. Then click on:

> **DATA** on the ribbon at the top of the *Excel* worksheet
> **TABLE**
> Click on the **COLUMN** entry
> In the **Fill Column** box, enter the first of the two columns you highlighted

This will create a table with 100 simulation results, each of which should be different, that you can analyze statistically in any fashion you want to with *Excel*.

## CHAPTER 8

Project Organization

Chapter Outline

Main Ideas Discussed

- Ways project personnel can be organized
- Different levels of project organization
- Features of matrix organization suitable for projects
- Factors favoring variations in organizational forms
- Desirable features of project managers

Working on information systems projects will expose you to many forms of organization and to many project managers. This chapter reviews the primary types of organization used for information systems projects and the reasons they are designed that way. The chapter also discusses features desirable in project managers—critical factors in project success.

The purpose of an **organization** is to coordinate the efforts of many to accomplish goals. Organizational structure shows reporting relationships. Figure 8–1 shows a small subset of reporting relationships in a large organization.

193

FIGURE 8–1

*Sample
organization chart*

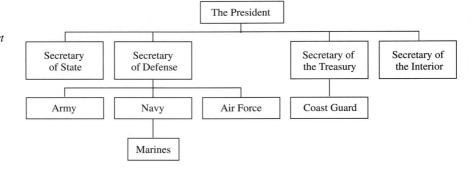

Alternate Organizational Structures

Organizational structures represent the hierarchical reporting and official communications networks within organizations. The management hierarchy consists of reporting relationships, the official chain of control or authority. This chain of authority deals with official activities, such as hiring, firing, and promotion. It also includes directing the activities of subordinates. Organizations can be grouped into major subdivisions on the basis of a number of frameworks.

Informal organization can exist in parallel to the official organization structure. Informal organization consists of the network of personal contacts within the organization, and it may also consist of cliques and groups of people who work well together and who may not work well with those outside of their subgroup. In organizations with high levels of professionalism (such as in information systems work), informal networks can be very powerful and positive forces. Informal communication is socially motivated. It is very fast, but is not necessarily thorough or dependable. Project managers, as we shall see, have relatively low levels of official authority. Galbraith[1] described three basic forms of project organization: functional, project, and matrix. Each form of organization has its own benefits, and each works well in certain types of environments. The appropriate organizational structure depends on the goal of the organization, the type of work it is supposed to do, and the environment within which it operates.

Functional Organization

Functional differentiation organizes elements by specialization (see Figure 8–2). This form of organization relies more on formal rules, procedures, and coordinated plans and budgets to control operations. In a project context, the project is divided into segments that are assigned to the appropriate functional groups, with each functional group head responsible for his or her segment of the project.

Functional organization works well in repetitive, stable environments. Organizational subelements are defined by activity or specialty function. All

FIGURE 8–2

Functional organization

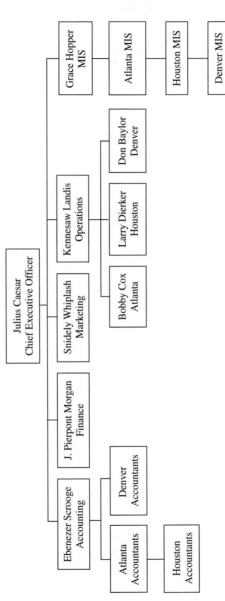

FIGURE 8–3

*Project organization
structure*

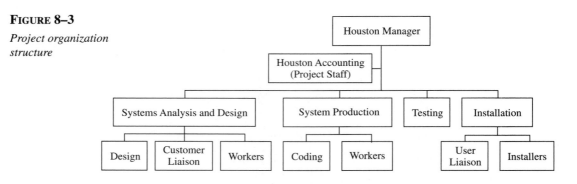

of the accountants in the firm are collected in one location, where they work together. The same is true for the functions of finance, marketing, and management information systems. Operations is a separate function, and operational sub-organizations are often grouped by geographic location, another optional form of organization. The primary benefit of the functional form of organization is that specialists work together and can develop professional skills in the most efficient manner. Accountants focus on accounting problems and become very well trained in accountancy. On the other hand, they gain little exposure to the problems of other organizational elements, such as operations or marketing.

Project Organization

Pure **project organization** involves creating a separate, independent organization specifically for accomplishing a particular project. One type of example would be the Olympic committees created to make each Olympic Games work. Another type of example are committees to elect someone, such as the infamous Committee to Reelect the President (CREEP), which did so much for Richard Nixon in 1972. Once the project is complete, there is no reason for the organization to continue (the next round of games or elections will involve other locations and candidates). Figure 8–3 demonstrates how skills can be grouped by project.

The project center is linked to the parent organization to draw resources and personnel as needed. In the case of Olympic committees, the permanent International Olympic Committee is available to provide continuity. In the case of committees for elections, there are permanent political parties to draw resources from. General Motors has created a task force (a temporary group of diverse specialists to accomplish a specific task) to develop ways to downsize, giving freedom to many of its workers to grow in other jobs. This task force draws resources from the ample supply of the giant General Motors organization. But it operates independently. Similar task forces are often created for relocation operations.

Sometimes project organizations are stand-alone organizations. These are newly created organizations for a specific mission, drawn from several organizations. Examples are large-scale public works, such as building Hoover Dam or the

Project Team Organization can be seen in committees such as the International Olympic Committee, who convene to make each round of Olympic Games work.

Dallas-Fort Worth International Airport. NASA space station development drew people from a number of organizations. Often stand-alone joint ventures are used in the construction business for very large projects beyond the scope of participating firms on their own.

Partial project organizations also exist. In this form, the project manager is responsible for some activities, while other activities that are more support oriented, such as accounting, remain with functional divisions. This is a common arrangement.

Matrix Organization

If an organization continually operates in a project mode (many organizations do in construction, in information systems, and in consulting), there is a need to quickly create large project groups. The **matrix organization** form is a gridlike structure of reporting and authority relationships overlaying traditional functional organization (see Figure 8–4). It is used within organizations that make more than minimal use of project teams or product groups. The improved coordination obtained from project organization is combined with the strengths for each specialty that are provided by functional forms of organization. The matrix form of organization was originally adopted by NASA and by the U.S. Department of Defense in the 1960s, when contracting practices required contractors to use project management. For each particular project, the contracting firm had to develop a project organization.[2]

FIGURE 8–4

Matrix organization structure

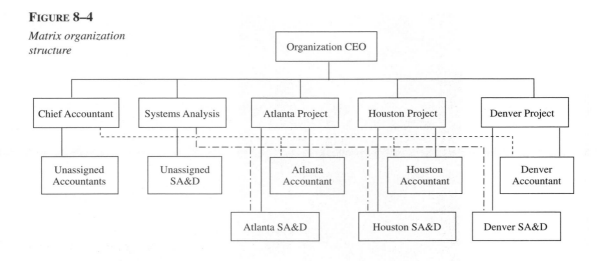

The key feature of a matrix organization is its multiple lines of authority. Specialists report to their functional managers with respect to issues involving their specialty and report to their project managers for specific assignments. Functional specialists are assigned to the project, which is usually physically located wherever the project is being implemented. These specialists make personal career decisions on the basis of their permanent functional homes. For example, the project accountant works with a project manager, and the project accountant's job is to keep the project manager informed of the cost performance on the project. Because the accountant will work on a number of projects during his or her career, the project accountant's promotion and raises are often decided by the chief accountant at the accountant's permanent organization. Project managers have some input, but the chief accountant would be the project accountant's permanent supervisor. Once the project was completed, the project accountant would return to the organization's accounting office, where he or she would await the next project assignment, or else undertake professional development such as training, or maybe stay with the accounting office on a permanent basis. The same is true of the project engineer. It could be true for the project manager and production personnel as well, although these people often go into the open market to another organization when the project is completed.

There are some problems introduced by the matrix form of organization. The dual reporting structure creates a state of confusion for those who like high levels of structure. It is said that no man can serve two masters. There also is a military principle of unity of command. The matrix system, with two potential sources of direction, has been found to lead to conflict because of incompatible demands and priorities from two managers of a specific individual.[3] Most people are able to cope with such mixed signals, but it causes distress in others. The ability of managers to compromise, and to deal with conflict, has proven very important in

Multiple lines of authority are at work in NASA's control center, where the matrix form of organization is adopted.

project management. While conflict can sometimes lead to improved performance, it needs to be managed carefully. Matrix forms of organizations call upon managers to do a great deal in a difficult environment.

The level of control used within a project organization should vary with the level of difficulty of the problems expected. If there are major technical issues, stronger centralized organization is merited, with a focus on technical lines of organization. For instance, if a major engineering problem is expected to be critical to the project, engineering components would be centralized under a project engineer. On the other hand, if no major engineering problems were expected, there might not be a project engineer, but rather independent engineers assigned to each work group that needed one. This independence would allow for focus on the tasks assigned to the work group rather than overall engineering coordination.

Comparison of Organizational Structures in Projects

There are many variations to the three basic organizational structures discussed so far in this chapter. The accompanying box demonstrates the effectiveness of innovative organization in a project environment. Cellular organization was used, where a small work group with people skilled in each required task were organized together.

Cellular Organization at AFLAC

American Family Life Assurance Company of Columbus (AFLAC) is an insurance company that has experimented with different organizational structures for their information systems projects. One of the strategies adopted by AFLAC was to use information systems products in innovative ways. They experimented with different organizational structures to effectively implement new information systems projects.

AFLAC's information systems had originally been organized by project. In an attempt to improve information systems project performance, the organization was redesigned based on processes. All project groups were eliminated. Three separate departments were created: business analysts, applications analysts, and programmers. The intent was to better use resources by maximizing the output of each of these three processes independently. This was the traditional functional organization. However, this approach did not meet expectations. Information systems workers were unable to see the entire project. Different functional groups would work on what was efficient for them, but their work did not necessarily consider the needs of their clients. Morale and communications problems appeared.

The next attempt to improve project performance was cellular organization. Six teams focusing on different types of information product requests were formed. These group teams were financial, claims, agency, troubleshooting, and two types of policy administration. This refocused information system attention on the needs of users. Within each group, analysts and programmers were cross-trained. A 140-project backlog was reduced to 60 projects within eight months, and the estimated time to finish this backlog was reduced from one year to three months. Production increased 1.5 to 2 times.

The cellular form of organization, similar to that used in manufacturing organizations, was highly successful in improving morale, as well as improving relationships with clients. The focus was now on getting the job done rather than on maximizing the amount of work accomplished.

Source: C. S. Stephens, "Producing the Information Systems Product: Can IS Learn from Manufacturing?" *Journal of Systems Management,* July 1993, pp. 25–28.

AFLAC started with a project structure but felt that the organization was not performing well technically. AFLAC therefore switched to a functional organizational structure to emphasize technical development. This led to each functional group focusing on their parts of the project, without considering overall project requirements. This is referred to as suboptimization. Finally, AFLAC adopted the cellular organization described, a variant of the matrix organization in which specialists are drawn together from diverse groups into a team. This approach proved highly successful in AFLAC's project environment.

There has been some research comparing the effectiveness of these forms of organization in various contexts. Marquis and Straight[4] studied 100 research and development projects and found that the functional matrix form provided better technical results, while a project matrix form had lower cost and schedule over-runs. Corey and Starr[5] surveyed 500 large manufacturing firms and found that project team and project matrix forms of organization were more successful in developing new products. Katz and Allen[6] studied 86 research and development projects and found that the balanced matrix organizational form had better results.

Hybrids

Larson and Gobeli[7] studied Project Management Institute members by survey, obtaining 547 respondents who were primarily involved in development projects. The organizational structures included in this study were the functional matrix, project matrix, and balanced matrix variants as well as the basic forms of organizational structure (functional, project team). Functional matrix and project matrix structures are hybrids of the three basic forms presented earlier.

A functional matrix organizational structure is used when a project manager is restricted to coordinated functional group assignments. Functional managers are responsible for technical work assignments. The project manager in this case acts as a staff assistant with indirect authority to expedite and monitor project activities.

In a project matrix form of organization, the project manager has more direct authority to decide personnel and work assignments. The functional manager is responsible for providing resources and advisory support to projects.

In the balanced matrix organization, project managers and functional managers have roughly equal authority and responsibility for the project. The project manager typically decides what needs to be accomplished, while the functional managers are responsible for deciding how work will be done and by whom.

The results of the Larson and Gobeli study are displayed in Table 8–1. Those organizational structures that were found to be superior in each category are shown left of the $>$ sign. The type of structure they were superior to are given to the right of the symbol. For instance, with respect to controlling cost, balanced matrix, project matrix, and project team structures were found to be superior to functional and functional matrix structures.

Larson and Gobeli also found that in research and development projects, functional and functional matrix forms of organization are inferior to the other

---

TABLE 8–1   Results of Larson/Gobeli Study

Controlling cost	Balanced matrix, Project matrix, Project team > Functional, Functional matrix
	Project matrix > Project team
Meeting schedule	Project matrix, Project team > Balanced matrix
	Balanced matrix > Functional, Functional matrix
Technical performance	Balanced matrix, Project matrix, Project team > Functional, Functional matrix
Overall results	Balanced matrix, Project matrix, Project team > Functional, Functional matrix

Source: E. W. Larson and D. H. Gobeli, "Significance of Project Management Structure on Development Success," *IEEE Transactions on Engineering Management* 36, no. 2 (1989), pp. 119–25.

forms of organization.[8] The project matrix form of organization was found to be superior to the project team form in controlling costs, while both of these forms were found to be better than the balanced matrix form at meeting schedules. Whether these relationships generalize to information systems projects is unknown, but a similar cultural style is present in both research and development projects and information systems projects. In both environments, independent specialty work is common, with loose degrees of control usually expected to be applied.

Organizational Structure for Different Risk Conditions

Projects can involve risks in a variety of forms. Couillard[9] studied Canadian military acquisition projects and drew some conclusions generalizable to a variety of projects. In the context of information systems projects, **technical risk** is the risk that the project will not perform as specified. **Cost risk** is the risk of exceeding a project's budget, something that is reported to commonly occur in information systems projects. **Schedule risk,** the risk of not meeting a project's deadline, is notoriously severe in information systems projects. Couillard found that when technical risk is high, project success was significantly influenced by the level of authority given to the project manager (as well as the ability to handle problems, to communicate, and to offer team support). Matrix forms of organization were found to be correlated with project success when technical risk was high because the matrix form of organization had more skilled assets available if needed. When the risk of cost overrun was high, project success was found to be significantly related to understanding of project goals, as well as project manager authority, team support, and communication. Projects that were riskier in terms of budget were found to require more formal planning, monitoring, and control. When schedule risk was high, project success was most closely correlated with project manager experience and the level of monitoring.

Levels of Project Organization

Projects involve a nontraditional form of organization. Traditional organizational design is much more rigid. While no organization is truly permanent, traditional organizational forms are designed on the assumption that they will continue into the foreseeable future. They are not very flexible, and they react slowly to change.

Projects, on the other hand, are organized with the understanding that they are temporary. Some projects can be very long in duration, such as the construction of a cathedral in the 11th to 14th centuries, taking hundreds of years. Other projects may last only weeks and therefore have very temporary lives. Projects involve very high levels of uncertainty and change, so project organizations need to be flexible and adaptive. In the traditional form, people can enhance their professional training and development. Many organizations that contract to undertake projects typically adopt a functional form of organization for permanent assignments, drawing people for individual projects from their permanent assignments to temporarily work with other specialists on specific projects. This is true in construction, engineering, and large accounting firms specializing in consulting, including information system consulting. Careers with such organizations involve a great deal of relocation because individuals leave their home base for the duration of projects to which they are assigned. Between projects, the organization may value their specialty skills enough to keep them on the payroll. Ultimately, however, new projects are needed in which these skills can be utilized.

Within project organizations, integrators are often used to facilitate communication. **Liaisons** are used to integrate two groups not part of the same organization. Liaisons are especially useful between the people who fund the project and the project team. **Task forces** are temporary groupings of individuals created to solve a particular problem. The task force idea comes from the military, where combining different types of units under a temporary leader for some specific mission is often practiced. In project organizations, individuals with different specialties are grouped together to develop a solution for a specific problem. Long-term task forces can be turned into permanent teams. Project **expediters** (or **coordinators**) are individuals whose job is to make sure that something happens. These individuals have no authority but are assigned to keep on top of problems so that they can inform project managers of the need for additional resources for specific activities.

Table 8–2 outlines the conditions for which a particular organizational form is most often appropriate. Other criteria that bear on the project type include uncertainty, cost and time criticality, and the uniqueness of the project. If the project involves high stakes, a matrix form or pure project form gives better control. If there are high levels of certainty, task forces and teams are appropriate because they involve less investment. If time and cost are not critical, task forms and teams are also appropriate. If the project is unique, a partial or full project form is appropriate.

Project Managers

It has been reported that more than 30 percent of new software projects are canceled before completion and that better than half are more than 180 percent

TABLE 8–2   Comparison of Organizational Forms

Type of Organizational Form	Project Size	Project Duration	Project Complexity
Task force	Small to medium	Short to medium	Low to medium
Project	All	All	Low to medium
Multiple Project Teams	Medium to large	All	Medium to high
Matrix	Medium to large	All	Medium to high

over budget. The most commonly cited reason is poor project planning and management. At the same time, there is a shortage of qualified, large-scale project managers.[10]

Project management involves getting work done through outsiders. In matrix forms of management, we have seen the dual lines of authority. Project managers are not in as powerful a position as managers in other forms of organization, and therefore they have to rely on influence and persuasion to get people to work toward project ends. Harrison[11] stated that the survival of a project manager depends a great deal on the strength of the alliances that the manager can make with powerful stakeholders and on success in competing for resources within the firm. The project manager's mission is to integrate diverse activities in a highly dynamic environment and to produce technical deliverables with a team whose members are temporarily assigned from different parts of the firm and therefore have other loyalties.[12] This must be done within the constraints of a budget for cost and for time, and meeting quality specifications.

The project manager has to make decisions, provide a sense of direction for the project organization, and serve as the hub for project communication. The ability to take on a number of roles is required. The project manager must be an *evangelist,* making sure everyone believes that the project will work. He or she must also be an *entrepreneur,* getting the necessary funds, facilities, and people required for project success. The project manager must also be a *change agent,* orchestrating diverse activities and facilitating these efforts to ensure project success.

The project manager has the responsibility of all managers: get the job done on time, within budget, and satisfying specifications. The job also includes planning and organizing and dealing with groups representing the owner and subcontractors. In addition to people skills, the project manager must understand enough technology to realize what is possible and what is not and to recommend project termination if things are not working out. The project manager needs to be personable and use a leadership style capable of motivating diverse people who do not work directly for the project manager. The project manager also needs to be able to understand budgeting.

Comparison: Functional and Project Managers

Project managers have to operate in a very turbulent environment. There are many differences between a project manager's job and that of a functional organization manager as seen in Table 8–3. The selection of a project manager should focus on a number of characteristics. Project managers need flexibility, leadership, confidence, and organizing skills. They should be generalists rather than specialists. They need to communicate well and be able to build trust and team spirit. They need general business skills, as well as technical understanding. Project management requires a well-rounded individual.

TABLE 8–3   Comparison of Manager's Positions

Functional Manager	Project Manager
Clear chain of authority	Often operates in matrix structure, low authority
Quasi-permanent relationships	Temporary, shared relationships
Can direct	Often must positively motivate
Established organization	Developing and changing organization
Long-term relationships	Short-term relationships
Directs a small set of skills	Directs a diverse set of skills

---

Team cooperation is critical in projects. Barker, Tjosvold, and Andrews[13] found that matrix organizations involved high levels of conflict, in large part because of the dual chain of authority found in matrix organizations. Project managers operating in that environment need to function without the authority often found in functional organizations. Within projects, compromise and dealing with conflict in a positive way are usually associated with reduced conflict intensity.

While not always given direct authority, the project manager has control over some resources. The primary source of authority, however, is often the respect gained from professional expertise—and sometimes charm and personality! Professional expertise can be gained from technical knowledge and administrative competence. Some have suggested that project managers try to appear powerful to workers so that they maximize their influence.

Project managers can be found either inside or outside of the organization. From within the organization, someone with experience and the right specialties is often impossible to find. Therefore, project managers may need to be found from outside the organization. However, this is also problematic, because it takes time to establish alliances and to learn the organization. But usually people with better organizational skills and experience are available in the broader market outside of the organization.

Summary

Organizational structure is a means to achieve goals and respond to problems. Project personnel are often organized into projects teams or into a matrix structure. These organizational forms are more flexible than functional structures, which tend to be more bureaucratic. The positive and negative features of alternative organizational forms and their variants need to be understood by top management so that they can select the organizational form most suitable for their situation. Understanding why these forms exist is also important to those working in them. The matrix form of organization is especially suitable for many projects for large organizations.

The project manager is central to control of the project. The project manager must integrate diverse elements to bring projects in on time, within cost, and with satisfactory performance. The project manager needs to be an individual capable of operating with diverse people and capable of understanding both technical and administrative aspects of the project.

Key Terms

cellular organization 199	organization 193
cost risk 202	project organization 196
expediter (or coordinator) 203	schedule risk 202
functional organization 194	task force 203
liaison 203	technical risk 202
matrix organization 197	

Exercises

1. What are the primary options in organizing?
2. What are the primary advantages of functional organization?
3. How does project organization differ from functional organization?
4. Describe a matrix organization.
5. What is a task force?
6. What does a project expediter do?
7. What is the best organizational form for a small, short project involving low levels of complexity?
8. What does the size of an organization have to do with the appropriateness of matrix organization?
9. What are the desirable features of good project managers?
10. Discuss the trade-offs between hiring managers from outside the organization as opposed to promoting managers from within the organization.

Microsoft Project Exercise

Identifier	Activity	Predecessor	Duration (days)	Resource
Perform Planning and Scheduling				
A1	Revise overall project plan	None	15	N,P1
A2	Complete detailed plan for detail design	A1	5	P1

Identifier	Activity	Predecessor	Duration (days)	Resource
A3	Revise skeleton and generic plan for rest	A1	3	P2
A4	Brief new team members	A2,A3	1	M,N,P1
A5	Complete phase estimate	A4	7	O,P1
A6	Review plan	A5	1	M,N,O,P1
A7	Revise plan	A6	10	O,P1
A8	Complete project schedule	A5 start + 3	4	N
A9	Milestone	A7,A8	0	

Prepare Database Design

B1	Document data models to catalog	None	15	B,P2
B2	Determine file structures for flat files	B1	12	B
B3	Prepare copylibs for flat file structures	B1	7	B
B4	Define each process	B2,B3	3	B,P2
B5	Review process access with database admin	B4	1	D,M,N,P2
B6	Physical database design	B5	20	B,R
B7	Review design	B6	1	B,D,M,N,P1
B8	Revise design	B7	15	B,R
B9	Conduct call pattern reviews	B6	10	B
B10	Milestone	B8,B9	0	

Prepare Physical Design Documents

C1	Prepare process-to-program specifications	B4	13	P2
C2	Determine security specifications	B9,C1	8	B,P2
C3	Prepare physical system flow	C2	12	B,P2
C4	Milestone	C3	0	
D1	Design programs and write specifications	A8,B9	18	B,P2
D2	Write data conversion and interface programs	D1	6	R, R(3)
D3	Revise documents	D2	30	R, R(3)
D4	Milestone	D3	0	
E1	Implementation	A8,B9,D3	5	B,P2,R
E2	Testing	E1	15	B,P2,R
E3	Final acceptance	E2	1	M,N,D
E4	Milestone	E3	0	

start July 1, 2000

5 day workweek
Holidays
   January 1
   3rd Monday in January
   3rd Monday in February
   July 4
   4th Thursday in November
   December 25

Resources	Cost/Day	Resources	Cost/Day
M Management representative	$500 (1)	R Systems programmers	$300 (3)
N Assistant	$150 (1)		
O Cost estimator	$300 (1)	D Database administrator	$600 (1)
P Systems analysts	$450 (2)	B Database designers	$400 (1)

Plan this project to stay within available resources. Assign individual names to resources, and use those in *Microsoft Project.* (You will have options as to which individual systems analyst to assign to each activity.) Level the project and turn in a Gantt chart printout, showing starting and finishing times for each activity, as well as assigned resources.

Outside of *Microsoft Project,* develop an organizational chart of resources used.

Endnotes

1. J. R. Galbraith, "Matrix Organization Designs—How to Combine Functional and Product Forms," *Business Horizons,* 1971, pp. 29–40.
2. _____, *Organization Design* (Reading, MA: Addison-Wesley, 1971).
3. J. Barker, D. Tjosvold, and R. Andrews, "Conflict Approaches of Effective and Ineffective Project Managers: A Field Study in a Matrix Organization," *Journal of Management Studies* 25, no. 2 (1998), pp. 167–78.
4. D. G. Marquis and D. M. Straight, *Organizational Factors in Project Performance* (Washington, DC: National Aeronautics and Space Administration, 1965).
5. E. R. Corey and S. A. Starr, *Organization Strategy: A Marketing Approach* (Boston: Harvard University Press, 1971).
6. R. Katz and T. J. Allen, "Project Performance and the Locus of Influence in the R&D Matrix," *Academy of Management Journal* 28 (1985), pp. 67–87.
7. E. W. Larson and D. H. Gobeli, "Significance of Project Management Structure on Development Success," *IEEE Transactions on Engineering Management* 36, no. 2 (1989), pp. 119–25.
8. Ibid.
9. J. Couillard, "The Role of Project Risk in Determining Project Management Approach," *Project Management Journal,* December 1995, pp. 3–15.
10. "Wanted: Project Managers," *Software Magazine,* December 1997.
11. F. L. Harrison, *Advanced Project Management* (Cambridge: Gower Publishing, 1992).
12. J. H. Graham, "Machiavellian Project Managers: Do They Perform Better?" *International Journal of Project Management* 14, no. 2 (1996), pp. 67–74.
13. Barker, Tjosvold, and Andrews, "Conflict Approaches of Effective and Ineffective Project Managers."

Project Implementation

Main Ideas Discussed

- Examples of project implementation
  success and failure
- Categories of project failure
- Critical success factors in
  information systems projects
- Reasons projects fail
- How planning can increase the
  probability of project success
- Outsourcing as an option for
  completing information systems
  projects
- The role of users in project
  implementation

In this book, we began with a discussion of the risks involved in accomplishing an information systems project. We then discussed what is involved in information systems project development. We now return to an overall perspective of what is involved in final implementation of information systems projects, with the intent of examining things that can be done to improve a project's prospects of success.

Information Systems Project Success

Not all information systems projects fail. We will begin with two information systems project success stories (see the accompanying boxes), looking at what was done at each project cycle step.

Railing and Housel[1] described TRW's implementation of a $45 million dollar project over a 4.5-year period that met all critical milestones while using only 90 percent of their original budget. This implementation was very successful, resulting in a network system providing valuable new technology for the firm. The TRW project was very carefully and thoroughly managed and controlled, resulting in successful implementation.

TRW's Network Infrastructure Implementation

Top management at TRW's Space and Defense Sector needed to reduce communications cost while maintaining profitable growth in a highly competitive field. Faster response capabilities were needed to respond to a rapidly changing market. In the early 1980s, TRW adopted a project to develop a new network infrastructure. After 2.5 years of planning, the system was implemented in 2 additional years. The system included a 30,000-line private branch exchange, 25,000 integrated voice and data digital lines, and security video services.

Project Approval and Planning

Once broad cost and benefit forecasts were evaluated, the data services and telecommunications departments of TRW were directed to develop a detailed analysis of current network needs. A project management team was organized consisting of internal technical, engineering, and project personnel from the affected organizational units. Procurement was organized to break large purchases into small units with subproject managers. Vendors were integrated into the cost scheduling control system, giving TRW added control over their participation in the project. A project baseline was developed to allow project management to monitor how well the project was staying on schedule and within budget.

Requirements Analysis

Detailed requirements analysis was used to accurately estimate costs and identify needed system performance standards. Current operations were studied to understand the system the network was to support. Data on users were gathered, and existing networks were identified so that the numbers and types of devices that would use the network could be estimated. Costs of current operations were gathered, and evaluative criteria for assessment of project success were established.

Cost Justification

The TRW process required that the project be justified either on the basis of a positive return on investment or that the net present value of the investment would exceed the firm's cost of capital. Decisions about leasing versus purchase and of capitalization versus expensing the investment were made for project components.

Requests for Proposals

Vendors were invited to bid on various parts of the project through requests for information. Initial vendor responses were the basis for very detailed requests for proposals, reflecting the network architecture, technical standards, environmental requirements, vendor relationships, and quality assurance criteria for each network component.

Proposals received from vendors were evaluated by the project team, supported by personnel from accounting, procurement, and cost analysts. After technical evaluations, risk analysis was conducted. Vendors were evaluated on their management plan, their ability to provide required resources on schedule, their ability to provide services or products required that were beyond their current area of expertise, and their inventory position. Total cost for each acceptable bid was carefully examined to develop a final price ensuring compliance with required technical standards. TRW Procurement was then given proposal evaluations to enable them to negotiate the best reasonable price for each component obtained from vendors.

Project Implementation

The requirements analysis and detailed requests for proposals formed the basis for the implementation plan. The implementation plan included

- Plan scope.
- Technical design criteria.
- Implementation phases.
- User requirements.
- Pre-installation preparations through user surveys.
- Organizational structure of the implementation team.
- Automation requirements (project management software).
- Conditional and final test plans.
- Facilities plans.
- Operations plans (transitioning to operation).
- User support plan (training).
- Security plan.
- Chargeback and accounting plans.
- Network configuration plan.

This detailed implementation plan enabled subproject teams to keep to their very tight schedules. Project management techniques that were credited with contributing to project success included:

Vendors submit proposals to the project team for evaluation. Upon approval, vendors discuss an implementation plan with the project team.

- Assigning responsibility to the subproject level.
- Very carefully maintaining project baseline schedule and costs.
- Development of a negotiations plan for dealing with vendors.
- Incorporating a wide involvement of firm technical expertise.

Source: L. Railing and T. Housel, "A Network Infrastructure to Contains Costs and Enable Fast Response: The TRW Process," *MIS Quarterly* 14, no. 4 (1990), pp. 404–19.

Successful implementation has been found to require mastery of the technical aspects of systems along with understanding of key organizational and behavioral dynamics.[2] Pinto[3] blamed most implementation problems on managerial and behavioral problems. The next case focuses on the perceptions of success for stakeholders within the firm affected by the project. Fowler and Walsh[4] reported implementation of an information systems project in England for a large project engineering organization. The focus of this study was more on the human side of project implementation. Care to involve users early in the requirements analysis proved to be very effective. While there was inevitable variance in the computer literacy of users, the comprehensive and carefully planned training program for the implementation of the new corporate-wide information system led to successful adoption of a more efficient and flexible system.

Company-Wide Information System

A major British nuclear firm adopted a new information system. This system focused on serving strategic business units, while providing information to all elements of the corporation. Fowler and Walsh interviewed system users and providers at all levels of the organization two years after the project was put into operation.

The firm had been privatized after its creation as a state-owned monopoly. In 1989 the firm developed a strategy based on the formation of small business units to focus not only on technical excellence, but also to provide products, services, and delivery to meet market demands. However, top management perceived that subunits had grown too autonomous. Therefore, a corporate-wide information system project was adopted. Project aims were to support corporate growth, as well as to support company expansion into alternative markets that were not related to nuclear energy. The proposed system therefore was designed with change in mind. The project manager was obtained from outside the organization, providing experience unavailable from within the company.

Planning Phase

A list of plans were developed for the major project phases of

- Project initiation
- System specification
- System design
- System development
- Acceptance testing
- Site preparation
- Implementation

In the early phases of this process, the notion of a central financial system was rejected. Therefore, an information systems project team was formed and visited corporate elements to establish system requirements. The new system was to be primarily package based, to be selected and implemented across the organization. Implementation was to be accomplished in a distributed manner to better support the different corporate elements. The project management approach of acceptance testing, data conversion, interfacing, training, hardware and networking, installation, and implementation was to be applied at each site.

The project included a common accounting structure with common reports and inquiry processes. Both a user manual and operations manual were developed for corporate-wide use. Software modules were made available for standard functions supporting accounting and business needs.

Implementation

Pilot implementation of the project as well as complete switchover to the new system (without any parallel operation) were both provided for in the implementation plan. Each site had its own implementation team (15 total). Training was considered a key success factor for the project and was carefully prepared for.

Perceptions of Project Success

Sixteen users of the system were interviewed two years after implementation. Consistent top management support was evident throughout the project. The project had been carefully managed and was completed on time and officially within budget. Corrective actions required were easily applied.

The implementation process at the lower levels of the corporation was found to have involved a number of problems. There was a wide variance in the complexity involved in project implementation among the 15 groups given implementation responsibility. A fixed target launch date focused efforts and was credited with fostering completion of the project on time. Pilot runs were credited with keeping the pressure on to complete the project on time by information systems personnel. However, users would have preferred parallel running of the new system with the old for safety, although it was recognized that this would have been more expensive.

Training was carefully planned and implemented. Training was focused on implementation teams, accounting users, and general users. Particular details of the training program were criticized, but overall the delivery of 2,500 training days was successfully accomplished.

Source: A. Fowler and M. Walsh, "Conflicting Perceptions of Success in an Information Systems Project," *International Journal of Project Management* 17, no. 1 (1990), pp. 1–10.

Information Systems Project Failure

There are many cases of information systems failing, for a variety of reasons. The implementation stage involves putting the system developed by the project into operation and turning the system over to the user. The major elements of implementation are system installation and conversion, user acceptance testing, and user training. If testing procedures are cut short as a means of recovering lost time, catastrophic failure often results.

Many information systems projects fail to some degree in terms of meeting design specifications or meeting time and cost estimates. Most project problems are not apparent until late in the project. The accompanying box demonstrates this phenomenon. This case involves an extreme instance of poor implementation of information technology. Adopting an enterprise resource planning project has proven very profitable for many firms. But information technology is not a cure for all ills. During project implementation, FoxMeyer encountered some radical changes in their business environment. Their reaction was in effect to increase their bet, hoping that information technology would again come to their rescue. This created such a turbulent environment that it was not possible to properly implement the proposed systems. Furthermore, when faced with a time-pressure problem, the firm cut many of the sound practices of the project process, resulting in further damage.

Information Technology Failure

FoxMeyer Drug Co. adopted a $65 million enterprise resource planning project in 1994. Within two years, the system failed to deliver, and the company filed for bankruptcy. Failure was blamed on unrealistic thinking about what information technology could do.

Some of FoxMeyer's bad luck can be attributed to external causes, such as losing a key customer accounting for 15 percent of its sales. But probably more pertinent were a series of risky management decisions arising from placing too much faith in the power of information technology. During implementation of the original project, FoxMeyer adopted a second information technology project to install a computerized warehouse, an $18 million project that encountered technical problems and led to inventory losses of more than $15 million. In trying to regain lost sales, FoxMeyer signed a contract for a new customer, assuming that the projected $40 million benefit from the enterprise resource planning (ERP) system would be realized right away. It wasn't. But to accommodate the new customer, FoxMeyer pushed the deadline for the ERP implementation forward 90 days, meaning that it could not reengineer business processes and reap savings. To meet the tighter deadline, testing of modules was cut short. While the ERP started on time, widespread data errors led to inaccurate customer sales histories, and only half the projected savings were realized.

Source: M. L. Markus and R. I. Benjamin, "Are You Gambling on a Magic Bullet," *Computerworld*, October 20, 1997, http://www.computerworld.com.

Project implementation involves applying the resources gathered to the activities scheduled in the planning stage of the project. A major consideration is that project plans are not rigid, and there usually is the need to change the plan to adapt to newly understood realities. The buffer concepts proposed by Goldratt[5] and discussed in Chapter 6 of this book should help. But nothing will avoid all of the potential changes that will arise in project implementation.

Technical validity refers to the system accurately doing the job it was designed to do. **Organizational validity** has to do with people using the system. Systems can be technically valid, but if there are reasons users won't use them (such as difficulty in using them), the system will have been a waste. **Organizational effectiveness** refers to how the system contributes to better performance by the organization. Information systems elements are meant to lead to better decision making, but the quality of decision making is impossible to measure except in very narrow contexts. Profit is often used as a measure of effectiveness, but rarely is only one factor responsible for changes in profitability. Probably the best measure of information system effectiveness is its use. Those systems that are used are probably successful, but even those may involve problems.

While it has been demonstrated that it is possible to successfully implement an information systems project, the FoxMeyer case demonstrated what can happen when projects fail. The many statistics we presented in Chapter 1 and elsewhere in this book demonstrate the scope of the problem of failure in information systems projects. Project failure can come in many forms (budget overrun, schedule overrun, technical inadequacy). Obviously some of these reasons are more critical than others. Lyytinen and Hirschheim[6] identified four major categories of project systems failure:

1. **Corresponding failure** alludes to the failure of the system to meet design objectives. This is a technical failure in that a computer code did not do what it was intended to do.
2. **Process failure** is failure to bring in a project system on time and within budget. The system may technically work, but it is no longer economically justifiable, or at least not within current business plans.
3. **Interaction failure** occurs when a system is not used as much as it was planned to be. This can arise when a system is built to technical specifications within budget and on time, but the intended users do not use it. This can be because of some bias on the users' part to continue to operate the old way, or because the planned system design really did not effectively deal with the problem.
4. **Expectation failure** occurs when the system does not quite match up with the expectations of project stakeholders. The system may perform technically, may be on time and within budget, and may be used, but it may not do the job as management was led to expect.

Ewusi-Mensah and Przasnyski[7] distinguished among **total abandonment** (complete termination of project activity before implementation), **substantial abandonment** (major simplification resulting in a project radically different than original specifications), and **partial abandonment** (reduction in original project scope without major changes in original specifications). Total abandonment was the most common case among the three. Sometimes managers became too committed to projects, extending their life when they should be canceled.[8] Project failure causes can be grouped into inadequate economic payoff, psychological factors (managerial persistence in expecting positive project prospects when they feel personally responsible), escalation factors (throwing good money after bad), social factors (including competitive rivalry), and organizational factors related to a project's political support.

Critical Success Factors

A **critical success factor** is something that the organization must do well to succeed. In terms of information systems projects, a critical success factor is what a system must do to accomplish what it was designed to do.

Morris[9] outlined a project life cycle of four stages and gave critical success factors in terms of drivers and inhibitors for projects by stage. The four stages and their success factors are listed in Table 9–1.

The presence of top management support is clear, showing up as a success driver in all four phases, and as a success inhibitor in the two intermediate phases. Clear objectives is present in the formation stage as a success driver, while problems with objectives is present as a success inhibitor in the build-up and close-out

---

TABLE 9–1   Project Life-Cycle Stages

Stage	Success Drivers	Success Inhibitors
Formation	Personal ambition **Clear objectives** **Top management support** Team motivation Technological advantage	Unmotivated team Technical problems Poor leadership Lack of funding
Build-up Leadership problems	Team motivation **Top management support** Personal motivation Technical expertise	Unmotivated team **Lack of top management support** **Conflict in objectives** Technical problems
Main phase	Team motivation **Client support** Personal motivation **Top management support**	Unmotivated team Deficient procedures **Lack of top management support**
Close-out	Personal motivation **Top management support** Team motivation Financial support	Poor control **Lack of objectives** Poor financial support Poor leadership

Source: P. W. G. Morris, "Managing Project Interfaces: Key Points for Project Success," in *Project Management Handbook,* D. I. Cleland and W. R. King, eds. (New York: Van Nostrand Reinhold, 1983), pp. 3–36.

phases. User involvement is present in the form of client support in the main phase. The relative importance of critical success factors was found to change as the project proceeded, with technological advantage being a success driver initially, technical expertise showing up in the build-up phase, and client support appearing in the main phase of the project. Thus, behavioral factors were found to outweigh technical factors in the Morris study.

Pinto and Slevin examined more than 400 projects, finding the following critical success factors in order of number of appearances:

- **Project mission**—clear goals and directions provided.
- **Top management support**—to ensure needed resources were provided.
- Plan/schedule—include detailed specifications.
- **Client consultation**—all affected parties given a hearing.
- Personnel—good people assigned to the project team.
- Technical tasks—needed expertise available.
- **Client acceptance**—sell the product of the project to the users.
- Monitoring and feedback—timely control during all stages of the project.
- Communication—network and data required are available.
- Troubleshooting—deal with crises and deviations.[10]

Three factors consistently appear as critical success factors for information systems projects. Top management support, client consultation (user involvement), and clear project objectives appear prominently in the studies discussed.

Primary Reasons for Information Systems Project Failure

A survey of information systems executives cited lack of user involvement as the chief reason information systems projects fail.[11] This was followed by lack of top executive support and lack of clear statement of business objectives. This survey confirms what many other studies, some outlined earlier in this chapter, have found.

Lack of Client Involvement

Heavy involvement on the part of users is needed for project success for two important reasons. First, systems analysts need user input to accurately identify the business system and what business problems are. Second, the project will not work if users do not use the computer system. If the users have been involved in identifying computer system problems, and have been consulted about proposed solutions, there is a much greater likelihood that they will accept the project.

Amoako-Gyampah and White[12] reported the system development of a project at a large manufacturing firm. The system affected 12 departments at five sites and 280 users around the country. A project team of 15 consultants, 10 people from the firm, and 2 project managers working for the firm was formed. A committee of top managers was created to provide oversight and met with the project team once a month. Weekly project meetings were held, chaired by the vice president for information systems. The project team encouraged user sign-offs at different phases of the project, such as software selection, and at the end of phases, such as changes to system components and development of screens. Different levels of users were involved at different phases to get users to buy into the system. Training sessions were provided, as well as pilot sessions where user suggestions were encouraged. However, the project was not a success. Four months after the system was installed, more than 1,000 requests for changes in the system had been received. Even though many means of encouraging user involvement had been applied, poorly defined lines of responsibility and communication resulted in failure of communication between users and systems designers. Users grew to feel that their input wasn't valued, and therefore they quit contributing.

This experience led Amoako-Gyampah and White to suggest steps, including the following, for building user consensus:

- Ensure project managers are highly visible.
- Include people with vested interest in the project outcome in project design.
- Identify these users early to avoid later conflicts.
- Allow users to make suggestions, and give them feedback.

- Remove communications barriers between system developers and user groups.
- Make the project team responsible for keeping affected parties informed of project progress.
- Use surveys for feedback.[13]

Lack of Top Management Support

Projects have a very difficult time succeeding if they are not "fostered" by top management. Project leadership is important too, but favorable views at the top, with control over purse strings, are probably more necessary for projects to succeed.

That is not to say that support within the project team is not important as well. The implementation team needs to develop team building and cooperation to succeed. Successful team characteristics include a clear sense of mission, understanding of interdependencies of system elements, cohesiveness of the system, and shared enthusiasm and trust within the project team. Within project teams, it is necessary to be flexible. It is also necessary to keep everyone informed.

While there is no one best leadership style, project managers should have the ability to motivate and inspire. This in great part is due to the fact that they have little coercive authority, especially within matrix organizations.

In addition to the project manager, another key role is the project champion. Project champions often have no authority, but are crucial to the success of projects. A comparison between project managers and champions is given in Table 9–2. Project champions have been found to be crucial at maintaining interest in information systems projects. This can be very positive. But it can also be negative if counterproductive projects are kept alive after their need has passed. This also has occurred when strong project champions have been present.

Lack of Project Definition

A **detailed project plan** needs to be developed, defining the system, user requirements, and system requirements. Part of this plan is a clear statement of the business objectives of the proposed system.

TABLE 9–2   Comparison of Project Managers and Project Champions

Project Manager	Project Champion
Technical understanding	Cheerleader
Leadership and team building	Visionary
Coordination and control	Politician
Obtain and provide support	Risk taker
Administrative	Ambassador

The *system definition* should identify the project team, including its leaders. Team members should be drawn from functional areas. Networks of the flow of information should be developed, along with identification of tasks and their relationship. Budgets need to be established, and policies need to be stated.

User requirements include performance measures. These measures are needed to determine the acceptability of the final product. For legal reasons, as well as for operational continuity, it is wise to have good documentation. This documentation becomes the ultimate reference for resolving issues that arise during the project.

System requirements are developed from user requirements. System requirements should clearly state the output of the system in technical terms. Typical information system specifications include the following:

- Compatibility with the larger system.
- Module interchangeability with existing modules.
- Cost-effectiveness measures.
- System reliability standards.
- Maintainability procedures
- Test standards.

These system requirements are the basis for a detailed list of user requirements and system requirements. Users should review this list to check for accuracy, completeness, and fit with the needs of the organization. Focus on system objectives needs to be maintained.

Quality Control in Project Implementation

Implementation planning involves developing plans and gathering resources to install the system and train users. **Quality control** is an important element in implementing the project. Management and control of software quality was studied by Phan, George, and Vogel,[14] using IBM's OS/400 R.1 project over the period from 1986 to 1988. This project involved generation of more than 50 million lines of high-level code. The final version consisted of more than 3.6 million lines of programming code, of which 1.2 million lines were reused from prior projects. It was imperative that the product be brought to market on time, with high quality.

Study of prior projects improved project quality. A large number of defects found after delivery were due to insufficient testing of many types of system configurations. Placing the need to obtain higher quality over traditional IBM secrecy, wide participation from customers and outside vendors was obtained in the requirements definition, development, and software testing phases. Written code went through three reviews and four tests. CASE and development support tools were used for development activities. User manuals were edited by professionals at independent editorial service companies. User surveys were used to obtain feedback, and telephone calls were made to each customer 90 days after installation.

TABLE 9–3   Ratio of Removal of Defects to Phase

Stage	Relative Cost of Defect Removal
Requirements definition	1
Design stage	3.5
Coding stage	10
Testing stage	50
After delivery	170

These steps resulted in an error rate below one per thousand lines of code at delivery, a significant improvement over prior operating systems. There was a decrease of about 50 percent in customer requests for software assistance. Documentation errors were reduced by 50 percent over earlier projects.

One reason that reported losses on information systems projects are so high is that many projects are canceled late in the project life. This is because most problems are not identified until the testing stage of a project, after much of the cost of the project has been expended. Boehm[15] provided relative estimates of the cost of defect removal. For large projects, the ratio of removing defects by phase was estimated to be as given in Table 9–3. It is obvious that correcting errors at an early stage is far better than later. To identify errors at early stages, early testing is required.

Reusable code and reused test cases made significant contributions to the high level of quality obtained in the OS/400 project. Key factors for obtaining high levels of software quality identified by Phan, George, and Vogel were

1. Well-defined quality goals, driven by market and end-user needs.
2. Good management of reusable code.
3. Good quality assurance planning and control.
4. Effective feedback.[16]

High levels of quality in any operation are obtained by quality inputs, careful production, followed by testing in realistic environments, and user feedback. The four factors identified by Phan, George, and Vogel match these general quality principles.

The Decision to Outsource

Nelson, Richmond, and Seidmann[17] stated that acquisition of software costs more than $250 billion per year in the United States. **Outsourcing** (hiring others to do work) is the most popular means of product development or product installation. Firms have the choice of developing systems themselves or purchasing software packages from vendors. Outsourcing can be beneficial in that the services of those more experienced in doing some activity can be acquired. Developing new expertise in-house can involve great expense, time, and risk. Clearly outsourcing is beneficial if the work in question requires high levels of expertise not currently resident in-house, and if the work is not expected to be something the company will be doing a great deal of in the future.

Outsourcing in the context of information systems is hiring others to develop (and possibly operate) systems. The basic rule is that organizations should *not* outsource operations involving their core competencies or the things that are key to their business strategy. Many other activities are judged to be less expensive and certainly less trouble if specialists are retained. International Data Corporation estimated that the health care field spent $800 million on computer outsourcing in 1995, and this number is expected to grow to $1.5 billion by the year 2000.[18] This sounds like a large figure. But Kelleher[19] reported that Computer Sciences Corporation signed an eight-year contract with Hughes Aircraft to handle all of its information processing for $1.5 billion. Dataquest was reported by Kelleher to have estimated worldwide outsourcing to reach $51 billion in 1998, exhibiting a growth rate of about 17 percent per year. A survey by G2 Research indicated that less than one-fourth of major U.S. companies have signed outsourcing contracts, but almost 75 percent are considering doing so.[20]

The primary reasons driving companies to outsourcing are speed and money. Companies can cut costs and time to develop computer projects at lower risk, relying on the provider firms to keep up with rapidly changing technology. Boath, Hess, and Munch[21] discussed the conditions appropriate for outsourcing in the pharmaceutical industry. Like many other industries, pharmaceuticals have found it very productive to implement information technology to more effectively and efficiently conduct their business. Boath, Hess, and Munch state that successful virtual organizations need to clearly define their core competencies required for sustainable growth, develop expertise in those areas, and outsource noncore activities to experts. Contracting out often reduces implementation time and can result in better quality products because of provider expertise. Companies that outsource gain the ability to focus limited resources on areas of strategic importance to them, while sharing information systems project development cost.

The Internal Revenue Service (IRS) has been heavily involved in outsourcing small projects as part of their overall efforts to modernize the tax collection system. As discussed earlier in this book, the IRS has not been totally successful in this endeavor. In 1998 the IRS made the decision to outsource management of the overall upgrading project. A call for bidders was issued in March 1998 for bids on an $8 billion, 15-year modernization project.[22] In December, Computer Sciences Corporation announced that they were going to head a consortium of contractors, including IBM, Unisys, and Lucent Technologies.[23] In this case, the difficulties of managing outsourcing is clear. Current IRS thinking is that outsourcing overall management of this massive information technology project is better than trying to manage it with internal assets. This project opens a new dimension in outsourcing scope.

Nelson, Richmond, and Seidmann[24] surveyed 186 system projects that were installed between 1967 and 1993. Subjects surveyed ranged from small companies to large, and the projects ranged from small personal computer applications to large, distributed systems. Using the two dimensions of in-house/outsource and custom/package application, 64 percent of the projects were in-house custom systems, 17 percent were outsourced custom systems, 11 percent were based on packages installed in-house, and 8 percent were packages installed by outsource firms.

The Nelson, Richmond, and Seidmann study found that systems using specialized technology or advanced development were more likely to be outsourced and were more likely to involve packaged software. Simpler systems, such as database management systems, were less often outsourced. Application type was not found to be a significant variable in explaining in-house development versus outsourcing or in the use of packages versus custom development. There was only weak evidence that strategically important projects were more likely to be developed in-house. Systems using specialized and advanced technologies for common applications tended to be outsourced. Systems using simpler technology for common applications tended to involve packages. Companies formerly had a strong predisposition to develop applications in-house, but this tendency has decreased over time.

Requirements analysis is a good stage to consider the option of outsourcing. If the project includes skills that the organization has not developed, outsourcing is an option that should be considered.

Outsourcing can be done at different levels. An organization could outsource specific operations, or it could outsource the management of information systems. The decision to turn over information systems management can be very effective from a cost aspect and can obtain access to newer technology. Outsourcing does involve risk. If entire systems are outsourced, organizations will place their entire information systems operation in the hands of others. If things should not work out, the cost of developing or obtaining alternative information facilities is liable to be very expensive.[25]

User Involvement in Project Implementation

The purpose of **user training** is to teach users how to operate, maintain, and service the new system. Training planning includes identifying the materials needed, the personnel to train, and the teaching techniques necessary. It is best to involve users in this planning. User approval of the training program expedites successful delivery of material. Training should show how the system fits into the organization's overall information system. All of those users affected by the system should be included in the training program, which should address concerns and not only show users how the system works but how it contributes to the welfare of the organization.

User acceptance testing is usually required before installation. Ideally, the user organization has been involved in testing throughout the development of the project. This can lead to identification of problems early so that they do not cause as much damage. If the first the user sees of the system is the final acceptance test, failure is almost guaranteed.

Actual installation of information systems can be accomplished in a variety of ways. Alternative strategies include parallel installation, pilot operation, and cold turkey approaches. **Parallel installation** involves running the new system in parallel with the old system. This is the most expensive approach because the resources required to operate both systems are used, but it is far safer than other approaches. The **pilot operation approach** involves running the new system on a limited basis. This does not expose the system to a full load. Obvious problems can be identified by this pilot approach, but problems due to work load will not be detected. The **cold turkey approach** is to place a great deal of faith in the new project, pull the plug on the old system, and turn on the new system. This approach is not recommended if it can be avoided.

We conclude this chapter by returning to a project we looked at in Chapter 1 (see accompanying box). The project had top management support, well-defined goals, and high user involvement. The project did not work well, however. In this case, there was a high degree of top management support for the project and attempts to have high levels of user involvement. There were clear goals on the part of top management, although some of these goals were insidious in that they were not clearly expressed to accountants (who were able to figure them out on their own). Goals, to be effective, need to be shared.

Integrated Requisitioning Information System

Kirby reported a project intended to design an integrated requisitioning information system for the requisition, purchasing, receiving, disbursement, and employee expense reporting processes for a U.S. food producer. This was to be a corporate-wide system, in effect an enterprise resource planning system. The new system was to interact with 36 previously developed information systems within the company's corporate headquarters and U.S. plants and sales offices. The system was to affect more than 3,000 employees, as well as incorporate suppliers to the firm. The system had a high level of top management support and was widely publicized and promoted through meetings and hot lines.

The project was started late in 1990 with the hiring of a reengineering specialist. By late 1991 an automated system was designed to deal with requisitioning and receiving operations. Early in 1992 four contracting firms were brought in to direct design, production, and implementation of the system. The project had 15 full-time people, supported by another 35 working on this project part-time. The project was in full-scale development by May 1992. Early in 1992 design meetings were held to define requirements and functional specifications. There was heavy user involvement in that each of the firm's plants and functional areas were represented in these meetings.

The system was divided into three phases. Phase 1 was to deal with check approval, check writing, and travel expense reporting. This module was to be released in November 1992 at corporate headquarters and to be installed in all U.S. plants within the next six months. Phase 2 dealt with requisitions, purchasing, and receiving, to be placed into operation by December 1993. Phase 3 was to integrate the new system with all other systems, as well as to deal with shipping orders, intercompany transactions, and electronic data interchange. Phase 3 was to be in operation by December 1993. Original cost estimates were about $3 million, including development, implementation, and training.

Phase 1 fell behind schedule because programmers had difficulties meeting functional specifications. There was increased turnover in project personnel. Cost estimates were revised to $5 million for the entire project. Delays were blamed in great part on the contracting firm responsible for delivering the software. In June 1993 this contracting firm was released, and the firm decided to write its own computer code. This required additional time to develop the necessary production teams. A scaled-back version of Phase 1 was pilot tested at corporate headquarters in early 1994, with the remainder of the project held up awaiting developments.

Blame for the project's failure was attributed to failure to adequately recognize the subjective nature of project management. Top management adopted a rational view, based on financial effect. A primary motivation for the project was that accounting staff would be reduced. This was not publicized. The project was expected to improve process efficiency and reduce the need for additional hiring. This was publicized. The system was intended to increase communications with plants and other facilities. The system was to provide sales representatives with a faster means of receiving reimbursement. An additional objective was to bring suppliers online and increase their dependence on the firm.

As prototype versions of the system were developed, it became apparent to many in accounting that they would no longer be needed. Users rationally enough questioned the value of the system to their own careers and did not provide many additional ideas for system improvement.

Plant representatives also saw the system as increasing the headquarter's ability to control their operations. What seemed rational and efficient to corporate headquarters was viewed as a way to more effectively increase regulations and corporate oversight.

Sales representatives viewed the new system as imposing added requirements on them and increasing their ties to their office computer. Sales personnel, like plant management, viewed the new system as a way for headquarters to increase its control over operations. Sales personnel, like accountants, saw the system as a threat to their jobs.

Kirby, who had been involved with project management on this project, concluded that people's perceptions of the project's effect were crucial. It is insufficient to demonstrate that a project is good for the company. Motivation to make the project work drops if it seems that the project is bad for the individual.

Source: E. G. Kirby, "The Importance of Recognizing Alternative Perspectives: An Analysis of a Failed Project," *International Journal of Project Management* 14, no. 4 (1996), pp. 209–11.

Summary

Four levels of project failure were presented. Studies of both information systems project failure and success were reviewed, intending to identify the circumstances that led to failure and using these bad experiences to identify procedures that can reduce the likelihood of failure. Additionally, a number of studies of information systems project failure were reviewed.

The primary causes of information system failure are lack of user involvement, lack of top management support, and lack of clear system objectives. Critical success factors in information system implementation were found to change with project stages, but to primarily involve motivation of the project team as well as the three primary factors of user involvement, top management support, and clear system objectives.

The decision to outsource is an important make-or-buy decision in information systems project management. Outsourcing can access more current expertise in the rapidly changing world of information technology. It also is quite often less expensive and may be faster. But outsourcing should only be applied for those activities that are not key to organizational strategy.

To avoid information systems project failure, a number of things are needed. Implementation planning, early system testing, and user training are required. Quality control should provide assurance of meeting project specifications. New system support and education are vital because they encourage the acceptance of new processes and systems. Training users is an important element in project implementation. While successful completion of an information systems project is challenging, the benefits are great.

Key Terms

cold turkey approach   224
corresponding failure   216
detailed project plan   219
expectation failure   216
interaction failure   216
organizational effectiveness   215
organizational validity   215
parallel installation   224
partial abandonment   216

pilot operation approach   224
process failure   216
project implementation   215
quality control   220
substantial abandonment   216
technical validity   215
total abandonment   216
user training   223

Exercises

1. What did FoxMeyer do with respect to risk management?
2. How could a project that performs according to technical specifications, and is completed on time and within budget, be considered a failure?
3. How did TRW develop their implementation plan?
4. What effect did a tight fixed-target launch date have in the British nuclear power firm's implementation of a company-wide information system?
5. Describe the four categories of project system failure outlined by Lyytinen and Hirschheim.
6. Discuss the primary reasons for information systems project failure.
7. Describe a project champion.
8. Morris outlined four stages of a project life cycle. Moving from formation through build-up and the main phase to close-out, describe the changes in success drivers.
9. Discuss the role of testing and of productivity tools in information systems project quality.
10. According to Boehm, what is the relationship of defect removal cost with project progress?
11. Compare information systems installation strategy options.

Microsoft Project Exercise

For the project entered in Chapter 4, identify expected cost of the original project.

To view *Microsoft Project*'s total cost projection, use the sequence:

Project	Project Information	Statistics

This provides a report of the project start, estimated completion, duration, and costs. For more detailed costs per task, use the sequence:

View	Table	Cost

This provides costs by task, giving baseline cost estimate, total cost, and variance.

After 25 working days, the following has been accomplished:

Activity	Completed	Percent Left
A1	17 days	0
A2	4 days	0
A3	6 days	0
A4	2 days	0
A5	0	100
A6–A9	0	100
B1	25 days	0
B2–B9	0	100
C1–C3	0	100
D1–D3	0	100
E1–E3	0	100

There have been the following revisions in estimated time:

Activity	New Estimated Duration
C1	20 days
C2	10 days
C3	20 days
D1	25 days
D2	10 days
D3	5 days

Work completed can be entered by clicking on each task in turn from the Gantt chart. Revised estimates can be entered directly in the duration column. Note that the baseline will not be changed.

When clicking on tasks, a task window is provided. In this window, the percent complete can be entered, as well as the duration. The percent completed is used to generate a bar reflecting actual work done. If 100 percent of work is completed, a check is generated in the "i" column by *Microsoft Project.*

What is the effect of work completed to date on project completion time? Cost?

Endnotes

1. L. Railing and T. Housel, "A Network Infrastructure to Contain Costs and Enable Fast Response: The TRW Process," *MIS Quarterly* 14, no. 4 (1990), pp. 404–19.
2. E. Oz, "Information Systems MIS-Development: The Case of Star*Doc," *Journal of Systems Management* 45, no. 5 (1994), pp. 30–34.

3. J. K. Pinto, *Successful Information System Implementation: The Human Side* (Upper Darby, PA: Project Management Institute, 1994).

4. A. Fowler and M. Walsh, "Conflicting Perceptions of Success in an Information Systems Project," *International Journal of Project Management* 17, no. 1 (1999), pp. 1–10.

5. E. M. Goldratt, *Critical Chain* (Great Barrington, MA: The North River Press, 1997).

6. K. Lyytinen and R. Hirshheim, "Information Systems Failures—A Survey and Classification of the Empirical Literature," *Oxford Survey of Information Technology* 4 (1987), pp. 257–309.

7. K. Ewusi-Mensah and Z. H. Przasnyski, "On Information Systems Project Abandonment: An Exploratory Study of Organizational Practices," *MIS Quarterly* 15, no. 1 (1991), pp. 66–86.

8. M. Keil, "Pulling the Plug: Software Project Management and the Problem of Project Escalation," *MIS Quarterly* 19, no. 4 (1995), pp. 422–47.

9. P. W. G. Morris, "Managing Project Interfaces: Key Points for Project Success," in *Project Management Handbook,* D. I. Cleland and W. R. King, eds. (New York: Van Nostrand Reinhold, 1983), pp. 3–36.

10. J. K. Pinto and D. P. Slevin, "The Project Champion: Key to Implementation Success," *Project Management Journal* 20, no. 3 (1988), pp. 15–20.

11. N. Engler, "Bringing in the Users," *Computerworld,* November 25, 1996, http://www.computerworld.com.

12. K. Amoako-Gyampah and K. B. White, "When Is User Involvement not User Involvement?" *Information Strategy,* Summer 1997, pp. 40–45.

13. Ibid.

14. D. D. Phan, J. F. George, and D. R. Vogel, "Managing Software Quality in a Very Large Development Project," *Information & Management* 29 (1995), pp. 277–83.

15. B. W. Boehm, *Software Engineering Economics* (Englewood Cliffs, NJ: Prentice-Hall, 1981).

16. Phan, George, and Vogel, "Managing Software Quality in a Very Large Development Project."

17. P. Nelson, W. Richmond, and A. Seidmann, "Two Dimensions of Software Acquisition," *Communications of the ACM* 39, no. 7 (1996), pp. 29–35.

18. C. Appleby, "Remote Control," *Hospitals & Health Networks* 71, no. 9 (1997), pp. 28–30.

19. K. Kelleher, "Move Over, EDS," *Financial World* 164, no. 12 (April 23, 1995), pp. 38–40.

20. Ibid.

21. D. Boath, P. Hess, and C. Munch, "Virtual R&D: A Core Competency Approach to Outsourcing," *Pharmaceutical Executive* 16, no. 6 (1996), pp. 72–78.

22. M. Hamblen, "IRS Takes Another Stab at Modernization," *Computerworld,* March 30, 1998, http://www.computerworld.com.

23. N. Weil, "CSC Tapped to Head IRS Upgrade Project," *Computerworld,* December 1, 1998, http://www.computerworld.com.

24. Nelson, Richmond, and Seidmann, "Two Dimensions of Software Acquisition."

25. Appleby, "Remote Control."

Project Control and Assessment

Main Ideas Discussed

- The importance of monitoring progress
- Methods to control risk
- The project control process
- The earned value budgeting concept
- Evaluation of project failure for future improvement
- The multiple project environment

The last topic of the book is control. Project control, like risk analysis and estimation, needs to be applied from the beginning of the project to the project's end. Control is concerned with keeping the project on target with respect to its objectives. **Assessment** is the means of monitoring project progress to identify problems requiring control action. The project, to be a success, should conform to the project plan as much as possible. Project management must adapt to new circumstances while simultaneously seeking to meet cost, time, and quality targets. This requires close coordination between the project manager and his or her superiors, whether they are part of the same organization or not.

Project Control Failures

Information systems projects face high failure rates. The risk of failure can be reduced by using sound development methods and tools. Even then there are uncertainties and risks that have critical influence on project success. There are a number of project features that can lead to problems. Lin and Hsieh[1] gave a number of examples of project control problems.

Corporate Culture.   A citrus fruit distribution company needed a new accounting information system in 1984. A new vice president was hired to head accounting and data processing operations. This vice president organized a task force to quickly develop the new system. Users were consulted early in the project but provided almost *no feedback*. The vice president assumed that all was under control, and in the summer of 1985, hardware and software were acquired and the new system implemented. During the implementation stage, the users began to complain. The system was brought online, and shortly thereafter the vice president resigned. In retrospect, it was inferred that the corporate culture had not been reached by the new vice president. Most of the users had been with the company for more than a decade, and worked together closely, but they were not open with outsiders. *The new vice president was simply ignored by the key user culture.*

Organizational Stability.   A Midwest manufacturing firm assigned three systems analysts to an information systems project to develop a production management system. The senior system analyst had experience in developing a similar system in another company. Throughout the development process, the production people were friendly, but *too busy to thoroughly review* all information sent to them by the project team. Before installation, key managers and primary users were asked to review the system. This *review found the system totally inappropriate*. The firm was undergoing a major reorganization, but this was not reflected in the new system.

Developer Experience with IT.   The finance department of a county wanted their payroll system, developed in the 1960s, to be upgraded. They tried several quick fixes, all of which failed. In early 1985 they began a development project estimated to take 10 months at a cost of $365,000. The *analysts assigned to the project were unfamiliar with the activities required* to build an online, integrated system. When completed two years later, the cost was $1 million.

Project risk increases as the project team's experience decreases. If no one in the organization is familiar with a complex undertaking, outside consultants should be hired. Vendors provide some assistance, but this is sometimes insufficient.

Developer Task Proficiency.   There have been many instances in which team personnel have been assigned to do things they have not been adequately trained to do. In 1991 an engineering company adopted a project management information system intended to monitor project costs. The existing system was simply a critical path method package without cost monitoring capability. A few days after the project was approved, the original project manager resigned, and a systems analyst was promoted to take his place. The *lack of experience on the part of the project manager* was blamed for the project taking 14 months when it was estimated at 6 months.

In all fairness, no one has experience until the first time they do something. But ideally, everyone should be given as much training as possible. Also, apprenticeship assignments should be used when possible.

Project Size.   The *larger the project, the greater the risk*. One strategy that works quite often is to split large projects into smaller subprojects and then develop one subsystem at a time. This method, of course, is slower. If the subsystems are developed in parallel, the overall project manager still needs to coordinate the development of these subsystems.

System Structure.   An application to automate routine data processing is highly structured and therefore low risk. Most information systems need to provide information for *decision making, which is quite unstructured*. In these unstructured environments, information requirements are difficult to specify and are frequently changed during systems development. Prototyping, which has the highest level of user involvement, is the best approach for such unstructured systems. Flexibility is also absolutely necessary.

These examples again demonstrate the need for user involvement and communication in accomplishing information systems projects. They also clearly show that experience improves the ability of project teams to accomplish tasks. Consideration of risk proved important as well.

Risk Management

We have seen that there are many potential problems that need to be anticipated in project management. Boehm[2] developed a list of the top risk items in software development projects. The actions to alleviate these risks are means of control. Actions need to be taken throughout the project and need to include continual monitoring to ensure that problems do not get out of control. Boehm presented a number of risk-resolution techniques.

Personnel Shortfalls

In the area of personnel management, Boehm discussed two techniques. The first is to *obtain quality people*. When operating in a matrix organization, people are obtained from the functional areas of the organization. Boehm recommended meeting with these functional managers to preschedule good people, by name, and then documenting these agreements. If people are obtained from either a matrix organization or from outside the organization, references should be checked to improve the probability that they will fit their planned roles.

The second personnel technique is *team building*. Proactive efforts should be taken to see that project management and team members share objectives. Participative planning and objective setting activities are useful to attain this aim, as well as group consensus techniques. Brainstorming, the nominal group technique, and Delphi methods, discussed in Chapter 3, are tools that can lead to group consensus by sharing ideas on the issue under consideration.

Controlling Dynamic Requirements

Project requirements sometimes change extensively. Some change needs to be accommodated—there are inevitable environmental changes that must be adjusted for. We have stressed user involvement. But once the scope of the project has been set, additional change (what systems people call *scope creep*) can be very detrimental to productivity. Some projects get out of control in the sense that requirements are constantly adjusted. One response to gain control over such a situation is to have a **high change threshold,** that is, not change plans until it is absolutely clear that they are needed. Risks are also reduced by deferring development of those project components that involve high probabilities of change. Another means of dealing with inevitable changes consists of determining major directions of anticipated changes in requirements and developing the system so that only minor revisions to the system are required (only one module would need to be replaced rather than revising the entire system).

Controlling Externally Provided Project Components

Combining system components obtained from multiple sources always creates risks of compatibility. These risks can be reduced by the activities of coordination and inspection. **Reference checking** involves contacting existing users of the component in question to verify features such as ease of use, ease of change, and other critical risk factors. **Pre-award audits** in the form of checklists and other techniques can be used to reduce the risk that outside vendors are incapable of delivering the component they are to provide. Other means of reducing the risk of failure in externally furnished components include use of award-fee contracts, soliciting competitive designs and prototypes, and involving outside providers in the project team.

Real-Time Performance Risk

The ability of the developed system to perform under actual working conditions is always uncertain until the system is implemented. There are a number of techniques available to reduce the risk of inadequate performance. **Benchmarking** involves placing the system under a representative workload and analyzing the system's ability to cope with this level of activity. **Prototyping** is another means of testing the critical performance features of a system. Instrumentation and tuning measure system performance in terms of bottlenecks. When bottlenecks are encountered, workload can be adjusted by changing task sequence, priorities, data distribution, and other workload characteristics to improve system performance. **Technical analysis** examines the ability of the system to function in environments such as distributed processing. The system's fault tolerance, security, and accuracy are also tested. Techniques supporting technical analysis include fault-tree analysis and failure modes and effects analysis.

Contingent Development Methods

Software systems should deliver functions needed by users. **Incremental development** allows organizations to test the functionality of system parts without wasting money on the entire project should it prove inadequate. *Prototyping* (discussed in Chapter 4) is a useful means of verifying the functionality of systems to users. Prototyping is also good for assessing the fault tolerance of systems. As the functionality of systems components is evaluated, those that are found lacking can be eliminated by **requirements scrubbing.** The cost/benefit methods discussed in Chapter 2 provide one basis for deciding on whether to keep a system feature or not.

    Mission analysis is the process of evaluating the contribution of a system component to accomplish an organizational objective. Mission analysis requires examination of the user's mission and the role of information systems support in leading to successful accomplishment of those missions. One of the key factors in information systems project success has been identified as clear statement of project objectives. Mission analysis would be a way of implementing this key factor. Tools to study the user's mission include identification of user tasks, data flows, and control procedures, as well as cost/benefit analysis.

Unrealistic Estimates

Chapter 5 discussed some of the difficulties in obtaining accurate estimates of cost and time in information systems projects. Boehm[3] recommended estimating a cost risk factor, which would serve as the basis for allocation of a reserve for risky items as needed. This is really the same concept (for budget) as Goldratt's buffers[4] (for time) discussed in Chapter 6.

    Another approach is to design projects to the available budget. The level of delivered functionality would be a variable. Software system components could be prioritized into mandatory, desired, and optional groups. The final design would have to include mandatory items, should include desired items, and would include optional items only if adequate time and budget were available. For instance, Sharpe and Keelin[5] demonstrated the method used by SmithKline Beecham for research project proposal evaluation (see Appendix 2A). Costs and benefits over time are calculated. Then two additional alternatives are generated— one a buy-up proposal with higher investment and increased features and the other a buy-down proposal with a scaled-down version of the project. The net present values and returns on investment for all three versions of the project are compared, and the version with the best return on investment is retained for comparison against other proposals.

The Control Process

There are some fundamental differences between **planning** and **control.** Planning focuses on setting goals and directions. Control is interested in guiding project effort toward attainment of these goals. Planning involves allocating resources to elements of the project hierarchy. Control seeks to ensure effective use of these resources. Planning requires anticipation of problems. Control requires correction of problems. Planning is a motivational effort, while control is more a matter of rewarding achievement.

Control requires understanding what is going on with a project. Project managers need to visit operations and see for themselves what is going on. Many actual problems do not show up in reports until it is too late for effective corrective action to be taken. Furthermore, a sense of the morale of members of the project team is better gained by actual visits.

Visits, in turn, do not reveal the details about performance that reports can. Reports of project progress should be as accurate as possible. Reports are used in a control sense by providing concrete measures of actual versus planned accomplishments of technical activities. Both time and cost reports are crucial to provide the project manager a clear picture of project performance. Major variances need to be understood by the project manager. There could be reasons beyond the control of anyone connected with the project. On the other hand, they could be the result of things that the project management team could correct. These variances also trigger a need for overall management to decide whether the project should be continued or dropped.

There are three general phases of the control process: (1) **Performance standards** are set at the beginning of the project. These provide technical specifications, budgeted costs, schedules, and resource requirements. Source documents include user specifications and the project plan. (2) Comparisons are made between actual performance and the plan during operations (assessment). Major project control elements include projected completion date and total estimated project cost. (3) When severe variances are experienced, the adoption of **corrective action** needs to be considered. There are many tools to control project development. We review three representatives here, in the area of personnel management, accounting, and work authorization.

Responsibility Assignment

A project team is formed to bring people with a variety of skills together to accomplish the project's objectives. A project responsibility chart is a simple device commonly used to clearly state who is responsible for each project activity. Table 10–1 is adapted from one presented by Andersen.[6] This chart can be used to clearly delineate the responsibilities of all parties involved. Also valuable is the information related to who must be consulted, informed, or is available for advice.

Budget

The traditional means of implementing cost control is **variance analysis**. Accurate measurement requires accurate identification of the quantities of work involved. Some costs are nonlinear, making it more difficult to estimate costs. This is especially true in information system projects, where progress is uncertain until testing is complete.

Cost control works most effectively when it is tied to work packages. **Work packages** include work descriptions, time-phased budgets, work plans and schedules, resource requirements, and assignments of responsibility. To make sense of cost reports, managers need to keep up with changes generated by schedule delay, and the differences in planned and actual times, as well as changes in the scope of work. The **earned value concept** is very useful to project management in this process. Earned value is the measure of the budgeted value of work that has been accomplished. Earned value indicates how much of the budget was planned to have been spent in order to do the amount of work done so far. This concept operates on the **standard time unit,** which measures work accomplished in terms of what a normal, prudent worker with average luck would accomplish in that time unit. Standard hours are traditionally used in manufacturing. Other time units, such as day or week, can be used as well. A standard week is probably more appropriate for information systems work. This can be useful in measuring the efficiency of a work unit. It also focuses on activity completion.

TABLE 10–1   **Project Responsibility Chart**

Activities: Develop Project Plan	*User*	*PM*	*CE*	*SA*	*PT*
A1 Initial project plan	A	I		X	
A2 Detailed plan of system modules				X	C
A3 Revise overall project plan	d	d			
A4 Complete resource, time, and cost estimates			P	X	C
A5 Review	d	d	C	C	C
A6 Final plan revision	I	I		X	I

Personnel:
User	who the system is to be built for
PM	project manager
CE	cost estimator
SA	systems analyst
PT	production team

Responsibility:
X—executes task
D—solely responsible for decision
d—shared decision responsibility
P—manages work & controls progress
C—needs to be consulted
I—needs to be informed
A—available for advice

Source: Adapted from E. S. Andersen, "Warning: Activity Planning Is Hazardous to Your Project's Health," *International Journal of Project Management* 14, no. 2 (1996), pp. 89–94.

In the example presented in Table 10–2, work packages A and B are completed, so the earned value is easy to calculate. The measures for unfinished activities are more problematic because it is difficult to accurately estimate the percentage of work completed. We have seen that in information systems projects, the final testing and debugging phases can include a great deal of unanticipated work. However, estimates of earned values can be calculated. In this case, credit is taken for half of the effort required on activity C and 75 percent of the effort required on activity D.

Relative efficiency can be calculated by dividing earned hours by actual hours. For example, if the actual effort expended on work package A was 25, it would have been rated as 20/25 = 0.80 efficient. If work package B took 8 units of effort, the efficiency rating would be 10/8 = 1.25, or 25 percent more efficient than expected. If activities C and D had actual expenditures equal to their earned value, the efficiency of this project component as a whole would be the total earned value (51) divided by total expended effort (54) = 51/54 = 0.94, or 94 percent of planned, on average. However, these measures need to be considered in light of conditions beyond the control of the project team. If late deliveries of materials or software cause work package A to run over its budget, the inefficiency could not in all fairness be attributed to poor performance on the part of those responsible for doing the work of package A. Project management needs to coordinate closely with the project team to understand the reasons for work lagging in time or running over in cost.

As we have stated before, people have a tendency to do the easiest work first, especially if it is important to appear as if they are making progress.[7] In project environments, this often leads to higher levels of progress reported than is actually the case. Projects are almost always reported to be on schedule until they are about 90 or 95 percent complete.[8] Some activities actually finish as scheduled. But many activities start to lag behind the planned completion date in the latter stages of their work. In information system projects one reason for this is that problems are often not identified until the testing stage. Progress reports in projects should be considered suspect until actual completion. That is the principal point of the **milestone** concept.

A primary role of the project information system is to monitor project progress. Data are collected from a variety of sources, including materials in-

TABLE 10–2 **Earned Value Example**

Work Package	Budgeted	Percent Complete	Earned Value	Actual
A	20	100	20	25
B	10	100	10	8
C	12	50	6	6
D	20	75	15	15
		Total earned value	51	54

voices, time cards, change notices, test results, and attitude surveys. Reports convey this information to key managers. All levels of management need to be provided the detailed information they need to identify problems and take corrective action. These reports need to identify variances. They also need to be published in a timely fashion.

Work Authorization

Authorization is a primary means of controlling projects. Upper management authorizes the project manager to proceed. The project manager in turn authorizes departments within the project management team to accomplish various elements of work through work orders. The authorization chain works its way down through the organization. Ensuring that expenditure and work activity do not proceed without authorization is a primary means of maintaining control over the project.

The **data collection process** works pretty much in reverse of the authorization flow. Work sections report their progress to their managers, who report up the hierarchy until ultimately the project manager receives summarized reports. These summary reports need to focus on problems and to identify accomplishments to date and current cost performance. The project manager needs to keep upper management informed. Upper management usually uses project information to merely keep informed of activities, unless things get so bad that canceling the project appears appropriate.

Because of the uncertain nature of information systems projects, change is to be expected. Management control through work authorization is a way to manage this change. Reasons for change include the following:

- Change in project scope and specification,
- Changes in design,
- Changes to improve rate of return,
- Changes to adopt improvements.

The owner may desire change in project scope and specification due to new circumstances. These can arise because of new regulations or changes in the market. Changes in design can occur if it is clear that the original plan won't work, or new technology may possibly be available now that is clearly better than what was known when the project was adopted. These changes can then arise because of errors, omissions, afterthoughts, or revised needs. Such changes can offer opportunities for improvement, but they may also open up opportunities for major foul-ups. Changes to improve the rate of return are a financial factor, where the owner has better things to do with the money required by the project.

Changes are troublesome for project teams. The more the project is completed, the more difficult it is to adopt changes. Changes can affect project scope, cost, and time, which, in turn, can lead to major sources of conflict. A change review process is a very good way to consider changes as rationally as possible. Changes should be avoided unless there are compelling reasons.

Project termination may be appropriate under a variety of circumstances. Sometimes the owner may determine that it is better to stop than to continue. This can be due to changes in the market, cost overruns, or depleted resources. When termination before completion occurs, there are a number of things that still need to be done. Final closeout activities need to be accomplished to ensure that the owner receives whatever he or she is entitled to and the project team gets their appropriate payment. There is also a need to coordinate with functional managers of the organization to return those individuals assigned to the project on a temporary basis. Other members of the project team may need to be reassigned, possibly to other projects.

Project Evaluation

Project evaluation is concerned with monitoring progress on a project. The ultimate output of project evaluation is the decision to continue with the project or to quit. There also is a need for after-action reports, providing a means to learn from the experiences of a project.

Formative evaluations refer to those that are used to control the project. Because projects involve so many interrelated activities, and are undertaken with limited resources, there can be many apparent reasons a particular activity or work package is not going well. Furthermore, it is very easy for management to think there is a problem when there really is not.

Meetings are very important in project control. Regular meetings in such an environment are well worth the time taken. There is a need within projects to maintain high levels of communication and coordination. Regularity leads to more thorough preparation on the part of participants. Helbrough[9] studied one project in detail, finding 368 meetings, ranging over time from the project definition phase through post-project evaluation. In this project, there were a total of 1,317 person-days of time exhausted in meetings. The largest meetings in terms of the number of people attending were in the early stages, during project design and planning phases. The most common type of meeting was for project assurance and quality review. There were repetitive project progress meetings, reviews at the end of milestones, and meetings driven by specific events.

Helbrough also discussed two distinct types of meetings that are used to manage projects. There are many *unstructured meetings* to coordinate activities, and fewer *structured meetings* to reach decisions.[10] Chapter 3 presented **group support systems (GSSs)** as applications of technology to hold meetings in a variety of forms, allowing project activities to progress more efficiently by increasing participation. Group support systems are especially good for brainstorming activities where there is a need to generate ideas. This type of meeting works best in a face-to-face environment, with computer software displaying comments as they are entered and allowing participants to score each comment. These scores can be used to sort ideas so that those receiving the most support can be considered first. Another form of group support system is a whiteboard system, where participants can post ideas at whatever time they find convenient. For meetings where the purpose is to inform, the whiteboard form of group support system can reduce or eliminate the time participants spend in meetings.

After-action evaluations involve first classifying completed projects into categories of success and failure. Management needs to understand why successful projects worked as well as they did. The reason could be especially favorable external conditions or could also be due to especially effective implementation by the project team. The key to success is to understand which is the truth for a given project.

It also is important for organizations that are continuously involved in projects of a given type to gather information about time and cost performance for specific work packages. These work packages should be measured in terms that occur across projects, so that the organization obtains knowledge about what doing a particular bit of work takes. This gives the organization a tremendous advantage over time relative to their competitors who either lack their experience or who fail to keep similar records.

Multiple-Project Environments

Many organizations have evolved into organizations that manage projects as the focus of their business. This has long been true in the construction industry, where firms develop skill and equipment expertise that can be applied to a type of work, giving them a competitive advantage. It has also been true for a long time in the accounting field, where large firms develop a pool of experts in various fields who can then be utilized on the problems of many firms. Information system project management has evolved from the accounting field, with many firms offering expertise that is available for hire. This is probably the most common form of outsourcing, applying expertise from consulting firms for specific problems within organizations. The matrix form of organization discussed in Chapter 8 is especially appropriate in this environment, with pools of experts trained to a high state of development in their specialty, available on call to cope with work as it is acquired.

Payne[11] found evidence that up to 90 percent of all projects occur in a multiple-project environment. Projects in this environment tend to be smaller than projects found in other environments. The reason for dealing with multiple projects is to share key resources, which would otherwise be underutilized. Critical resources of this type would be the bottlenecks that Goldratt[12] used as the top priority in scheduling. The scheduling of projects subject to resource smoothing was discussed in Chapter 6. In addition to the complications involved with scheduling critical resources, there are additional sources of change in multiple-project environments. As new projects are obtained and old projects encounter difficulties, the priority for use of critical resources is liable to change. For instance, a key production crew might have originally been scheduled to work on a project for the first three weeks in March. After one week of this work was completed, an emergency requirement might arise where this crew could help. Top management has to decide whether to disrupt this current project to fix the problems on the one with the emergency. It often makes economic sense to have one project suffer for the greater good of the firm overall. Management is responsible for setting priorities and determining which projects will receive top priority.

To demonstrate the problems involved in multiple-project management, assume a consulting firm performs work requiring three crews (design, production, and training). To simplify matters, assume the firm's projects all involve three activities, performed in sequence. Therefore, for each project, the design crew performs its work, which must be completed before the production crew can start its work, which, in turn, must be completed before the training crew does its work. Currently the firm has three projects in progress, as shown in Table 10–3. The current schedule selected by management (showing only 30 weeks) is shown in Table 10–4. After the second week, the firm has completed its work as planned, and obtained two new jobs as shown in Table 10–5.

This plan is unfeasible within available resources. Therefore, another production crew, the critical resource, is developed. New people are to be hired and trained, a three-week process (indicated by the letter "t") required before they can begin productive work (see Table 10–6):

In weeks 3 and 4, problems were encountered in the production of project C, which appear to require an additional three weeks. This forces rescheduling production for project A. Once training is announced, it can be delayed, but it cannot be shifted back because trainees need to coordinate their schedules. Therefore, training has to be left as scheduled. Rescheduling production for project A to keep it within its schedule shifts production for project E back. Project E is then delayed beyond its deadline. The firm has meanwhile picked up projects F and G (see Table 10–7).

At this stage, it is clear that the firm is losing much of its slack resources. Project D will not be completed on time even if everything goes according to schedule (or earlier). After week 6, two new projects (H and I) have been obtained, but project F has been canceled. Training on project C has been delayed for two weeks because of trainee scheduling conflicts (see Table 10–8).

TABLE 10–3   Example Firm—Three Projects

Project	Design	Production	Training	Deadline
A	4 weeks (completed)	7 weeks	3 weeks	Week 20
B	3 weeks	5 weeks	1 week	Week 10
C	1 week	4 weeks	1 week	Week 10

TABLE 10–4   Current Schedule

	W	e	e	k																									
	1	2	3	4	5	6	7	8	9	10	11	12	13	14	15	16	17	18	19	20	21	22	23	24	25	26	27	28	29	30
Design	C	B	B	B																										
Production	A	C	C	C	C	B	B	B	B	B	A	A	A	A	A	A														
Training						C					B						A	A	A											

TABLE 10–5   New Jobs and Schedule

Project	Design	Production	Training	Deadline
D	5 weeks	9 weeks	3 weeks	Week 30
E	4 weeks	6 weeks	3 week	Week 20

Week	1	2	3	4	5	6	7	8	9	10	11	12	13	14	15	16	17	18	19	20	21	22	23	24	25	26	27	28	29	30
Design	C	B	B	B	E	E	E	E	D	D	D	D	D																	
Production	A	C	C	C	C	B	B	B	B	B	A	A	A	A	A	A	E	E	E	E	E	E	D	D	D	D	D	D	D	D
Training						C					B						A	A	A				E	E	E					

TABLE 10–6   Additional Production Crew

Week	1	2	3	4	5	6	7	8	9	10	11	12	13	14	15	16	17	18	19	20	21	22	23	24	25	26	27	28	29	30
Design	C	B	B	B	E	E	E	E	D	D	D	D	D																	
Production 1	A	C	C	C	C	B	B	B	B	B	A	A	A	A	A	A	A	D	D	D	D	D	D	D	D					
Production 2						t	t	t	E	E	E	E	E	E																
Training						C					B				E	E	E	A	A	A						D	D	D		

TABLE 10–7   Addition of Projects F and G

Project	Design	Production	Training	Deadline
F	2 weeks	5 weeks	2 weeks	Week 30
G	4 weeks	7 weeks	3 week	Week 30

Week	1	2	3	4	5	6	7	8	9	10	11	12	13	14	15	16	17	18	19	20	21	22	23	24	25	26	27	28	29	30
Design	C	B	B	B	E	E	E	E	D	D	D	D	D	F	F	G	G	G	G											
Production 1	A	C	C	C	C	C	C	C	C	B	B	B	B	B	E	E	E	E	E	E	D	D	D	D	D	D	D	D	D	
Production 2						t	t	t	A	A	A	A	A	A			F	F	F	F	F	G	G	G	G	G	G	G		
Training									C					B	A	A	A			E	E	E	F	F				G	G	G

TABLE 10–8   Addition of Projects H and I

Project	Design	Production	Training	Deadline
H	5 weeks	9 weeks	4 weeks	Week 40
I	3 weeks	6 weeks	2 week	Week 30

Week	1	2	3	4	5	6	7	8	9	10	11	12	13	14	15	16	17	18	19	20	21	22	23	24	25	26	27	28	29	30
Design	C	B	B	B	E	E	E	E	D	D	D	D	D	G	G	G	G	I	I	I	H	H	H	H	H					
Production 1	A	C	C	C	C	C	C	C	B	B	B	B	B	E	E	E	E	E	D	D	D	D	D	D	D	D	D		H	H
Production 2					t	t	t	A	A	A	A	A	A				G	G	G	G		G	G	G	I	I	I	I	I	I
Training									C					B	A	A	A			E	E	E				G	G	G	D	D

We leave the schedule at this point. Projects D, E, and I clearly have trouble meeting their deadlines. At the added cost of training new crews, some of this could be alleviated, but not necessarily at the lowest cost. The point overall is that multiple-project environments have high levels of uncertainty because new jobs are acquired (and possibly canceled) that make optimized and densely packed resource schedules highly unrealistic. Here we only hypothesized minor duration extension, whereas in reality, delays can occur of much greater consequence. Added complications of redirecting experienced crews to priority projects in the middle of work tasks can create additional chaos. Overall, operating in a multiple-project environment is an extremely interesting endeavor.

Summary

Project control is a means to guide project efforts toward achievement of project goals. A primary means of control is to compare actual work with planned accomplishments. This requires accurate data collection and efficient dissemination of project reports.

There are many reasons for project failure. Consideration of the failures of others is needed to increase the probability of success of a specific project. High levels of uncertainty and change require flexible project management. Experience and preparation help increase the odds of project success.

Project risk management needs to be applied throughout the life cycle of the project. Consideration of risk is important when the project is initially considered for adoption and is implemented by estimating what could go wrong in developing the project. In the organization stages of the project, there are a number of things project management can do to ensure that good people are assigned, that estimates are realistic, that contingency options are available should problems arise, and that project components delivered by those outside the project organization are received in a timely fashion and perform to specifications. During the building of the project, original time and cost budgets need to be compared with actual performance to determine if problems are arising. It is important not only to understand that problems exist but to plan for ways of dealing with the problems that are identified.

Project control should clearly identify responsibilities for work packages and use these work packages as the basis of cost accounting. The authorization process ensures that management retains control over the project. There is a need to constantly update projected performances so that that top management has a complete picture and is capable of making decisions to continue the project based on sound, objective information.

Project evaluation provides organizations that deal with a continuous stream of projects the ability to develop a database of knowledge by work package. This gives such an organization a tremendous edge relative to competitors unable to do the same. Furthermore, careful analysis of post-action success or failure enables organizations to better understand their work environment.

The problems of managing multiple projects arise in most large organizations. The biggest difference in one large project versus many smaller projects is that in the large project, the project team is able to focus on attaining one set of objectives. In a multiple-project environment, scarce resources need to be shared by many competing projects, and hard decisions have to be made to further overall organizational goals rather than focusing on the goals of specific projects.

Key Terms

after-action evaluations   241
assessment   231
authorization   239
benchmarking   234
control   236
corrective action   236
data collection process   239
earned value concept   237
formative evaluations   240
high change threshold   234
incremental development   235

mission analysis   235
performance standards   236
planning   236
pre-award audits   234
reference checking   234
requirements scrubbing   235
standard time unit   237
technical analysis   235
variance analysis   237
work packages   237

Exercises

1. How would the systems failure method discussed in Chapter 3 provide a tool to better control projects?
2. When is prototyping an appropriate method to develop systems intended to support decision making in unstructured environments?
3. Discuss the different tactics required to obtain good project personnel in a project organization as opposed to a matrix organization.
4. How can the Delphi technique contribute to team building?
5. Are there any conflicts in the aims of design flexibility and having a high change threshold?
6. How would designing projects to a given budget help manage risk?
7. When would requirements scrubbing be appropriate?
8. What is the relationship between risk assessment and resource buffers used in project scheduling?
9. Discuss the difference between planning and control.
10. What role do standards play in control?

11. What is the role of variance analysis in control?
12. Describe the concept of earned value.
13. Given the following data concerning budgeted and accomplished work, calculated earned value.

Work Package	Budgeted	Percent Complete	Rate	Earned Value
Systems analysis	8 weeks	100	$600/wk	
Programming	15 weeks	80	$500/wk	
Testing	4 weeks	50	$700/wk	
Install	2 weeks	0	$650/wk	

14. If actual times in Problem 13 were 12 weeks for systems analysis, 12 weeks for programming, and 3 weeks for testing, calculate estimated efficiency at this point.
15. How does authorization provide control?
16. What is the role of meetings in project control?
17. A firm is considering installation of an enterprise resource planning system to serve the entire organization. The current proposal involves initial expenditure of $400,000 (for the basic software module, along with six weeks of training). This option would require the firm to hire three additional people, whose cost including fringes and support the first year would be $300,000. This expense is expected to increase 5 percent per year over the five years of project evaluation. The benefit of this system is that it is expected to eliminate the need for an estimated $400,000 worth of projects per year (to be inflated at 10 percent per year). It is estimated that there will be a 0.9 probability that there will be no installation or implementation problems. If there are problems, the cost to the company would be $800,000 in Year 1.

A buy-up alternative would cost $750,000 initially and would involve added personnel expense of five people, or $500,000 the first year, inflating at the rate of 5 percent per year. The benefit is expected to be reduction of an estimated $600,000 per year in projects, inflating at 10 percent per year. There is an estimated 0.95 probability that no problems will be encountered in installation and implementation, with the same cost of $800,000 in Year 1 if problems are experienced.

The buy-down alternative would cost the firm $100,000 the first year. Only two people would need to be hired at a cost of $100,000 the first year (inflating at the rate of 5 percent per year). Benefits from this approach would only be $250,000 per year (inflating at 10 percent per year). There would be a 0.7 probability of successful installation. If installation and implementation failed, the same cost of $800,000 in Year 1 would be experienced.

The marginal value of capital for the firm is 15 percent.

Microsoft Project Exercise

Enter the original plan for the multiple projects demonstrated in this chapter in *Microsoft Project*. Enter each project as an activity.

For the project entered in Chapters 3 and 4, and updated in Chapter 9, generate a "Who Does What" table using the following sequence:

View	Reports	Assignments	Who Does What

This chart displays all activities by resource.

For the project entered in Chapters 3 and 4, and updated in Chapter 9, identify expenditures to date.

View	Reports	Costs	Budget

Endnotes

1. E. Lin and C.-T. Hsieh, "The Seven Deadly Risk Factors," *Journal of Systems Management,* November/December 1995, pp. 45–52.
2. The following discussion is based on B. Boehm, *Software Risk Management* (Washington, DC: IEEE Computer Society Press, 1989).
3. Ibid.
4. E. M. Goldratt, *Critical Chain* (Great Barrington, MA: The North River Press, 1997).
5. P. Sharpe and T. Keelin, "How SmithKline Beecham Makes Better Resource-Allocation Decisions," *Harvard Business Review,* March–April 1998, pp. 45–57.
6. E. S. Andersen, "Warning: Activity Planning Is Hazardous to Your Project's Health," *International Journal of Project Management* 14, no. 2 (1996), pp. 89–94.
7. Goldratt, *Critical Chain.*
8. F. P. Brooks, Jr., *The Mythical Man-Month: Essays on Software Engineering,* anniversary edition (Reading, MA: Addison-Wesley, 1995).
9. B. Helbrough, "Computer Assisted Collaboration—The Fourth Dimension of Project Management," *International Journal of Project Management* 13, no. 5 (1995), pp. 329–33.
10. Ibid.
11. J. H. Payne, "Management of Multiple Simultaneous Projects: A State-of-the-Art Review," *International Journal of Project Management* 13, no. 3 (1995), pp. 163–68.
12. Goldratt, *Critical Chain.*

MICROSOFT PROJECT 2000 UPDATE

Microsoft® Project 2000 is the sixth Windows® operating system. A companion product, Microsoft Project Central, has been introduced as a web-based collaboration tool. New features of Microsoft Project 2000 are intended to provide added support in the following areas. Microsoft can provide details for additional enhancements and their capabilities.

IMPROVE TEAM PRODUCTIVITY

Collaborative Planning

    Personal Gantt charts can be developed for each team member's own tasks across multiple projects.

    View Nonworking Time: Team members can report nonworking time such as vacation or sick leave.

    Workgroup: Project managers can assign task responsibilities and track project status across workgroups.

Collaborative Tracking with Microsoft Project Central

    Status Reports: Users can create custom report formats.

Easy Access to Project Information

    Offline Capabilities: Team members can take timesheets and status reports offline.

INCREASE USEFULNESS OF PROJECT DATA

Flexible Viewing

    Grouping: Users can categorize task and resource information as needed.

    Network Diagram: (Former PERT Chart)—new filtering and layout options

    Fiscal Year in Timescale:

Flexible Analysis

    Task Outline Level: Much easier to expand and collapse task outline structure.

    Task Calendars: Task-specific calendars can be used to affect only selected tasks.

    Materials Resources: Users can specify consumable resources.

    Deadline Dates:

    Cross-Project Critical Path:

    Custom Fields—Value Lists: Users can define pick lists to restrict values that can be entered.

    Custom Fields—Formulas: Conditional testing and functions can be applied.

    Estimated Durations: Users can indicate that a duration is tentative.

    Month Duration: Can specify months as time unit.

    Contoured Resource Availability: Time-phased resources can be used.

    Leveling: Better control and faster performance.

Task and Project Priority: Now 1,000 unique priority levels.

Work Breakdown Structure: Can format and number WBS.

Scaling and Printing: More efficient printing, new printing and scaling options.

Enhanced User Confidence

Adaptive Menus: Only items users often use are prominently featured on the menu.

Autosave: Can set time interval for automatic backup.

Project Management Across the Organization

Improved database performance

Improved resource pooling

Improved ability to insert projects

Improved Visual Basic for Applications (VBA)

Microsoft Project

Chapter Outline

Main Ideas Discussed

- Basic introduction to *Microsoft Project* features

The past two decades have seen the development of many excellent project management software products. *Microsoft Project* is easy to use and is widely available. *Microsoft Project* provides excellent quantitative support in the form of critical path and PERT, develops network graphs automatically, and has very good report generating facilities. It also has resource usage and cost accounting capabilities. The manager can use *Microsoft Project* to do sophisticated analysis of alternatives through resource leveling.

This chapter is meant to provide a brief introductory guide to *Microsoft Project*. There are a number of versions of *Microsoft Project*. Each may involve slightly different syntax. A book takes about two years to print. The author was hoping that this book would last a few years after publication. Over that period, there will be many new versions of *Microsoft Project*, as well as many other good new competing products. The general procedure of *Microsoft Project* is fairly similar for all versions. For details, please refer to *Microsoft Project* help, as well as the manual.

251

Getting Started

The first step is to set up the project time frame. The project start date can be entered by clicking on the Project menu, and then clicking on "Project Information." There is a box for the start date and for the finish date if there is a deadline. The standard base calendar works Monday through Friday, 8:00 A.M. to 5:00 P.M. (eight working hours), and uses early start scheduling. These settings can be changed. Working days can be specified through the project calendar. On the Tools menu, click on "Change Working Time." You are presented one monthly calendar. Other months can be accessed by the down arrow or up arrow. For any particular day you wish to declare a holiday, you click on the day and are given a window including a radio button for "*non-working time.*"

Project information can be entered and manipulated in a variety of views. There are two types of views: task views and resource views. Task information can be entered, changed, or displayed in a number of ways. The default is to set the current date as the project start date, as well as the start date of the first task.

Tasks

The **Gantt chart** view gives the task form on the left, with a list of project tasks with room for durations and time units, predecessor activities, and a bar chart (Figure A–1). Tasks can be entered by row, entering the name and duration for each task in the appropriate column. Tasks can be inserted or deleted using the Edit menu. There are columns for start time, finish time, and predecessors (which may be hidden and can be uncovered by sliding the task form to the right). Duration unit syntax is the number followed by the time unit. The abbreviations are as follows:

m = Minutes
h = Hours
d = Days
w = Weeks

To enter a duration of 6 weeks, the entry would be **6w**. Elapsed time units can be entered to disregard weekends and other nonworking periods. If you need to schedule a task over a continuous period of time that includes nonworking time, an elapsed duration can be used. If a task is to take 10 calendar days, beginning on Monday and ending on the following Wednesday, the elapsed time would be 10 elapsed days. Elapsed durations are entered by preceding the time units with the letter "e." For instance, if a task is to take 10 calendar days, the entry for duration would be **10ed.**

The approach just presented in the figure is fixed duration. Fixed duration is obtained by selecting the Fixed check box on the task form or typing yes in the Fixed Field of a task table. Task durations can be based on the amount of work

Figure A–1

Gantt chart view

		Task Name	Duration	Predecessors
1		Identify products available	1 wk	
2		Literature search	2 wks	1
3		Contact vendors	3 wks	1
4		Analyze literature	2 wks	2SS+1 wk,3SS+
5		Identify needed features	0 days	
6		Interview managers	2 wks	5
7		Interview systems manage	3 wks	5
8		Develop systems specificat	6 wks	6,7
9		Identify costs	6 wks	3,8
10		Obtain vendor bids	9 wks	9
11		Develop in-house estimate	12 wks	9
12		Management selection	1 wk	10,11
13		Decision	1 wk	12
14		Systems analysis	0 days	13
15		Impact on existing system	2 wks	14
16		Needed equipment	3 wks	15,18,20
17		Network	2 wks	16
18		Needed software	3 wks	14
19		Programming	5 wks	17
20		Data access	4 wks	14
21		Design reports	6 wks	14
22		Installation	2 wks	19
23		Testing	2 wks	22
24		Acceptance	1 wk	23
25		Training	0 days	13
26		Develop Program	6 wks	25
27		Print manuals	2 wks	26
28		Deliver training	4 wks	27
29		Monitor use	12 wks	24,28
30		Modification	6 wks	29

required and the number of resource units assigned to it if resource-driven scheduling is used. If this is not done, when multiple resources are assigned to a task, *Microsoft Project* will divide the entered duration by the number of resources assigned. This is appropriate in many other environments but is generally not appropriate in information systems projects. Therefore, resource-driven scheduling should be turned off. This may require clicking on each task on the Gantt Chart view, and clearing the "Effort Driven" box for each task.

Predecessor relationships (along with durations) are all that there is to the critical path model. The conventional predecessor relationship is finish-to-start (a following activity cannot start until all predecessors are complete). In reality, other relationships might be appropriate, such as start-to-start (SS), where a following activity can start as soon as its predecessor begins; finish-to-finish (FF), where a following activity cannot finish until its predecessor finishes; or start-to-finish (SF), where a following activity cannot finish until its predecessor starts. All of these relationships can be used in *Microsoft Project*. In the Predecessor column, list the number of all predecessor activities. If activity 1 is a predecessor to activity 2, for activity 2 the predecessor is 1. The default is finish-to-start, and this does not have to be specified. For any of the other three relationships, specification is entered using the two-letter qualifier. For instance, if there is a finish-to-finish relationship, the predecessor for activity 2 would be 1FF.

Sometimes following activities can start before the predecessor activity is completed. For instance, if activity 2 can start after five days of activity 1 is completed, the predecessor relationship for activity 2 would be 1SS+5d. There is also a Lag column that can be used on the Task Information window that can be accessed by double clicking on the activity and selecting the Predecessors tab.

Tasks can also be entered on the PERT Chart, the Task Form, or the Task Sheet. The **critical path** is the set of activities on a connected path that must be completed as estimated, or the project completion time will be delayed. The critical path can be identified by using the Gantt Chart Wizard button on the top menu. If not in the Gantt Chart view, on the View Bar select Gantt Chart. Then click on the "Gantt Chart Wizard," a button with a wand on it. The initial screen has a "NEXT" button to click. You are then presented with a set of options, including a radio button for Critical Path Tasks. Click this radio button on, and select "FINISH." The Gantt Chart will now display critical tasks in a distinctive color or bar code as in Figure A–2.

The **PERT chart** view gives a network diagram of tasks and task relationships (Figure A–3). On the PERT chart, tasks can be entered and related to other tasks using the mouse. Tasks that are critical are displayed in red. Milestones are displayed in double boxes. The PERT chart view gives the best graphical description of predecessor relationships. Within each box the task identification number, duration, start time and finish time are reported.

FIGURE A–2

Gantt chart view with critical path

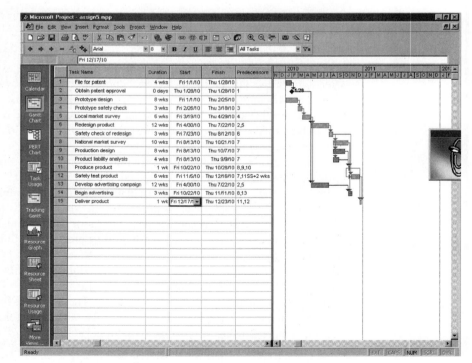

The Task Sheet is a spreadsheet format. It can be used to quickly create a list of tasks and information and to assign resources. It also can be used to review progress by comparing planned and actual progress. You can enter task start dates and finish dates directly if you want, but these will lock that activity into the given time frame. Usually, project management intent is best met by letting the software calculate the start dates and finish dates from the duration and predecessor input.

The Task Form allows you to enter task name with duration, one task at a time. The Task Form is displayed to the left of the Gantt Chart on the prior page. There are boxes to enter the task information, including the percentage complete. Resources required can also be entered on the Task Form.

The Task PERT Chart is a focused view of the PERT Chart, showing the immediate predecessors and successors for a specific task.

To use the PERT method, you need to calculate estimated durations by hand and enter those. The probabilistic PERT approach is covered in the *Microsoft Project* assignment in Chapter 7. You also can do critical path with *Microsoft Project* by inserting columns and selecting "Early Start," "Early Finish," "Late Start," "Late Finish," and "Slack" from the menu of columns.

Calendar

The Calendar view gives a monthly calendar showing tasks and durations (Figure A–4). This view can be used to show the tasks scheduled in a specific time period.

FIGURE A–3

The PERT chart

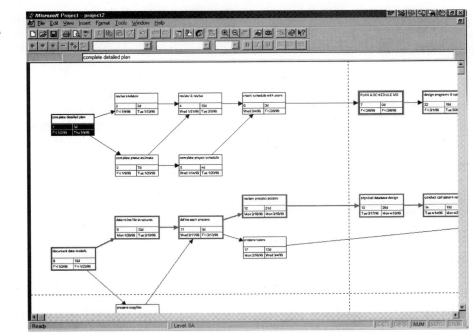

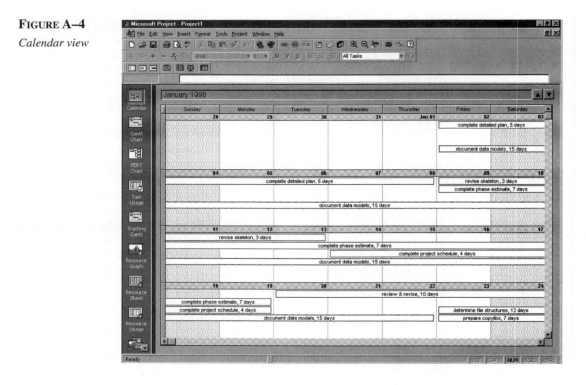

The Calendar view is obtained from the View menu. The Calendar can be used to review tasks scheduled on particular time periods, to enter tasks and durations, and to assign resources.

Nonwork days are shaded. Unfinished activities are shown on weekends in this view, but work is not accomplished on those days (see complete detail plan, scheduled for five days of work, on the 2nd, 5th, 6th, 7th, and 8th, but not the 3rd or 4th. If you want to enter January 1 as a holiday, you can adjust the calendar).

To select a calendar, select the Options menu, and choose "Base Calendars," "Standard," and the "Edit" button. You can scroll up or down to other months. To change selected days to working days, use the Tools menu item, and select "Change Working Time." Click on the specific day in question, and days can be made working or nonworking by clicking the appropriate radio button. In this case, holidays for January 1, January 19, November 26, and December 25, 1998, can be made nonworking days.

Resources

The Resource Sheet shows data about each resource in the project in a spreadsheet view. Resources can be entered, modified, or sorted (Figure A–5). Cost, usage, and work information can be entered. Insert and Delete commands can be selected

FIGURE A–5

Resource sheet

	Resource Name	Initials	Group	Max. Units	Std. Rate	Ovt. Rate	Cost/Use	Accrue At	Base Calendar	Code
1	asst	a		1	$150.00/d	$0.00/h	$0.00	Prorated	Standard	
2	SA	s		1	$450.00/d	$0.00/h	$0.00	Prorated	Standard	
3	est	e		1	$300.00/d	$0.00/h	$0.00	Prorated	Standard	
4	MAN	M		1	$500.00/d	$0.00/h	$0.00	Prorated	Standard	
5	dba	d		1	$500.00/d	$0.00/h	$0.00	Prorated	Standard	
6	dbd1	d		1	$400.00/d	$0.00/h	$0.00	Prorated	Standard	
7	dbd2	d		1	$400.00/d	$0.00/h	$0.00	Prorated	Standard	
8	p1	p		1	$300.00/d	$0.00/h	$0.00	Prorated	Standard	
9	p2	p		1	$300.00/d	$0.00/h	$0.00	Prorated	Standard	
10	p3	p		1	$300.00/d	$0.00/h	$0.00	Prorated	Standard	

from the Edit menu. The Resource Sheet includes columns for full resource name, initials, a group to assign the resource to, the maximum units for each resource, and standard and overtime cost rates. In this case, costs were entered by day. No overtime was used. If overtime rates were paid, the rate can be entered in the Ovt. Rate column.

Resources may be assigned by *Microsoft Project* in an effort-driven mode. This means that if you have multiple resources assigned to an activity, *Microsoft Project* will take the liberty of dividing the duration you entered by the number of resources. You can turn off effort-driven scheduling from the Tools menu, clicking on "Options," the "Schedule" tab, and clearing the box for "New tasks are effort driven."

The Resource Graph shows resource allocation of a particular resource by time (Figure A–6). This view shows the user which resources are overallocated, and by how much, as well as showing the percentage of usage capacity for those resources not overallocated.

Overscheduled resources are shown in red on *Microsoft Project*. In this case, we can see that the one systems analyst available is overscheduled. In fact, we need three systems analysts in mid-January.

There is a resource graph for each resource. The arrow buttons at the bottom on the left scroll through these resources. The arrow buttons at the bottom on the right scroll through time. The drop-down menu on the top allows selection of a particular resource.

FIGURE A–6

Resource graph

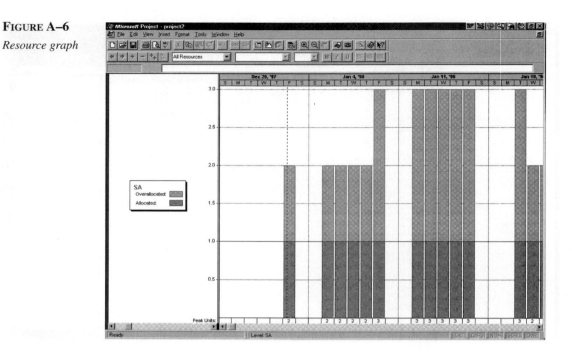

Resource Usage lists resources showing allocation, cost, or work information by time (Figure A–7). The rate at which resources are used each day is shown. In this case, overused resources can be detected in tabular form whenever more than eight hours are scheduled in a given day. In this case, resource SA is over-scheduled.

Reports

Microsoft Project allows printing of views and of reports. Views that can be printed include the Gantt chart, the PERT chart, Resource Graph, Resource Sheet, Resource Usage, and Task Sheet. Views can be customized by tables, filters, and sorting. There are seven basic reports to print.

The Project Summary report covers all tasks (Figure A–8). It is accessed by the View menu item and then selecting "Reports." A set of options are provided, the first of which is Overview. This option contains, in addition to the project summary, reports that can be obtained for top-level tasks, critical tasks, milestones, and working days. The other options besides Overview are Current Activities, Costs, Assignments, Workload, and Custom.

You can set up pages and add legends, headers, and footers.

FIGURE A–7

Resource usage

FIGURE A–8

Project summary report

Leveling Resources

One of the most powerful tools available in *Microsoft Project* is **resource leveling.** You have options to prioritize tasks and have the ability to specify tasks that are not to be delayed because of resource shortage. The standard leveling method checks predecessor relationships, slack time, dates, priority, and task constraints to select tasks to delay. You have the ability to set priorities. To change resource leveling criteria, select the Options menu, and "Leveling." The Automatic option will level resources as soon as they become overallocated. If you want to bar delaying the project completion date, the "Delay Only Within Slack" box can be checked. The "Order" box gives you the ability to change criteria.

Automatic leveling delays tasks that have not been given a constraint of Must Start On, Must Finish On, or As Late As Possible. Automatic leveling will not delay tasks if Do Not Level has been selected for the task. Those tasks that have been started are not delayed. Delays are assigned considering slack time, start date, priority, and task constraints.

Manual leveling can be set by selecting the Options menu, "Leveling," and "Manual." If this option was selected, the "Level Now" command can be selected from the Options menu. The user can then delay activities to alleviate resource overusage. You can also resolve resource shortages by assigning overtime, or adding resources.

Updating Project Progress

Schedules can be updated on the task and resource forms. Before updating, it is wise to save the original project plan under a unique file name. A **baseline** plan can also be saved using the Set Plan command from the Options menu. A baseline contains the original schedule, resource usage and cost estimates. Updating a baseline plan can be accomplished on the Task Form to the left of the Gantt chart view. Place the cursor on the task to be updated, and type Shift-F2. This gives the Task Form where the percent complete can be entered in its box, and the total revised estimated time can be entered in its box. Note that these two parameters need to be carefully calibrated so that the intended effect is obtained. Another way to update task usage is from the View bar, selecting "Task Usage," View menu, "Table," "Tracking," dragging the divider bar to the right to view the Actual Work field, and typing the updated work value and duration as appropriate.

Work completed can be entered in the task form under % Complete. The duration can be changed to reflect new circumstances. Changes in durations can be made in the duration column. The percent complete can also be set on the Gantt chart using the mouse. From View, select "Gantt chart." Point to the left edge of a scheduled duration bar or the right edge of the progress bar. Drag the mouse until you have the percent complete you desire. You can also update using a percentage complete for each task (Figure A–9).

	Task Name	Duration	Start	Finish	% Comp.	Cost
1	complete detailed plan	5d	Fri 1/2/98	Thu 1/8/98	100%	$3,000.00
2	revise skeleton	3d	Fri 1/9/98	Tue 1/13/98	100%	$1,350.00
3	complete phase estimate	7d	Fri 1/9/98	Tue 1/20/98	100%	$5,250.00
4	review & revise	10d	Wed 1/21/98	Tue 2/3/98	70%	$9,000.00
5	complete project schedule	4d	Wed 1/14/98	Tue 1/20/98	100%	$1,800.00
6	check schedule with users	3d	Wed 2/4/98	Fri 2/6/98	0%	$3,300.00
7	PLAN & SCHEDULE MS	0d	Fri 2/6/98	Fri 2/6/98	0%	$0.00
8	document data models	15d	Fri 1/2/98	Fri 1/23/98	100%	$6,750.00
9	determine file structures	12d	Mon 1/26/98	Tue 2/10/98	33%	$4,800.00
10	prepare copylibs	7d	Mon 1/26/98	Tue 2/3/98	86%	$2,800.00
11	define each process	3d	Wed 2/11/98	Fri 2/13/98	0%	$2,550.00
12	review process access	21d	Mon 2/16/98	Mon 3/16/98	0%	$35,700.00
13	physical database design	20d	Tue 3/17/98	Mon 4/13/98	0%	$16,000.00
14	conduct call pattern reviews	10d	Tue 4/14/98	Mon 4/27/98	0%	$8,000.00
15	check plan with users	3d	Tue 4/28/98	Thu 4/30/98	0%	$3,750.00
16	DATABASE DESIGN MS	0d	Thu 4/30/98	Thu 4/30/98	0%	$0.00
17	prepare specs	13d	Mon 2/16/98	Wed 3/4/98	0%	$5,850.00
18	determine security specs	8d	Fri 5/1/98	Tue 5/12/98	0%	$6,800.00
19	prepare physical system flow	12d	Wed 5/13/98	Thu 5/28/98	0%	$10,200.00
20	check db design with users	2d	Fri 5/29/98	Mon 6/1/98	0%	$3,100.00
21	PHYSICAL DESIGN MS	0d	Mon 6/1/98	Mon 6/1/98	0%	$0.00
22	design programs & specs	18d	Fri 5/1/98	Tue 5/26/98	0%	$15,300.00
23	write data conversion	36d	Wed 5/27/98	Wed 7/15/98	0%	$32,400.00
24	test	15d	Thu 7/16/98	Wed 8/5/98	0%	$20,250.00
25	check pd with users	2d	Thu 7/16/98	Fri 7/17/98	0%	$3,400.00
26	PROGRAM MS	0d	Wed 8/5/98	Wed 8/5/98	0%	$0.00
27	implement	20d	Thu 8/6/98	Wed 9/2/98	0%	$15,000.00
28	test	15d	Thu 9/3/98	Wed 9/23/98	0%	$20,250.00
29	TURNOVER	0d	Wed 9/23/98	Wed 9/23/98	0%	$0.00

Bars are shown on the Gantt chart to indicate work completed, which gives a good graphical view of the status of project tasks. For instance, activities 4 and 9 are running behind schedule. On the other hand, activity 10 is running ahead of schedule.

Milestones are points in the project that indicate completion of a significant block of activities and provide another way to monitor project progress. Milestones can be entered in *Microsoft Project* as tasks with zero duration, with those tasks finishing the block as predecessors.

Different versions of the package may have different ways to enter the data. The help facility will tell you how to update work complete. A way that works with the most recent version is to ask for Views from the top ribbon, More Views from the menu list, Task Form from the next menu list, and click on the "Apply" button. There will be a task form for each activity, with a % Complete window on the right side of the form, second row. Percentage complete can be entered directly in this window. There are "NEXT" and "PREVIOUS" buttons to move to other activities.

The software also includes a great deal of filtering ability. At the right end of the standard toolbar ribbon across the top of the *Microsoft Project* window is a formatting toolbar for filtering, which initially lists "All Tasks." This filtering can be used to get views of specific activities, such as those that are completed, or those that are over budget. Options available are accessed by clicking on the down arrow to the right of "All Tasks."

Summary

Microsoft Project is a valuable project management tool. It provides one of the most flexible and user-friendly systems for generating critical path analysis. There are a variety of views to determine project status, and resource usage. It has a variety of printing functions that give the user the ability to communicate this same information to others.

This material was meant to get you started on *Microsoft Project*. There is a great deal more information in system help, documentation and other materials produced by the developer of *Microsoft Project*.

Key Terms

baseline	260	milestone	261
critical path	254	PERT chart	254
Gantt chart	252	resource leveling	260

Exercises

1. Use the software to develop an initial schedule for the following project, to include an early start schedule. (Use January 2, 2010, as the first day of the project, working five days per week, with holidays on January 1, July 4, the 4th Thursday in November and December 25.)

Identifier	Activity	Predecessor	Days	Resource
A1	Identify products available	None	5	Asst
A2	Literature search	A1	10	Asst
A3	Contact vendors	A1	15	Asst
A4	Analyze literature	A2, A3	10*	Asst
A5	Milestone A	A4	0	

NOTE: Activity A4 can start 5 days after the start of both A2 and A3

B1	Interview managers	None	10	Asst
B2	Interview systems management	None	15	Asst
B3	Develop system specifications	A5, B1, B2	30	SA1, SA2
B4	Milestone B	B3	0	
C1	Identify costs	A3, B4	30	CE1
C2	Obtain vendor bids	C1	45	CE1
C3	Develop in-house estimate	C1	60	CE1
C4	Management makes selection	C2, C3	5	Mgr, CE1, SA1
C5	Milestone C	C4	0	
D1	Decision	C5	1	Mgr

Identifier	Activity	Predecessor	Days	Resource
Systems Analysis				
E1	Impact on existing system	D1	10	SA1
E2	Needed equipment	E1, E4, E6	15	SA1, NI1
E3	Network	E2	10	NI1
E4	Needed software	D1	15	Asst, SA1, Pr1
E5	Programming	E3	25	Pr1, Pr2, Pr3
E6	Data access	D1	20	Asst, SA1
E7	Design reports	D1	30	Mgr, Asst, SA1
E8	Milestone E	E5, E7	0	
F1	Installation	E5	10	SA1, NI1, SI1
G1	Testing	F1	10	Asst, SA1, NI1, Pr1, SI1, QC1
H1	Acceptance	G1	1	Mgr, Asst, SA1, NI1, SI1, QC1
Training				
I1	Develop program	D1	30	Asst, Tr1
I2	Print manuals	I1	10	Tr1
I3	Deliver training	I2	20	Tr1
I4	Milestone I	I3	0	
J1	Monitor use	H1, I4	60	Asst, Tr1
K1	Modification	J1	30	Mgr, SA1, QC1

240 working days per year

Resources	Cost/day	Resources	Cost/day
Mgr management representative	$500 (1)	Prn system programmers	$300 (10)
Asst assistant	$150 (1)	SIn software installer	$350 (2)
CEn cost estimator	$300 (2)	QCn quality control	$450 (3)
SAn systems analyst	$450 (5)	Trn trainers	$250 (2)
NIn network installer	$400 (3)		

    a. Schedule the project leveled to the currently available resources.

    b. Based on this plan, what is the expected project cost? (Labor is billed by time used on project: Assume low vendor bid for software of $100,000 at this time, and materials cost of $50,000, both of which must be added to personnel costs.)

    c. Are there any additional resources required? Make suggestions for how to do this.

    d. If the value of this system to the company was $250,000 per month, beginning with January 1, 2011, do you have any suggestions?

2. For Problem 1, assume that you have hired three additional assistants at $150/day each. Also assume that it has been decided to expedite activity B3 to 15 days total at an extra cost of $20,000.

    a. To expedite activity C3 to 40 days total at an extra cost of $10,000.

    b. To hire a training consultant to do activity I1 in five days at a cost of $30,000 (you will not have to use your trainers at $250/day, although you will need your assistant for activity I1 for 5 days).

    c. Reschedule the project. What is the expected cost now? What does this plan save over the original plan, in light of value to the company?

3. For the last revision of the project in Problem 2:

Assume that three months into the project (65 working days), the following has happened:

Activity		Expected	Actual	Status
A1	Identify products available	5	5	Done
A2	Literature search	10	8	Done
A3	Contact vendors	15	21	Done
A4	Analyze literature	10	19	Done
B1	Interview managers	10	12	Done
B2	Interview systems management	15	17	Done
B3	Develop systems specifications	15	15	Done
C1	Identify costs	30	30	67% done

The rest of the project is still pending. You have spent $17,000 in materials to date as planned, plus the prorated contracted amounts to speed up operations as planned.

Identify cost to date, and report on expected time completion and cost.

4. Develop the early start schedule for the following governmental project, to begin January 2, 2010.

Identifier	Activity	Predecessor	Duration (weeks)
1	Decision staffed and recorded	None	60
2	Environmental impact study	1	70
3	Licensing study for nuclear materials	1	60
4	Nuclear regulatory commission review	1	30
5	Conceptual design	1	36
6	Assure compliance with regulations	5	70
7	Site selection	1	40
8	Construction permit obtained	4, 6, 7	0
9	Construction	6, 8	100
10	Procurement	6SS, 9SS+5	70
11	Install equipment	9	72
12	Operating permit obtained	11	0
13	Cold start test	11	16
14	Readiness test	13	36
15	Hot test	14	16
16	Begin conversion operations	12, 15	0

Identify the Early Start, Early Finish, and Total Slack for each activity. (Insert a column, selecting Total Slack from the menu.)

5. Develop the early start schedule for the following product marketing project, to begin January 2, 2010.

Identifier	Activity	Predecessor	Duration (weeks)
1	File for patent	None	4
2	Obtain patent approval	1	0
3	Prototype design	None	8
4	Prototype safety check	3	3
5	Prototype approval	4	0
6	Local market survey	5	6
7	Redesign product	2, 6	12
8	Safety check of redesign	7	3
9	Local test	8	1
10	National market survey	9	10
11	Production design	9	8
12	Product liability analysis	9	4
13	Approve product	10, 11, 12	0
14	Produce product	13	1
15	Safety test product	14SS+2w	6
16	Approve production output	15	0
17	Develop advertising campaign	2, 6	12
18	Begin advertising	10, 17	3
19	Deliver product	16	1

Identify Early Start, Early Finish, and Total Slack for each activity.

6. Schedule the following project to install a supercomputer.

Identifier	Activity	Predecessor	Days
A1	Request for network connections	None	1
A2	Request for system connection	None	1
A3	Request multi-mode fiber connector	None	1
A4	Ethernet and fast ethernet installed	A1, A2, A3	3
A5	Request PO for electrical connections	None	2
A6	Install electrical connections	A5	5
A7	Request serial cable for console	None	1
A8	Make serial cable	A7	4
A9	Schedule down time	None	2
A10	Move MVS for supercomputer	A9	3
A11	Setup supercomputer	A4, A6, A8, A10	5
A12	Milestone	A11	0
B1	Verify hardware supported by Linux	None	1
B2	Obtain console hardware	B1	4
B3	Obtain Linux	B4	1
B4	Plan Linux installation	B1, B2	3
B5	Determine subsystems to be installed	B4	2

Identifier	Activity	Predecessor	Days
B6	Install Linux	B3, B5	3
B7	Configure	B6	2
B8	Test	B7	5
B9	Obtain and install necessary software	B7	12
B10	Deploy	B8, B9	2
B11	Connect to supercomputer	A12, B10	1
B12	Milestone	B11	0
C1	Create supercomputer platform in Claim	B12	1
C2	Create three accounts and tie to supercomputer	C1	1
C3	Tie student account to CAF funding	C2	1
C4	Tie Claim server to supercomputer manager	C3	2
C5	Setup system accounting on supercomputer	C4	5
C6	Pre-load overhead account	C5	2
C7	Sub-allocate three Claim accounts	C6	2
C8	Merge supercomputer accounts into system	C7	4
C9	Milestone	C8	0
D1	Setup basic NQS on supercomputer	B12	4
D2	Configure MISER	D1	2
D3	Integrate MISER in NQS	D2	2
D4	Configure checkpoint/restart	D1	2
D5	Integrate checkpoint/restart in NQS	D3, D4	2
D6	Milestone	D5	0
E1	Determine disk layout	B12	5
E2	Create disk layout	E1	1
E3	Install backup software and configure	B12	3
E4	Install SSH	B12	1
E5	Install TCP_wrappers	E4	1
E6	Install Tripwire	E5	1
E7	Install Crack	E6	1
E8	Install Tiger	E7	1
E9	SLM integration	B12	5
E10	Install third-party software	B12	9
F1	Create policies	B12	16
F2	Announcement of new system	E8	1
F3	Update web pages	E8	3
F4	Review short courses	E8	3
F5	Review user guides	E8	12

Provide a schedule by activity, and identify the critical path.

Glossary

After-action evaluations review of projects with the intent of identifying need for system changes 241

Assessment comparison of actual and planned system performance 231

Authorization control device where work is not started until authority approves starting 239

Baseline permanent record of initial plan, saved to compare with changed plans as the project develops 260

Baseline schedule synonymous with Baseline above 12

Benchmarking placing a system under a representative workload for purposes of evaluation 234

Brainstorming generating new ideas within a group by sharing ideas on an issue 67

Buffers time built into a schedule to allow for anticipated contingencies 150

Capability maturity model system developed by the Software Engineering Institute to identify the level of software development maturity of an organization 96

Cellular organization organization grouping specialty skills required to accomplish a specific set of work 199

Checklist project evaluation method using a list of minimum requirements 32

Checkpoint reviews meetings held at the conclusion of each project phase to determine if the rest of the project should be completed, or if modifications to the project are required 126

Coding (or acquisition) phase phase of a software project where the software is developed or purchased 108

Cold turkey approach implementation of a new system after disconnecting the old system 224

Conceptual design   description of the intended system in terms of its functional components   60

Conceptual integrity   inherent consistency within an object, focused on the object's purpose   129

Constructive cost model   software project estimation method based on a nonlinear regression against lines of code   134

Control   guiding efforts toward attainment of goals   236

Corrective action   modification of planned activities to respond to situations requiring change   236

Corresponding failure   failure of a system to meet its design objectives   216

Cost/benefit analysis   evaluation of benefits and costs in monetary terms, either as a ratio or a difference   12, 34, 109

Cost risk   project risk with respect to cost overruns   202

Crashing   compressing an activity duration at a cost   153

Critical activity   activity which has no slack   126

Critical path   chain of activities with zero slack that must be completed on time in order for the project to meet its scheduled completion time   126, 147, 262

Critical path method   procedure to identify the early start schedule and slack for a project   126, 145

Critical success factors   those things that an organization must do well to succeed   13, 216

Data collection process   gathering numbers measuring organizational or system performance   239

Data conversion   transformation of data into a consistent, complete format usable by other systems   109

Data mining   exploring large quantities of detailed data in an attempt to identify marginal competitive advantages   102

Data warehousing   large-scale database technology to organize and store vast quantities of data, enabling data mining analysis   102

Decision support system (DSS)   computer system used to evaluate alternative decision choices   102

Delphi method   a process of pooling expert opinion by sharing initial opinions anonymously, and iteratively obtaining revised opinions   68

Detailed project plan   definition of system, user requirements, and system requirements   219

Detailed task list   listing of work packages briefly describing work to be done   119

Discounted cash flow   conversion of cash flows into their worth as of some base period, usually the present   31

Distribution   the statistical distribution best fitting a given set of data   176

Early start schedule   schedule designed to accomplish each task as early as possible   146

Earned value concept   use of budgeted value of work accomplished, to be compared with actual expenditures   237

Enterprise resource planning system   large-scale system intended to serve all of the organizations computing needs   103

Executive information systems   systems designed to provide focused reports on critical success factors for an organization, as well as providing the ability to explore data for details   102

Expectation failure   failure of the system to meet stakeholder expectations   216

Expected duration   duration calculated assuming it is the weighted average of the minimum, most likely, and maximum estimates   174

Expediter (or coordinator)   individual who monitors problems in an organization and works on alleviating them rapidly   203

Extranet   semi-private network connection across organizations for the purpose of allowing these organizations to work together online   61

Feasibility study   analysis to determine whether or not a system can successfully be built, or if it is expected to be profitable   105

Feeding buffers   buffers added to a project to protect the task in question from delays in completion of predecessor activities   150

Formal specification   detailed description of work to be accomplished, clearly stating what needs to be done, hopefully with required test measures   61

Formative evaluations   evaluations used to control a project   240

Function point analysis method   software project estimation method based on the functions the software is designed to accomplish   131

Functional organization   organization by type of work group members do   194

Gantt chart   bar chart of project tasks plotted against time units   149, 252

Group support system (GSS)   software used to improve group communication and decision making   61, 102, 240

High change threshold   having a low tendency to modify plans   234

Implementation phase   project phase in which a tested system is put into action   110

Incremental development   use of modular system development (independent development of system components)   235

Independent slack   slack in an activity that is not shared with other activities   148

Intangible benefits   outcomes of value that are not accurately measurable in monetary terms   26

Interaction failure   failure of the organization to use the system as planned   216

Internal rate of return (IRR)   that marginal value of capital that yields a net present value of zero for a stream of cash flow   37

Internet commerce   doing business over the Internet   103

Intranet   network of computers linked within an organization   61

ISO 9000   set of standards for an organization's processes   95

Late start schedule   schedule designed to accomplish each task as late as possible while maintaining expected project completion time   146

Learning curves   mathematical functions predicting production rates as a function of experience   141

Liaison   individual assigned to provide personal coordination across groups   203

Lines of code   software project estimation method based on extrapolation from the estimated lines of code required   130

Logical design   description of the control operations of a system   60

Make or buy decision   analysis comparing the costs and benefits of developing a system in-house versus outsourcing   105

Management control   systems providing management with the information needed to monitor organizational performance   102

Matrix organization   grid-like structure of dual reporting relationships combining functional and project organizational features   197

Milestone   distinct event signifying completion of a block of tasks   126, 238, 261

Mission analysis   evaluation of how the proposed system contributes to organizational goal attainment   235

Monte Carlo simulation   analytic technique assuming the values of probabilistic events by generating a random number and converting this value to the input distribution   177

Multiple criteria analysis   study of alternatives in terms of tradeoffs among different criteria   42

Negative disasters   cancellation or massive modification of a project because it is viewed as having failed   69

Nemawashi   a Japanese group decision approach involving a coordinator designing a solution based on interviews with group members, and obtaining individual approval prior to an official meeting   64

Net present value   the worth, in today's terms, of a stream of cash flow over time, assuming a given marginal cost of capital   36

Network   sketch showing the predecessor relationships among project tasks   146

Nominal group technique   structured process to elicit group participation in generating new solutions for dealing with an issue   68

Optimization models   models capable of identifying the best possible decision   46

Organization   structure created to coordinate the activities of people   193

Organization chart   hierarchical sketch of reporting relationships among the people in an organization   123

Organizational effectiveness   check if the system makes the organization perform better   215

Organizational validity check if the system is accepted by the people in the organization 215

Outsourcing hiring outside organizations to develop systems or to perform work 106, 221

Parallel installation implementation of a new system while the old system still functions 224

Partial abandonment reduction of original project scope without changing specifications 216

Payback method of evaluating project proposals in terms of the time required to recover investment 35

Performance standards specifications, budgets, and resource requirements set at the beginning of a project 236

PERT (Program Evaluation and Review Technique) critical path analysis incorporating optimistic, most likely, and pessimistic duration estimates 174

PERT chart in *Microsoft Project,* a project network chart showing predecessor relationships 254

Pilot operation approach implementation of a system tested on a partial load of work prior to disconnecting the old system 224

Planning setting goals and directions 236

Planning process the process of anticipating activities to accomplish, resources required, and time to accomplish project work 118

Positive disasters projects that are completed and implemented, but do not perform acceptably 70

Pre-award audits use of checklists and other techniques to assure outside vendors are competent 234

Process function accomplished by a software system (or by humans) 95

Process failure failure to finish the system on time and/or within budget 216

Program computer code usable by its producer 127

Programming product computer code refined to the point that it can be marketed 128

Programming system computer code usable by the general using public 127

Programming system product computer code refined over time 128

Project a unique, one-time activity to develop something new 3

Project buffers buffers added to a project after its final task to ensure against delay in project completion time 150

Project champion influential person within an organization who maintains support for a project 15

Project failure insufficient performance of a project, on a variety of scales and according to the perspective of a variety of individuals 9

Project implementation putting a product produced by a project into effect 215

Project management system software used to plan a project and monitor its progress 8

Project manager individual assigned the responsibility of managing a project 8

Project organization organization by project task or groups of tasks 196

Project profile   a display of expected project performance on important criteria, allowing comparison of alternative projects   32

Project team   personnel assigned to work on a project   8

Prototyping   development of a small-scale version of a system to be tested for evaluation of system features   90, 235

Quality control   monitoring performance of the system to ensure that it performs as designed   220

Random number   number generated by computer reflecting the input distribution and parameters specified   178

Rapid prototyping   development methodology applying intensive effort (including prototyping) to quickly develop a piece of software   92

Reference checking   contacting users to verify system performance   234

Request for proposal   a set of specifications upon which outside entities can develop a bid to do work   12, 107

Requirements analysis   study of the resources and features required of the proposed system   60

Requirements scrubbing   deletion of unnecessary system features   235

Resource buffers   buffers added to a project before a task to ensure that the resources it requires are available   151

Resource leveling   adjustment of project schedule to stay within given resource levels   158, 260

Resource smoothing   adjusting a schedule to make the use of resources more uniform, minimizing resource usage peaks and valleys   160

Responsibility matrix   chart identifying individuals responsible for project tasks   122

Risk evaluation   assessment of project elements likely to involve problems   13

Schedule risk   project risk with respect to time overruns   202

Screening   a method of implementing a checklist for project evaluation by listing the worst acceptable performance on a list of criteria   31

Shared slack   slack that is common to two tasks (if one of these tasks were to be late, it would exhaust its own slack, as well as the slack of the sharing task)   148

Simulation   use of models (usually with random numbers) to analyze probabilistic problems   173

Slack   extra time available to accomplish a task beyond the time scheduled, while still allowing the project to be completed as scheduled   126, 147

SMART   simple multiattribute rating theory, a means of objectively comparing the values of projects considering multiple criteria   42

Specification phase   project phase where initial requirements are specified   105

Spiral model   software development methodology involving iterative risk analysis and prototyping for development of highly risky projects   91

Staff meeting   meeting of the people on a team assigned to accomplish an activity   126, 272

Standard time unit   quantity of time a unit of work is planned to take   237

Statement of work   document describing what a system is to do in terms of functionality   105, 118

Status review meetings   meetings to update project participants about project status, as well as to gather cost, quality, and time information   126

Strategic resource buffers   buffers added to projects in multiple project environments to ensure that key resources are available for critical activities   151

Substantial abandonment   major modification of the project providing less than original specifications   216

Surgical team   software project team designed around the concept of using a small number of specialists focusing on supporting the activities of the chief system developer   129

System   a collection of entities responsible for accomplishment of interrelated activities with a common purpose   7

Systems analysis   determination of what software components are required to accomplish required functions   88

Systems design   design of the software system to accomplish specified functions   88

Systems development approach   systematic procedure to develop software   104

Systems failure method   method to gather as many similar cases as possible with the intent of identifying problems, so that similar problems can be avoided in the current project   69

Tangible benefits   outcomes of value accurately measurable in monetary terms   25

Task force   temporary grouping of people of diverse skills with the intent of accomplishing a specific job   203

Technical analysis   examination of the system to perform designed work   235

Technical risk   project risk with respect to the quality or performance of project output   202

Technical validity   check if the system does what was intended   215

Testing phase   project phase where the initially produced system is thoroughly tested   110

Time value of money   value of cash flow discounted by cost of capital   36

Total abandonment   cancellation of a project prior to completion   216

Transaction processing   use of computers to do repetitive, highly structured work   102

User training   system training for those who are to use the system   223

Validation   process to assure that the list of requirements generated accurately reflects user information needs   60, 89

Value analysis   analysis of a proposed project by comparing subjectively described benefits versus estimated costs   40

Variance analysis   identification of problem areas through comparing actual and planned performance   237

Verification   the process of determining whether or not the software components function properly   89

Waterfall model   systems development methodology consisting of a sequence of standard project activities   89

Wavefront model   systems development methodology using informal problem analysis and description, followed by prototyping and testing to study system feasibility   94

Work breakdown structure   hierarchical chart of tasks required to accomplish a project   119

Work packages   units of activity in a project   237

Index